T0329053

Knowledge for justice

Critical perspectives from southern African-Nordic
research partnerships

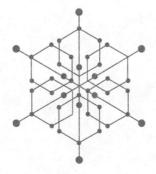

Knowledge for justice

Critical perspectives from southern African-Nordic research partnerships

Edited by Tor Halvorsen, Hilde Ibsen,
Henri-Count Evans and Sharon Penderis

Published in 2017 by

African Minds
4 Eccleston Place, Somerset West, 7130, Cape Town, South Africa
info@africanminds.org.za
www.africanminds.org.za

and

The Southern African-Nordic Centre
University of the Western Cape, Private Bag X17, Bellville, 7535
Tel: +27 21 959 3802
http://sanord.net

 2017

ISBNs
978-1-928331-63-6 Print
978-1-928331-64-3 e-Book
978-1-928331-65-0 e-Pub

Copies of this book are available for free download at
www.africanminds.org.za and http://sanord.net

ORDERS
For orders from Africa, please contact:
African Minds
Email: info@africanminds.org.za

For orders from outside Africa, please contact:
African Books Collective
PO Box 721, Oxford OX1 9EN, UK
Email: orders@africanbookscollective.com

Contents

Frequently used acronyms and abbreviations

CDM	Clean Development Mechanism
CEO	chief executive officer
DFID	Department for International Development
ECTS	European Credit Transfer System
FDI	foreign direct investment
GCIs	green campus initiatives
GIS	geographic information systems
IAU	International Association of Universities
ICT	information and communications technology
IPPE	International Programme in Politics and Economics
ITMOs	internationally transferred mitigation outcomes
IWRM	integrated water resource management
LEMS	Literacy Education in Multilingual Settings
MDGs	Millennium Development Goals
MSRDT	Multidisciplinary student and research development teams
NOQA	Nordic Quality Assurance Network in Higher Education
NPM	new public management
NRF	National Research Foundation
OECD	Organisation for Economic Co-operation and Development
PISA	Programme for International Student Assessment
PPPs	public–private partnerships
PRP	Primary Reading Programme
PUPs	public–public partnerships
SANORD	Southern African–Nordic Centre
SAQMEC	Southern and Eastern Africa Consortium for Monitoring Educational Quality
SDGs	Sustainable Development Goals
SDSN	Sustainable Development Solutions Network
SWOT	strengths, weaknesses, opportunities and threats
UNDP	United Nations Development Programme
UNFCCC	United Nations Framework Convention on Climate Change
UNRISD	United Nations Research Institute for Social Development
VoB	Voice of Business
WIL	work integrated learning
WHO	World Health Organization
WTO	World Trade Organization

Introduction

Tor Halvorsen, Hilde Ibsen, Henri-Count Evans
and Sharon Penderis

THIS IS THE THIRD BOOK IN A SERIES that has evolved out of conferences hosted by the Southern-Africa-Nordic Centre (SANORD), where researchers from the southern African and the Nordic countries have met to discuss aspects of knowledge production relevant to sustainability. This 2017 volume also marks SANORD's tenth anniversary as a network that candidly and critically engages with the ideologies and knowledge systems that span the two regions and within the different member institutions.

Since the early 2000s, international academic networks have grown phenomenally and are increasingly acknowledged to be a critical part of the work done in universities and research institutions. From its inception, SANORD had a head start, in the sense that many of its founding institutions had already forged close relationships over previous decades through numerous cross-regional linkages and collaborative projects. Of course, the southern African and Nordic countries have followed very different trajectories related to modernisation and development, but as relationships between the two regions have evolved, the similarities between them have come to the fore. Framed by our positions in the global economy, and within the international geopolitical balance of power, we have numerous common interests as 'small-states'. In a world dominated by large economic blocs such as the OECD, OPEC and BRICS, our two regions represent a different set of interests and can therefore articulate a range of alternative ideas about how a sustainable world can and should be developed.

Certainly, we have a long way to go before academics from higher education institutions in southern Africa and the Nordic countries are able to consistently work closely together on long-term projects and benefit from the co-created knowledge that comparative research supports. Nevertheless, SANORD bridges cultural barriers and tries to promote and facilitate interdisciplinary work. Ten years in, progress is being made. Since 2007, SANORD's different nodes have enabled scholars to learn from one another about who we are and how we can do better in terms of knowledge co-creation. As collaborative research drives academic co-operation down new pathways, future publications will no doubt provide increasingly useful theoretical and empirical studies of the similarities and differences between our regions, thus offering new and important perspectives on how we might close up the North–South divide.

The contributors to this third book in the series take this process forward. Critical perspectives on the United Nations' Sustainable Development Goals (SDGs) (UN 2015b) have guided the collection, and all the contributors have brought their knowledge and competence to bear to critically review the intentions of the SDGs in relation to their own areas of expertise.

One of the fundamental ideas underpinning the SDGs, although arguably the least developed, is that no country should aim to implement them in ways that prevent other countries from doing so too. A crucial step, then, is to overcome the knowledge cleavages between North and South, that have been created over many years by structural inequalities and poor leadership. The contributors show how cross-regional research networks can contribute to shifting the conditions that create unequal development and, in almost every chapter, suggest alternatives to the one-size-fits all solutions that render the twenty-first century's dominant neo-liberal paradigm so limited and so dangerous.

As a network of academic institutions, SANORD has an important role to play in meeting the challenges of academic freedom and the decolonisation of knowledge. It is pertinent to raise awareness about knowledge independent from politics and economic interests, and create a climate for the SDGs to be discussed openly, critically and creatively.

Unpacking the SDGs

In 2015, heads of state and government representatives from around the world adopted the 17 SDGs and the associated 169 targets with the aim of eradicating extreme poverty, reducing inequalities, building a just and more equal society and achieving economic development, social inclusion and environmental sustainability. The SDGs are based on the principle of 'leaving no one behind'. Turning principle into practice is the real challenge.

The SDGs' call for transformation presents opportunities and challenges for the academic world generally and higher education institutions in particular. Questions that urgently require answers involve how our institutions and networks will contribute to the collective journey set out in the SDGs, while also reaffirming the vision of unity set out in the preamble to the United Nations' founding charter back in 1945.

In terms of the SDGs, higher education institutions have been given responsibility for developing models for global justice and for mobilising a critical mass of academic support (see UN 2015b). For real change to occur, however, action must take place at the global, national, regional and local levels, and across borders, regions and continents. The success of the SDGs undoubtedly requires a deeper understanding of the problems facing the world and of the kinds of skills and abilities that will enable governments, the private sector, academia and civil society to collaborate in addressing these.

Taken together, the 17 SDGs particularly call into question the so-called development model propagated by the North for so long, most recently in the guise of neo-liberal reforms. But will we really see global development initiatives taking the issues of climate change adaptation and mitigation seriously and reducing both inequality and carbon emissions in ways that actually leave no one behind?

Idealism writ large?

Importantly, the process of determining the SDGs was more inclusive and collaborative than the formulation of the Millennium Development Goals (MDGs), in that it included not only the world's wealthy nations, but also middle-income and low-income countries (Abel et al. 2016; Sachs 2012). In implementing the SDGs, the United Nations envisages a participatory process between multilevel stakeholders and the fostering of global partnerships between governments, the private sector, NGOs, aid organisations and local communities (Prescott and Stibbe 2016). In this regard, the United Nations General Assembly Resolution that was adopted in September 2015 on the SDGs states:

> We are determined to mobilize the means required to implement this Agenda through a revitalized Global Partnership for Sustainable Development, based on a spirit of strengthened global solidarity focused on the needs of the poorest and most vulnerable and with the participation of all countries, all stakeholders and all people. (UN 2015: Preamble)

Unlike the MDGs, the SDGs reflect the United Nations' attempt to offer a more integrated approach to sustainable development, bringing together the economic, social and environmental dimensions (Sterling 2016). In deciding on a new global agenda, the United Nations' argument is that progress made towards achieving the Millennium Development Goals proved that humanity can work together to achieve common goals. Although many had seen the MDGs as too idealistic and unrealistic, significant progress was made towards fulfilling them. The consensus, therefore, was that 'when much is dared, much can be achieved'. In addition, the wider applicability of the SDGs was seen as signalling a new era for global politics and development.

As emphasised by many who were involved in drafting the goals, the implementation of the SDGs will require new knowledge, and this places the universities and the process of knowledge production in the spotlight. Clearly, politicians and policy-makers will never recommend political solutions in line with the shifts required by the SDGs unless they have critical and evidence-based research to guide and inform them of how critical such shifts have become. Universities have the duty to provide quality research and the necessary knowledge-base for sound, informed policy choices that take global realities into account and address the global inequalities that lie beneath them.

Taken together, the SDGs also have the potential to restore a level of power and legitimacy to the political sphere. The basis of this authority is embedded in the 'theory of development' that the combination of goals appeals to, and which differs considerably from the authority held by the G20 and similar entities. The SDGs' theory of development holds that *all* activities, including economic activities, must take into account their social and environmental impact and long-term consequences. This vision carries within it an appeal to the academic profession to come up with viable alternatives when hegemonic powers resist change. The viability of this global authority, and the validity of this theory of development, will depend on whether alternative ways of running the local, national, regional and global economies can be developed and implemented. Without this, the SDGs will never be realised.

In many ways, the central question here is posed precisely by the existence of the contemporary hegemonic global regime (as touted by the World Bank, the OECD, the G7 and the G20): how is it possible to delink economic growth from an unsustainable energy system, and either create enough jobs or redistribute resources in ways that secure the livelihoods of the most vulnerable people in the world?

Those who currently hold economic and political power in the world seem to prefer to avoid this question, and we seem to lack the knowledge relevant to answering it. However, turning the SDGs into reality depends on our ability to challenge and change the workings of the global economy at every level. Of course, this is not the task of knowledge or the producers of knowledge alone, but without such knowledge alternatives, the future of the planet looks bleak.

In a UNDP/UNRISD publication titled *Global Trends: Challenges and Opportunities in the Implementation of the Sustainable Development Goals* (Dugarova and Gülasan 2017), two clear arguments are made. The first is that new and critical kinds of knowledge are crucial for the implementation of the SDGs. The second is that if the SDGs' most fundamental value 'leave no one behind', is to be honoured, the voices of those who are most deeply affected by the achievement of the goals all over the world must be present in the development of this knowledge. Participatory approaches to development are essential, as is knowledge production that involves the collaboration of researchers, policy-makers and communities themselves. The 'engagement of all stakeholders' has to be seen as a 'pre-condition for success' (Filho et al. 2017:1). Central to this engagement is the recognition that solutions to the problems of sustainability must come from, and be defined by, communities themselves, not by scientists, economists, technocrats, policy-makers or politicians who live elsewhere.

The knowledge we need

In the late 1980s, Jürgen Kocka estimated that there were 5000 to 6000 disciplines in higher education, many of which started out as a combination of disciplines, but have since evolved their own orthodoxies (Kocka 1987). In our view, the critical need for new knowledge means that it is time to loosen up the feudal structure of university disciplines, with their tribes and territories. As Leal Filho et al. (2017: 1) argued, what is urgently needed is multi-, trans- and interdisciplinary research which has as its objective 'to jointly find solutions and design strategies that can contribute to creating good lives for the community today and in the future'. For the achievement of the SDGs, a non-hegemonic approach to knowledge is crucial.

If knowledge production occurs along existing disciplinary lines, we risk losing the relationships that are so important to understanding the legitimacy and potential of the SDGs. A similar argument applies to the compartmentalisation of politics, and the segmentation of the state. Crosscutting links must be made explicit through a common knowledge discourse and the ongoing commitment of the academic community. If the SDGs are to foster new ways of thinking about development, and used as a basis for universal mobilisation, they have to be of concern to everyone. Development is no longer an issue of, for example, 'poorer regions catching up' (as the World Bank typically argues), but a way of living into the values of a 'good society'.

The role of networks like SANORD is to contribute to this new knowledge production. As academics, we have to use existing knowledge differently and work across disciplines to better understand how economic goals can be refocused in ways that strengthen social and environmental imperatives. To manage this, we have to change curricula so as to make space for new meetings between established disciplines, but also create room for new 'cross-disciplinary' disciplines to emerge.

About this book

The chapters in this collection reflect a number of key issues related to SDGs and their targets. The contributors to Part I focus primarily on the realities and challenges facing academics and professionals in the context of neo-liberal hegemony. In Chapter 1, Tor Halvorsen reminds us of the importance of academic responsibility from a philosophical and ethical perspective. The SDGs represent ideals and visions, but are also open to interpretation and contestation. If global justice is the grand global challenge, and if the knowledge taught and produced in universities matters, Halvorsen argues that scholars must take responsibility for the knowledge they produce and the potential consequences of that knowledge for a world in which the logic of neo-liberalism and academic capitalism still reign supreme.

In Chapter 2, Henri-Count Evans and Rosemary Musvipwa warn that international processes intended to address climate change and poverty are embedded in the very same neo-liberal principles that perpetuate inequality, and are leading to the rise of a kind of green imperialism. They suggest that neo-liberalism fundamentally influences how world leaders seek to solve humanitarian problems related to climate change and the use of natural resources, and call for a deeper search for alternative perspectives.

In this context, however, the decline of academic freedom in many countries poses a major threat. In Chapter 3, Jens Stilhoff Sörensen and Erik Olsson use the sobering but enlightening case of Sweden to illustrate the kinds of pressures higher education institutions are under to function according to the new public management (NPM) model. While Sweden is often seen as a bastion of liberal democracy, Sörensen and Olsson reveal how university reforms introduced since 2011 are dismantling collegiality and institutional autonomy. In addition, the introduction of shadow management systems ensure that, even though academic freedom is protected by legislation, these laws can easily be bypassed for reasons of economic or political expediency. They argue that such shadow management is typical of neo-liberal reform processes that are dismantling public institutions piece by crumbling piece throughout the world.

In Chapter 4, Carina van Rooyen demonstrates how this same neo-liberal logic turned a not-for profit bulk water utility in South Africa into a profit-seeking business that prioritises efficiency over effectiveness, while effectively dispossessing its poorest clients and jeopardising affordable and universal access to water in the areas it serves.

Critical perspectives on educational goals and basic knowledge are the main focus of Chapter 5, in which Hilde Ibsen, Sharon Penderis and Karin Bengtsson explore how global ideas about education and knowledge are expressed via South Africa's and Sweden's basic education curricula. Global educational goals reveal good intentions and might have rhetorical impact, but in practice they do little to challenge the structural inequalities embedded in the neo-liberal political economy. Ibsen, Penderis and Bengtsson thus argue that education institutions should lead the way in giving situated and indigenous knowledge its rightful priority from basic education up to university level.

Of major concern to Suriamurthee Maistry and Erlend Eidsvik, the authors of Chapter 6, is that NPM's universalistic apparatus will also dominate the implementation of the SDGs. They depart from a critique of universal targets and indicators, and raise the important question of how to develop a socially inclusive pluriversal perspective on knowledge.

The chapters in Part II reflect a common concern with the value and validity of North–South research partnerships and shared knowledge production.

In Chapter 7, Kate Rowntree and Roddy Fox assess what was achieved via a long-term academic exchange programme between a South African and two Swedish universities. They outline what they see as the key factors that contributed to the success and longevity of the programmes that they helped to establish and run.

In Chapter 8, Thembinkosi Mabila and Rachel Singh suggest that North–South research collaborations and academic exchanges would be more effective if project partners were to prioritise co-operation and reciprocity from the earliest stages of a collaborative process and especially when defining project objectives.

Stephen Mago, in Chapter 9, steps back a little to describe how the geopolitics of research collaboration has the potential to negatively affect processes and outcomes, but also offers some suggestions about how to overcome this challenge through more innovative staff and student training and the effective use of academic networks.

In Chapter 10, Robert Martin, Regina Krause, Martha Namutuwa, Evgenia Mahler and Hartmut Domröse, consider the role of North–South collaboration as a way of responding to industry demands and improving student employability. They describe experiences based on a pilot project between a university in Namibia and Germany, where student teams from different disciplines worked on a business idea or problem. Lessons drawn from the project led to the 'Voice of Business Programme' which aimed at strengthening the curriculum of the institutions involved in the project.

Part III contains a set of small-scale case studies that provide rich and valuable insights for cross-regional research programmes, while still highlighting the value of co-created knowledge. Related to SDG 3 (good health and well-being), SDG 4 (quality education) and SDG 15 (sustainable land use), the chapters reveal possibilities and obstacles for collaboration across and within regions, highlighting the importance of comparative research and local knowledge.

In Chapter 11, Mubiana Sitali-Ngoma and Emmy Mbozi turn our attention to need to avoiding formulaic generalisations and one-size-fits-all solutions. In a study of life satisfaction among elderly persons in Zambia, they show how theories of aging developed in the North cannot be universally or uncritically applied, and that local circumstances and local contexts are vital in any intervention. Chapter 12, by Anne Marit Vesteraas Danbolt, Dennis Banda, Jørgen Klein and Geoffrey Tambulukani, is on home–school relations and the crucial role that parents can play in reinforcing indigenous knowledge as their children acquire early literacy and learning skills. In the final chapter, Antti Erkkilä and Nelago Indongo analyse farming practices in Namibia, focusing on a seldom-researched but effective agro-forestry practice that is characteristic of north-central Namibia. They show that the use of more modern and permanent building materials have the potential to undermine the practice and thus impact negatively on soil fertility as well as fruit and grain production.

Perhaps the central thread woven through all the chapters is how to find solutions we can all agree are appropriate, effective and justly share the burden. This discussion must go on, no doubt through future conferences and perhaps through future SANORD publications.

Acknowledgements

No less than four peer reviewers were generous enough to share their insights and knowledge and strong praise is due to them all for accepting the difficult task of reviewing all or part of this collection. Your comments contributed enormously to improving the rigour and focus of the chapters and your skilful and timely assistance is much appreciated.

All of the contributors to this volume have patiently tolerated long delays and urgent deadlines, email systems that crashed and the usual difficulties of long-distance communication. We thank you all for responding to requests so diligently and with such equanimity, especially given all of the other demands on your time.

All three books published in this series have been funded via SANORD's central budget, and the support of the SANORD board and member institutions in this regard is much appreciated. The assistance of the staff of its secretariat at the University of the Western Cape, Leolyn Jackson and Maureen Davis has been immeasurable.

As with the previous books, we could not have managed without freelance production manager and copyeditor, Mary Ralphs, whose hard work and useful suggestions have improved the book tremendously. Our thanks also to assistant copyeditor Carrie Schwartz for helping us meet our deadline and to Peter Bosman for his design and typesetting wizardry. Our publisher at African Minds, François van Schalkwyk, has enabled SANORD's publications to achieve a global reach and impact we otherwise never would have managed.

We hope you can make use of the fruits of these combined efforts and wish you good reading.

References

Abel G, B Barakat and W Lutz (2016) 'Meeting the Sustainable Development Goals leads to lower population growth' *Proceedings of the National Academy of Sciences* 113 (50): 14294–14299.

Dugarova E and N Gülasan (2017) *Global Trends: Challenges and Opportunities in the Implementation of the Sustainable Development Goals.* New York and Geneva: UNDP and UNRISD. This is under UNDP/UNRISD on p.36.

Kocka J (1987). *Interdisiplinarität.* Franfurt-am-Main: Suhrkamp.

Leal Filho W, U Azeiteiro, F Alves, P Pace, M Mifsud, L Brandli, SS Caeiro and A Disterheft (2017) 'Reinvigorating the sustainable development research agenda: The role of the Sustainable Development Goals' *International Journal of Sustainable Development and World Ecology* Published online, 28 June.

Sachs J (2012) 'From Millennium Development Goals to Sustainable Development Goals' *Lancet* 379: 2206–2211.

Prescott D and D Stibbe (2016) *Partnering for the SDGs: Building up the System of Support to Help Mainstream Collaboration for Sustainable Development.* Oxford: Partnering Initiative.

Sterling S (2016) 'A commentary on education and Sustainable Development Goals' *Journal of Education for Sustainable Development* 10 (2): 208–213.

UN (United Nations) (1945) 'Preamble' in: *Charter of the United Nations,* signed 26 June, San Francisco. Available online.

UN (2015a) *Global Sustainable Development Report: 2015 Edition* (Advance unedited edition). New York. Available online.

UN (2015b) *Transforming our world: The 2030 agenda for sustainable development.* Resolution 70/1 adopted by the UN General Assembly, 25 September 2015. Available online.

PART I: KNOWLEDGE AND NEO-LIBERALISM

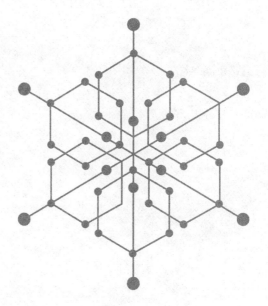

The Sustainable Development Goals, knowledge production and the global struggle over values

Tor Halvorsen

SINCE THE KNOWLEDGE PRODUCED AND REPRODUCED by universities matters more than ever, it should not be surprising that politicians are increasingly debating how to prioritise and make the best use of knowledge, as well as how to guide, evaluate and control the work of professionals and academics. It may seem paradoxical that some of the world's most highly educated experts are increasingly subject to high levels of monitoring and control, while their work is considered worthy of less and less respect, particularly by politicians.[1]

In fact, this is not a paradox at all. It is a sign of how much power and knowledge depend on, and yet are also in opposition to, one another in our modern age.

The 'power of knowledge' matters today in ways humans have probably never experienced before, and control, over both the content and holders of knowledge is crucial to those who aim to influence social development. The power inherent in the control of knowledge is particularly clear as we confront the global environmental crisis, and attempt to create a global discourse about how to understand and respond to it.

In the Western world, over the past century or so, neither academics, nor the professionals they have trained, have adjusted well to the power they hold and the ethical questions it raises. Rather, a range of unhealthy adjustments have undermined the ethical responsibility that academics and professionals are expected to take for the types of knowledge they pursue, how their data is used, and the wider consequences of these actions. Here, I am referring not only to engineers or the arms industry but to every single discipline and profession. The positivist notion that knowledge is 'technical' and 'objective', and therefore neutral and 'true', seems to have shielded academics and professionals from seeing and taking responsibility for effects of our actions.

Rather than perpetuating this situation, it is necessary to renew and rebuild trust in the ability of the academic profession to *mediate knowledge in ways that presuppose democratic interaction*. Academics and professionals still have the power to influence how the global challenges facing our planet are defined, understood and addressed. We must therefore be much more explicit about the potential influence of our research, and much clearer about taking responsibility for this.

Everyone involved in knowledge production and research has some crucial questions to answer. Why are we developing the knowledge we are developing, and for whom? What consequences might this have? Who might use this knowledge, and what do we know about their intentions and ethical standards? How do we prevent the misuse of knowledge and make provision for any unforeseen harmful consequences? While a number of ethical standards already exist (and are overseen by research ethics committees as well as organisations such as UNESCO, the EU, etc.), these have proven insufficient given the critical turning point that the world has reached.

In this regard, the United Nations Development Programme, and its Research Institute for Social Development (UNRISD) identified six megatrends (UNDP and UNRISD: 2017; UNRISD 2016): poverty and inequality, demography, environmental degradation and climate change, shocks and crises, development co-operation and financing, and technical innovation. Others, such as the G7 or the OECD, might focus on a different set of trends, but global debate around these issues led to the formulation of the 17 Sustainable Development Goals (SDGs). Through this, a common discourse with immense legitimacy seems to have been established, albeit one that is also having something of a standardising effect, as discussed later in this chapter.

Taken singly, all of the SDGs are crucial; together they starkly define our situation at a global level. As argued in the Introduction, the 17 SDGs (and their associated 'indicators' or sub-goals) represent a *new kind of global authority* – a new discourse that legitimises political action that supports social and environmental sustainability. Based on this authority, academics must take a new level of responsibility for developing a shared lexicon and deeper insights, and for highlighting what is left out (or left behind) as goals, norms and standards are institutionalised, thereby legitimising and favouring particular discourses over others.

Re-embedding economic development

Through the adoption of the SDGs, most of the world's governments ostensibly committed themselves to developing their economies in ways that put social and environmental values first. This runs contrary to the so-called *financialisation* of the global economy, which has seen economies becoming increasingly dependent on international finance and disengaged from local social and political agendas. That is, governments have agreed to shift back towards re-embedding social, economic and technological development within society and nature in ways that acknowledge that human survival relies on nature being able to flourish, and even to have 'veto powers'. That is, *if implemented, the SDGs will reframe the purpose of economic development as both social and environmental;* this will entail transforming the resource and energy base of many of the world's economies and putting an end to forms of development that threaten biodiversity.[2] Thus, although the SDGs do not explicitly refer to the Anthropocene (the view that the earth has moved into a new geological period), they are based on an understanding that humanity and the planet have reached a turning point. This demands new kinds of knowledge, new ways of legitimising knowledge, and new behaviours from those who produce and use knowledge.

When debates about the SDGs began, those leading the process proposed that they be both shaped and implemented in a context of close co-operation between researchers and policy-makers. In the foreword to the 2015 *Global Sustainable Development Report*, Wu Hongbo, United Nations Under-Secretary-General in the Department of Economic and Social Affairs noted that 'the scientific community has provided valuable guidelines in the formulation of the SDGs, and it will need to remain closely engaged as the world moves towards implementing the new agenda and reviewing our progress.' He added that 'more than 500 independent scientists and experts from many UN entities and affiliated organizations located in all regions of the globe have contributed to the report' (UN 2015: i; see also ICSU and ISSC 2015). Many universities and research institutions are taking this seriously and are already contributing in many ways;[3] hopefully, professional associations, especially those working at post-national level, will quickly follow suit. The ethical challenge is to find a way out of the contemporary growth paradigm, which creates wealth for a few at great cost to nature and the poor while insisting that wealth will eventually trickle down to everyone if we all seek economic growth. Despite much evidence that shows this to be false, a blind faith in the relationship between free trade and widespread prosperity continues to be proclaimed. Reducing inequality is an important aspect of the SDGs, particularly SDG 10 (reduced inequalities) but, so far, little has been said about the consequences this must have for those who are benefitting from the global economic system while keeping others poor and doing so much to destroy the biosphere.

The sad history of leaving too many behind

This turning point in history must also make us ask how knowledge has contributed to our situation. If knowledge has been a driving force in creating a world that is no longer viable, should we then place our hope for a better future in the hands of the very same knowledge producers and professionals? My suggestion is that *ethics*, based on a democratic polity and processes of popular participation, should guide the knowledge that is produced for the interpretation and implementation of the SDGs.

For example, the *basic* social commitment made in the SDGs: 'leave no one behind' – essentially the notion that everyone has the right to a decent life – was, until recently, ridiculed by science. In his book, *Race, Eugenics and American Economics in the Progressive Era*, Thomas Leonard (2016) describes how, in the last decades of the nineteenth century, economists who dominated both the academic institutions and offices of public administration in the United States, used the so-called science of eugenics to justify white male supremacy. The consequences of this are all too evident today in the behaviour of Donald Trump and his supporters. The ethical conviction behind the work of these economists and policy-makers, then as now, was 'America first'.

In the 1930s and early 1940s, eugenics was brutally applied in Germany with help of all kinds of professionals. We all know the story. Less widely known is what became of many of those who put their skills and knowledge as lawyers, doctors, natural scientists, engineers and civil servants to work so as to more efficiently murder people with disabilities, the so-called ethnically 'unclean', refugees, etc. Kjartan Fløgstad (2016), in his book *'Etter i saumane: Kultur og politikk i arbeideklassens hundreår'* (part 2 on 'Science' in particular), shows that, after the war, many of these same professionals were employed within Germany's public sector, the media and other institutions. Fløgstad shows how these academics and professionals not only made the Nazi system work, and never took responsibility for their actions, but also created a kind of continuity between the Nazi regime and the Adenauer era. Effectively, until very recently, they blocked studies that exposed how intertwined knowledge and politics had been in the Nazi period.

Following Fløgstad's lead, other contemporary historians such as Konrad Jarausch are researching the lives of academics who were active in the Nazi era. According to Jarausch (1990), more lawyers who supported National Socialism were employed within West Germany's public sector in 1952 than during the Nazi era. Jarausch's study of the Nazi regime reveals that the majority of Germany's doctors and lawyers supported National Socialism – doctors more out of scientific conviction (believing in the 'truth' of Hitler's views on race), and lawyers due to a lack of ethical awareness. After 1945, some even secured academic careers based on work they had done during the war. One example is that of ornithologist Obersturmführer Günther Niethammer, whose PhD about birdlife in Auschwitz in 1941 marked the start of an illustrious career in science. From 1968 to 1973, Niethammer chaired Germany's ornithological society, and when he died, he was celebrated as a distinguished and reputable scientist, a man of 'truth' (see Fløgstad for details).

A similar situation occurred in South Africa, where lawyers, social scientists and biblical scholars, in particular, formed an alliance with the ruling party. Together they reinforced the foundations of colonialism and created the ideology of apartheid, which legalised and justified racial repression and exploitation on biblical grounds for over forty years. In the culmination of a long struggle, dating back to the start of the colonial period, apartheid rule was overthrown in a largely peaceful political revolution that occurred between 1991 and 1994. However, cultural and economic transformation has yet to follow. As this unfolds, the ways in which academics and professionals in all fields used their knowledge and skills to help policy-makers and public officials to entrench and uphold apartheid at every level will have to be unveiled.

Learning to value knowledge again

What these examples show is that human rights is an ideal that professionals and academics have too often sacrificed to serve their own ethnic or national interests. In the First World War, Europe's democratic regimes, with the help of a *professional* military elite, in alliance with a range of other professionals forced their working populations into the trenches, creating a vast killing field. When the International Association of Universities (IAU) was created after the Second World War in 1948, its aim was to secure a stronger ethical voice among the academic community and broaden scholars' commitment to universal values. Their aim was to prevent anything similar to the development of the gas chambers and the atomic bomb from happening again. After this, a belief in knowledge gradually emerged that had seldom been seen before (Halvorsen 2012b). Indeed, the idea that no one should be left behind, is one that some say the human rights movement deserves credit for, in that it reflects the crucial and *positive* contributions since made by the legal profession.

Today, notwithstanding the rise of the new right, the real challenge facing the world is a global economy that promises prosperity for all, while, in fact, destabilising the earth's heat balance, causing mass extinctions and leaving more and more people vulnerable to poverty. For decades, Talcott Parsons, one of the United States' leading sociologists, suggested that the inclusion of academics into economic organisations would create a morally conscious capitalism that would be marked by values other than utility maximisation

(Halvorsen 1992). Gradually, the knowledge society emerged, and Jürgen Habermas (inspired by Parsons)[4] could criticise Marx's base and superstructure theory by showing that the professions cultivated in the universities (part of superstructure) brought ethics and moral commitment into the world of work, technology and market calculations.

In the 1970s, Daniel Bell (1973/1999) took these views further in his writing on knowledge societies and knowledge economies. Also from the 1970s, increasing numbers of professionals began to be employed in the public sector in many parts of the world, and ideas developed about how bureaucrats could make decisions not only by following legislation and rules but also by using their knowledge and initiative. Slowly, public servants came to a deeper understanding and awareness of the consequences of their actions, thus opening up the public sector to using knowledge for purposes other than law enforcement through bureaucratic means.

Thus, by the beginning of the 1980s, when neo-liberalism started to change everything, academics and professionals were widely trusted. They were expected to be able to transform the 'iron cage' of capitalist bureaucracy into regulated and well-intentioned houses of reason, in which the weak and vulnerable would be listened to, not left behind. As many Northern countries shifted towards welfare-state rights and a public service that had to treat everyone equally, it is probably fair to say that most citizens in higher-income countries, and the elites in lower-income countries, could be reasonably secure that their basic rights were protected.

Learning to question knowledge

As Fløgstad revealed, between about 1880 and the mid-1940s, few academics or professionals in the West seem to have reflected on the role of knowledge or questioned the interests of those who put it to use. The West's post-war apparent success story of growing numbers of jobs for an increasingly highly educated and prosperous workforce left little room for questions about who or what knowledge should be for, or about how professions were being shaped to serve the perceived needs of clients in the capitalist nations. It is impossible to know what alternatives were lost along the way, and how these might have created a world that would have been more aware of and responsive to wider social and environmental issues. What is clear is that the research and knowledge that was supported simultaneously led to a myriad of other avenues of research and knowledge being closed off.

In hindsight, and given the values implicit in the SDGs, it is difficult to identify even one of the 17 goals where the pursuit of alternative avenues of knowledge would not have been more beneficial. In our own era, as historians

Christophe Bonneuil and Jean-Baptiste Fressoz show in *The Shock of the Anthropocene* (2015), crucial knowledge choices have been made that have massive consequences for the present and the future. These choices have led to the situation in which it is possible and even acceptable to some that the wealthiest 1 per cent of the world's population annually consume (or waste) one-and-a-half times what the planet is able to annually produce in a sustainable way. This consumption requires and sustains the building of dams at massive environmental cost, the emission of excessive amounts of greenhouse gas, the overfishing and acidification of the ocean, mono-cropping that depletes the soil and leads to the mass extinction of plants and animals, the building and operating of heavy industry that heats and poisons the atmosphere, and the generation of massive amounts of plastic and other waste that is contaminating our rivers and water supplies. Collectively, humanity is responsible for creating a global economic system that has forever changed the earth. The Anthropocene period can be seen as having begun with industrialisation and modernity. As Bonneuil and Fressoz (2015) point out, since it began, there have been warnings of its shortcomings, risks and dangers.

Through uncontrolled development, humans have initiated changes to the biosphere on a global scale and unleashed consequences that are far beyond human influence. To stand any chance of survival, Bonneuil and Fressoz argue that humanity has to change; and to do this, we need to know more about our own history. We need to see that alternative knowledge exists and understand why it has been suppressed, despite (or perhaps because of) having identified the potentially destructive consequences of industrialisation and modernity, and despite being more trusted by knowledge 'of the life world' to use a Habermasian expression.

> We have passed the exit gate from the Holocene. We have reached a threshold. Realization of this must revolutionize the views of the world that became dominant with the rise of industrial capitalism based on fossil fuel. What historical narratives can we offer of the last quarter of a millennium, able to help us change our worldviews and inhabit the Anthropocene more lucidly, respectfully and equitably? (Bonneuil and Fressoz 2015: xiii)

Relearning social values

What we need now is a focus on the actors, institutions, knowledge and decisions that have produced the 'global challenges' we face. Instead, what is often foregrounded is an ahistorical notion of science's 'discovery' of global warming and climate change. This means we risk replacing one set of (old modernist) experts with a new set, who see improved governance (based on Western ideals, obviously) and new technologies (including their production, marketing and sale, meaning 'economic growth') as the *only* possible solution.

While it is important to be wary of parallels that may not be valid, it is important to prevent a recurrence of what happened after the Second World War, when fascist academics simply slipped into new positions and continued to build careers without anyone questioning how the ethical positions and convictions they had held before continued to influence their work.

Western values and systems of knowledge production, reproduction and exploitation appear to be beyond debate despite overwhelming evidence from the United Nations' own global research on their environmental consequences. Instead of a concerted search for a new paradigm, the impression often created is that all that is required is improved governance, based on the extension of Western hegemony regarding knowledge and knowledge production. All too often, scientists (even natural scientists) present themselves as being at the vanguard of geo-engineering and high-tech solutions.[5]

Of utmost importance for our future is that the engineering profession becomes more engaged, vocal and independent. What we don't need is engineers at the vanguard of a new technocracy. Instead, as history shows, the strengthening of democracy is more likely to deliver the kinds of knowledge relevant to the broadest spread of the population, rather than just the elite and the 1 per cent.

Democracy should entail governance by the many, including the oppressed, and promote the basic value of equality. This means it has the potential to be a voice for the many who see nature not as a resource to be exploited, but rather an environment to inhabit. It is worth highlighting that one of the liveliest debates in contemporary Europe is about whether capitalism and democracy are different and (under neo-liberalism) contradictory value systems; of course, this question is central to debates on sustainability. As Merkel (2014:109) explains:

> Capitalism and democracy follow different logics: unequally distributed property rights on the one hand, equal civic and political rights on the other; profit-oriented trade within capitalism in contrast to the search for the common good within democracy; debate, compromise and majority decision-making within democratic politics versus hierarchical decision-making by managers and capital owner. Capitalism is not democratic, democracy not capitalist.

For example, in relation to SDG 10, it is only fair to ask why social and political scientists have not done more to challenge the economic theories that have done so much to foster inequality, concentrate wealth in the hands of so few, and entrenched the hegemony of the global economic powers.

In a book that focuses on the history of the economics profession in the United States, Britain and France from the late nineteenth century, Marion Fourcade (2009) shows how alternative economic thinking has at times brutally been suppressed in favour of the kinds of economic reasoning that has led to the financialisation mentioned earlier. Writing about the contemporary era, Philip Mirowski shows how neo-liberalism evolved and even strengthened after the 2008 financial crises. He points out that the economics profession has been shaped by a view that conflates the market with 'nature', seeing it as a force that 'will never be adequately comprehended by human science'.[6] He argues that

> for neoliberals, humans can never be trusted to know whether the biosphere is in crisis or not, because both nature and society are dauntingly complex and evolving; therefore, the neoliberal solution is to enlist the strong state to allow the market to find its own way to the ultimate solution. (2013: 336)

For neo-liberal economists, the only way to solve the environmental crisis, if such a solution ever existed, is for the state to create secure markets in the environmental sector. The only really true science is economics, but of a particular kind (see also Evans and Musvipwa, this volume).

Instead of supporting an economic system capable of reproducing democracy, neo-liberalism reproduces power relations that, as 2016 Holberg Prize winner Jürgen Kocka (2016) observed, undermine democracy at all levels, particularly when democracy asks for alternatives to the knowledge that the market allows to develop.

When I want to be controversial, I often argue that London's financial district has a higher ratio of crooks per square metre than any other place on earth. The main role of its bankers and brokers is to find ways of placing money in tax havens, to speculate against 'bad papers', and avoid public oversight over large financial deals, including those that will inevitably create greenhouse gas emissions. In London, on Wall Street, or in any other financial centre, career progression is often linked to an ability to find loopholes in laws created to control 'market externalities' (a category neo-liberals have no use for). Do they really do this, in the conviction that they are merely allowing natural market forces to operate, and that this is the best and most ethical way for them to use their knowledge, skills and insights?

Universities that educate accountants, lawyers and economists seldom seem concerned about the destructive consequences of the 'free market' or the 'ethics' of their graduates. Ethics courses taught in universities seldom inform the practising of professions in ways that humanise or democratise capitalism – at least, not in the ways that Parsons, Habermas and Bell hoped they might. The age of enlightenment has little bearing on late modernity. These three highly revered social scientists got it all wrong, never anticipating the strength of neo-liberalism and the many think tanks that now spread its gospel.

Responsible consumption and production

This leads us to SDG 12 (responsible production and consumption). Without constantly expanding consumption, capitalism cannot survive. This was a worry for economists a hundred or so years ago. As human needs were satisfied by industrial production, what demands would remain to stimulate further growth? The answer, of course, is that not all needs are a given, many are socially constructed. Industrialists then sought help from psychologists who studied consumer behaviour and fed this knowledge to the advertising industry.

Psychologists and marketing professionals have, through advertising, played a huge role in cultivating many of the consumer behaviours we take for granted, especially in higher-income countries and regions. This behaviour, often expressed in terms of 'individual freedom' and 'freedom of choice', has created habits and personalities that have not only saved capitalism from stagnation, but created the basis for our present crises of both environment and identity. This is a highly under-discussed aspect of the much-debated book by the great German social philosopher, Axel Honneth about individual freedom, *Freedom's Right*. Honneth's major concern is how capitalism in its present form undermines constitutional democracies by making states instrumental in and subject to the global economy. Yet, on the other hand,

> Free market participation, self-aware democratic citizens and emancipated family members – all of whom correspond to ideals institutionalized in our society – mutually influence each other, because the properties of the one cannot be realized without those of the other two. (Honneth 2011: 330)

Although Honneth argues that, of these three institutions, democracy holds first position since it alone is primarily reflexive (that is, a realm in which knowledge developed within academia matters in the form of 'better arguments'), he does not discuss the role of knowledge in shaping 'unfree' citizens into consumers. Neither does he discuss the role of knowledge in constructing the notion of the free market as a 'force of nature' to which we have to adjust. Is democratic participation in the 'free-market' even possible? Only, it seems, in Honneth's world, if the market is re-embedded.[7] To this,

I would add, only if the academic professions commit themselves to such a project in alliance with the democratic forces Honneth refers to, and in ways that these forces can trust in knowledge as a force for change in line with the SDGs, and particularly with the achievement of SDG 1 (no poverty).

This construction of needs fulfilment as a way of realising success (and forming a view of the self as successful), is so integrated in contemporary culture in so many parts of the world, that the idea of responsible consumption (among the wealthy) is fiercely resisted by many as an attack on their freedom, culture and identity as individuals. It is difficult to see any alternatives emanating from psychologists or marketing professionals (except perhaps in Argentina where psychoanalysis is valued more highly than behaviourism).[8] In the developing world, the argument is, why should these long-suffering nations not 'catch up' with the rest; why deprive them of owning their own oil-refineries and petrol-driven cars or air-conditioners and coal-fired power stations? As long as economic growth and shareholder value remains the key priority, the same kind of development that has blighted and blinded the rich world must trickle down to the suffering masses of the poorer nations; or at least, that is, until the rich nations want to start talking about 'sharing the burden' created by the environmental crisis.

Human 'needs' – and the associated resources needed for their satisfaction – are of course very unequal in the world, as are the consequences for energy consumption and pollution. On average, US citizens consume many times more energy and resources and create many times more carbon emissions and other waste than Amazonian Indians for example (who consume next to nothing). And if everyone in the world were to consume the same amount of resources and energy as the average US citizen, all the psychological problems linked to consumerism would count for nothing compared with the speed of global destruction.

However, no mechanism exists to equal things out in a way that values or protects the lives of Amazonians or their environment. So, while real living alternatives to consumerist culture still exist, they tend to be portrayed either as fringe elements or as lost and vulnerable communities that need to be rescued and set on the path towards the kind of 'freedoms' enjoyed by high-end consumers. Such alternatives are seen as losing what Western culture perceives as humanity's 'battle with nature', and the need to 'free society from nature', as if humans are not part of nature too.

The question is, how do we secure a good-enough life for all, in which 'no one is left behind', while still opposing the blind consumerism that capitalist accumulation requires and presupposes? According to Bonneuil and Fressoz (2015), no evidence exists of the West revising its basic ethical framework, and the alliance between behavioural psychologists and economists remains solid as they continue to seek ways of conquering nature for the sake of the 'free market'. As noted, in *The Shock of the Anthropocene*, Bonneuil and Fressos show that alternative voices have figured in history, but many alternative economic models were destroyed by imperialism that was, in turn, justified by science that kept itself 'above' popular knowledge.

> Economic growth and the social model of the Western industrial countries would have been impossible without this unequal exchange. Economists have recently shown that two–thirds of the growth of the Western industrial countries has been due simply to an increasing use of fossil fuel, with only one-third resulting from sociotechnical progress…The Great Acceleration thus corresponds to a capture by the Western industrial countries of the ecological surpluses of the Third World. (Bonneuil and Fressoz 2015: 249)

The other side of SDG 12 is responsible production. For this, we need to shift our focus onto the engineers, whose job is to innovate, and whose success is often measured by their ability to make production cheaper and more effective or create products that stimulate new consumption. SDG 9 (industry, innovation and infrastructure) also speaks directly to engineers.

Today, as in the early days of industrialisation, engineers are being touted as the creators of technological solutions to our biggest challenge: how to delink economic growth from unsustainable and polluting energy use. If this were possible, engineers would have an opportunity to stand out as the green profession par excellence, but are they willing to take this on? Engineers still seem to be playing an ideological role in the debate rather than putting forward any real and convincing solutions (Klein 2015). For example, global energy companies are applying pressure on governments to allow them to combine resources and begin mining the ocean floor to which the endless frontier of knowledge is now apparently obliged to contribute in order to secure further economic growth. Only the most sophisticated engineering knowledge can make mining in the deep-sea areas possible. Therefore, it is engineers who have to say no to the risks that this poses for the life in and of the ocean (see SDG 14: life under water). But will they, if strong economic actors see prospects for profit?

In the West, engineers have long been at the forefront of conquering nature, as if this was the real purpose of life. So far, the battle has been brutal and life threatening for most life forms on the planet. Financial capital sustains and promotes the most energy-consuming (and polluting) companies but without having to reflect on this because the abstraction known as 'shareholder value' is what counts. Despite their growing enthusiasm for alternative energy technologies, very few engineers raise their voices to reflect on the role of *real economics*, that is the real costs of what is produced as opposed to financial economics, which is about the circulation of money and credit.

Numerous attempts have been made to develop alternative technologies in parallel with the invention of fuel engines,[9] suburban urban planning with the associated household energy and transport needs, Fordist factory technologies, the arms industry, oil pipelines, and so on. Few have survived the logic of more convenience = bigger markets = larger profits. As big oil now prepares to industrialise the ocean floor, very few voices are heard speaking about the ethics of the SDGs. The idea that any production must first of all support social values related to reducing inequality within and between nations, ensuring that all citizens have an equitable influence on decision-making, enhancing gender equality, reducing or at least not increasing pollution levels, mitigating the impact of climate change (see SDG 16's sub-goals), seem to be absent from the discussion.

As early as 1921, Torstein Veblen saw the struggle within the engineering profession as crucial for democracy (1921/2012). Foremost among those who have spoken out since, is Jack Ellul (1964). Hannah Arendt and Herbert Marcuse are among many who have promoted his admittedly pessimistic ideas. Ellul wrote: 'In the modern world, the most dangerous form of determinism is the technological phenomenon. It is not a question of getting rid of it, but, by an act of freedom, of transcending it. How is this to be done? I do not yet know' (1964: xxxiii). Fifty years later, we are no wiser.

Bell (1973/1999), Habermas (1981) and Parsons (in his writing on professions – see Halvorsen 1992) tended to see engineers as a reflection of the technologies they created, leaving little room for ethical or environmental awareness, much less the courage to stand against the destruction wrought by capitalism and imperialism. Perhaps this occurred because alternative voices had so little space within the profession, but also because the profession gradually lost its independence within capitalist enterprises? In a book chapter titled 'Thanatocene power and ecocide', Bonneuil and Fressoz (2015) show how weak the engineering profession is if evaluated in terms of ethical values, and how alternative options have been repressed. They also highlight the roles of other professions in the technological complex, such as that played by geographers and environmental scientists during the Vietnam War.

Agriculture

Despite the agriculture industry's greater proximity to nature and clear awareness of environmental feedback, several parallels exist between it and the

in the oven, you could still be a birdwatcher. Not anymore. Not only is the decimation of the bird population likely to cause you alarm, but you have to link this insight to the general consequences of industrialisation, globalisation, and power dynamics that have made and continue to make genocide possible. Nazi scientists and engineers excused their own actions based on the neutrality of science and the political expectation of obedience (see Jarausch 1990).

A second ethical principle foregrounded by the SDGs debate is to think through the new kinds of knowledge we need about how humans and nature interact, and consider the implications of this for knowledge development. The professions themselves must be more alert to how the knowledge and assumptions embedded in existing practices predetermine the outcomes of this interaction. We must commit ourselves to acting more ethically towards both other humans and nature, the practicalities of which will come to the fore as professionals define and make plans to operationalise the 169 indicators embedded in the SDGs, and preferably in ways that allow for quantitative measurement.

Our societies are built around systems of classification, with indicators and evaluation measures. If the SDGs are to be taken seriously, dramatic reclassifications will be necessary. All academic fields will be affected. Some will probably resist. Those whose identity and prestige is bound up in disciplines as they are currently construed will be threatened. Nevertheless, the SDGS invite debate around this issue – debates that require academics not to remain specialists within established knowledge categories, but rather to dialogue across disciplines to capture a new human–nature paradigm.[12]

This implies the adoption of a third ethical principle related to achieving the SDGs; that is, to form an alliance with the universities to defend knowledge against political and economic actors who ask specialists to solve specific problems, but refuse to address the systemic causes of those problems. Psychologists might well be capable of helping each and every neurotic child, but it is important to question how their neuroses relate to our knowledge about other phenomena – such as how, in some parts of the world, humans have become totally alienated from nature, especially nature that is not 'pre-packaged' and 'consumable'.

This leads to the fourth ethical principle: to integrate knowledge development into processes that empower people, and thus contribute to building active democracy. At present, research councils, dominated by bureaucrats and budgets, act as a fortress against democratic influence other than as formally debated in parliament. If researchers are also to be committed to reproducing the social and environmental goals of the SDGs within all economic activities, they will require a much more vibrant and democratic process in relation to setting knowledge priorities. Here we need some reorganisation as a political tool to create a societal university as Honneth (2011) argued. For economists and accountants, who often perceive themselves as contributing only by managing the means of achieving given goals, this will be a big challenge. They have to see that the means that they present as neutral may in fact be contradictory to achieving the SDGs.[13]

But this is also a general point; professional associations, in alliance with the universities, have to be aware of the power of knowledge in times of critical transition like the one we are in now, and take responsibility not only for how knowledge is used (in relation to clients, for example), but also for preventing its misuse. The City of London should not be able to exist as a knowledge hub without being ethically embedded in better-intentioned tax policies, attempts to abolish tax-havens, the need to train financial experts and brokers to understand the consequences of continuing to invest in coal and oil, beyond widening their and their shareholders' profit margins.

Universities and the role of academics

The global challenges we all face also present challenges of global proportions to the universities. This is particularly so since the adoption of the 17 SDGs. Without university-based knowledge, the goals will not be achieved in time. In the debates that led up to the formulation of the SDGs, participants asked that the close relationship between knowledge and politics be acknowledged.[14] In other words, it is up to universities, the academic profession, and the professionals we train, to make ourselves heard by the political leaders in our countries. To use knowledge to influence how the different goals and sub-goals address and offer solutions to the global challenges we face is a task academics must be particularly concerned with.

As actors seeking to contribute to the implementation of the SDGs, the universities face challenges at all levels. From dealing with the politics of knowledge in international arenas to how we mediate knowledge within our own states, to changing how we teach, research and manage our own campuses sustainably.

The process of change has already begun: many universities and scholarly networks have created centres for global studies, focusing on the SDGs. Master's and doctoral students are being encouraged to submit research proposals related to the goals. Discussions are taking place about how to reform curriculum content and teaching practices to bring them more in line with the global challenges. There seems to be consensus that universities must take more responsibility for bringing different kinds of specialists and experts into contact with one another. The knowledge that evolves out of inter-disciplinary work, should – for the sake of *university-based* influence on the implementation of the SDGs – be at the centre of how universities promote themselves as actors for global change.

Another area of consensus is that the students, at their own insistence, should be more involved in both curriculum change and in building course content. Their engagement will be crucial. Such students will undoubtedly be sought after, particularly among firms that see they have to become more socially and environmentally responsible in line with the SDGs, and in line with the general argument that those who (previously) caused the most damage must now take the lead in making amends.

As a development strategy that takes global cultural variations seriously, the SDGs do seem to carry a new kind of authority and a much wider level of legitimacy. The OECD countries are no longer being held up as the model for development or providing a roadmap for modernisation. In fact, in the attempts to reach the SDG indicators, Norway scores badly in relation to energy and technology policies, while Malawi scores very well in terms of per capita energy consumption. The US, once seen as the epitome of modernity and development scores low in many of the SDG indicators, including, for example, on inequality, access to health and education, energy consumption and poverty levels (Sachs et al. 2016).

Perhaps the most important role for universities, both as separate institutions and in networks, is to contribute to affirming the global mandate of the SDGs and the moral commitment made by most nation states to implementing them. The SDGs offer universities and professional associations a new opportunity to develop knowledge and practices that support the idea of development only having value when it reduces social and economic inequality and is beneficial to the environment (or at least does no further harm). The universities also need to ask critical questions about the role of the SDGs – about the processes leading up to their formulation and about how their implementation will be measured? Methodological questions about how to measure achievements and progress will be crucial in relation to how we learn from new practices.

In addition, as argued above, more often than academics tend to do, we have to explore the consequences of the knowledge and the detailed data we produce, and take responsibility for this in terms of its ongoing impacts and effects. For example, the links between technological development and poverty, the industrialisation of agriculture and biodiversity loss, urbanisation and food insecurity, product development and energy consumption have to be made clearer, and conscious choices have to be made. All actors and stakeholders involved in research need to focus more on producing solid evidence-based knowledge while being explicit about the ethics and politics of this knowledge production. North–South knowledge networks offer unique opportunities for the revival of alternative forms and systems of knowledge that have the potential to change the way we understand how knowledge should be developed, and shared or not. In this respect, Susanna Koch and Peter Weingart (2016) have warned of 'the delusion of knowledge transfer'. They not only show how bad knowledge transferred via experts can be, but also what must be done to make the *co-creation* of knowledge possible. This co-creation of knowledge is what the implementation of the SDGs relies upon (see Halvorsen and Nossum 2016). It is also crucial if we are to achieve SDG 1 (no poverty), and meet the greatest social and political challenge of all: to transform the global economic system and secure better lives for everyone whose living conditions cannot now be described as good. This is our common challenge, both within countries where inequality is growing and between countries where power imbalances are growing faster than ever.

Fortunately, some of the world's best brains have started reflecting on these challenges. I will end by describing just one inspiring example: the work of Finnish philosopher Pekka Himanen who has collaborated with academics around the world, in particular from South Africa, to promote the concept of 'dignity as development'. Himanen argues that dignity is a globally valid value in a multicultural world, and one around which we can categorise, measure and evaluate what a 'good life' means. Using elaborate models, he developed alternatives to the standard models that measure 'gross domestic product' and economic growth. His model relies on and allows for human, environmental and economic sustainability. While using the tools of our information society to facilitate this shift in understanding, he suggests using a Dignity Index to measure progress (Himanen 2014). This focus on dignity is important because it offers an effective alternative to the OECD's destructive but massively hegemonic views on growth (so well described by Schmelzer 2016; see also Halvorsen 2012a, 2017). His work also opens up debates about broader understandings of knowledge, and the need to link what we call scientific knowledge to other forms of knowledge about living with nature.

As Bruno Latour (2013: 8) so succinctly said, 'Between modernizing and ecologizing, we have to choose.' Our challenge then is to develop the power of knowledge in relation to new ethical and social standards to which the academic communities are committed. The debate about the role of knowledge in relation to the SDGs is thus also a debate about this new and democratic kind of knowledge society that must urgently turn modernity to face ecology.

Notes

1 Stefan Collini, for example, observed that 'universities across the world in the early twenty-first century find themselves in a paradoxical position. Never before in human history have they been so numerous and so important, yet never before have they suffered from such a disabling lack of confidence and loss of identity. They receive more public money than they have ever done and yet they are more defensive about their public standing than they have ever been.' (2012: 3)

2 This is already taking effect at the level of policy change in many countries; Norway's 2017 White Paper is an interesting example of one government's response to the SDGs (see Government of Norway 2017).

3 See (UN 2016). In terms of academic networks taking up the SDGs, see for example, the Worldwide University Network (https://www.wun.ac.uk), which has prioritised the SDGs in networking activities and research collaborations; the same is true for the Southern African Nordic Centre (SANORD). The International Association of Universities held a conference in Thailand in October 2016 on how to support universities so that they align with the priorities of the SDGs. The UN's Sustainable Development Solutions Network (UNSDSN) also devotes most of its attention to its network of universities (see http://unsdsn.org).

4 This is a recurring topic for Habermas that is, in my view, best expressed in his work on university reforms, democracy, modernity and post-modernity, *Kleine Politische Schriften,* in which he confronted Daniel Bell among others; see 'Die Moderne, ein unvollendetes Project' in that collection (Habermas 1981).

5 For example, Hamilton (2013) argues that, in the Anthropocene era, the role of scientists is to guide society towards environmentally sustainable management, while Crutzen (2002: 23) affirmed that 'this will require appropriate human behaviour at all scales, and may well involve internationally accepted large-scale geo-engineering projects'.

6 As Mirowski put it, 'The market can dependably sanction success or failure of human endeavor because it is the Rock upon which the complex chaotic maelstrom dashes; the market is the zero point from which all motion and change is measured. The market itself is never chaotic; because it exists outside of time. The market must be generic and unwavering, because if it were completely embedded in historical time (like society, like nature), then it could in principle be just as clueless about the true telos of human striving as any deluded human being: in other words, it could get things wrong' (2013: 335).

7 Honneth himself seems to be in doubt about free-market idealism when he argues that 'Whereas eighty to hundred years ago, we could point to concrete events that demonstrated the class-specific selectivity of the state apparatus, today the bias of the state in favour of capitalist profit interests seems to be entirely hidden from public view, because the corresponding government measures are either not addressed in parliament at all or are justified with reference to *objective constraints*...The only way out of this

crisis of the democratic constitutional state would be to bundle public power or organizations, social movements, and civil associations in order to put coordinated and massive pressure on the parliamentary legislature, forcing it to take measures to ensure the social re-embedding of the capitalist market' (2011: 326, emphasis added). Since Honneth does little to highlight the ethical role of the academic profession, it must be said that the so-called 'objective constraints' he mentions are often the result of categories, standards, indices and types of qualifications set up and legitimised by a particular set of neo-liberal economists and accountants, whom Honneth describes as of the 'ordo-liberal' type.

8 The *Argentinian Independent* of 10 July 2009 quotes from Mariano Ben Plotkin's introduction to his book, *Freud in the Pampas*, as follows: 'One of the things that foreign visitors to any major city in Argentina find most surprising is the enormous presence of psychoanalysis in the urban culture. Anyone who questions the existence of the unconscious or of the Oedipus complex at a social gathering is made to feel as if he or she were denying the virginity of Mary before a synod of Catholic bishops.'

9 Rockefeller himself owned an electric car in about 1914, which can be seen at the house he lived in on the Hudson River in New York State.

10 The evidence of the harm done by such fertilizers is overwhelming, but only now that it is seen as a scarce resource, is its use declining (see GPRI 2010).

11 For example, Bonneuil and Fressoz explain how Emil Durkheim, one of the founders of the social sciences, helped to construct this break (2015: 31). With the exception of geography, almost all the research objectives of the social sciences were defined in ways that assiduously removed them from nature. Accordingly, social and cultural anthropology were separated from physical anthropology, creating a watertight division between society and the natural environment.

12 This issue is likely to dominate future debates about the SDGs. Its importance is already evident in French sociology. The work of Pierre Bourdieu (and particularly his 1984 book) is a common reference point. To me, Alain Desrosières' work, *The Politics of Large Numbers* (1998) is more significant, but see also Beckert and Musselin's 2013 text, which reflects the breadth of the French debate around categorisations, quantification and valuations. They write: 'The catégorie socio-professionelles in France have increasingly developed into a kind of statistical basic unit, categorizing French society according to socio-demographic variables... This also demonstrates the claim made by Durkheim and Mauss that classification system represents a whole by establishing the relationship between the parts of a social system. But contrary to Durkheim and Mauss, existing classification systems do not simply represent a social order, but also constitute it within the praxis of classification – a point made specially forcefully by Pierre Bourdieu (1972, 1977, 1990)' (Beckert and Musselin 2013: 7). In other words, as academics suggest new classifications and measurements for the sake of achieving the SDGs, they may also have to reclassify themselves and their own categories of knowledge. Of course, as those

of us working in the cross- and interdisciplinary space know too well, this is a dangerous process: in the existing paradigms, if you fall between categories you are lost.

13 For a more elaborate description of how the World Bank, and many international donor organisations, use the term 'technical expert' to hide the value orientations of their preferred brand of educational economists, see Koch and Weingart (2016).

14 Universities have not yet figured strongly as such. In the document that sets out the SDGs, *Transforming Our World: The 2030 Agenda for Sustainable Development* (UN 2015), universities are not mentioned. The United Nations mostly refers to the need for 'experts', but has appointed a team to follow the implementation of the goals, most of whom are university-based. Other references to university-based knowledge have however steadily increased. For example, the United Nations University, a global think tank and post-graduate teaching organisation headquartered in Japan that encompasses 13 research and training institutes and programmes in 12 countries across the world, notes that 'The SDGs will rely upon good scientific input in a number of different ways. Scientists were crucial in providing important inputs at the Rio+20 conference in 2012 and into the process at the Open Working Group meetings, which formed the content of the SDGs. However, the role of scientists and scientific communities does not end with these inputs. It will be necessary for these actors to help shape the SDGs at all levels, to integrate sustainability concerns into other decisions. Implementation, monitoring and reassessment of the SDGs will require continual engagement with science and scientific communities'. See their webpage at https://ias.unu.edu/en/events/archive/symposium/science-and-the-sustainable-development-goals.html#overview (accessed September 2017).

References

Beckert J and C Musselin (eds) (2013) *Constructing Quality. The Classification of Goods in Markets*. Oxford: Oxford University Press.

Bell D (1973/1999) *The Coming of Post-Industrial Society: A Venture in Social Forecasting*. New York: Basic.

Bonneuil C and J-B Fressoz (2015) *The Shock of the Anthropocene*. London: Verso.

Bordieu P (1984) *Distinction: A Social Critique of the Judgement of Taste*. Oxford: Routledge.

Brown W (2015) *Undoing the Demos: Neoliberalism's Stealth Revolution*. New York: Zone.

Collini S (2012) *What are Universities for?* London: Penguin.

Crutzen PJ (2002) 'Geology of mankind' *Nature* 415: 23.

Desrosières A (1998) *The Politics of Large Numbers: A History of Statistical Reasoning*. Cambridge, MA: Harvard University Press.

Ellul J (1964) *The Technological Society* (translated by John Wilkinson). New York: Knopf.

Fløgstad K (2016) *Etter i saumane: Kultur og politikk i arbeideklassens hundreår*. Oslo: Gyldendal.

Fourcade M (2009) *Economists and Societies*. Princeton, NJ: Princeton University Press.

Government of Norway (2017) 'Felles ansvar for felles fremtid. Bærekraftsmålene og norsk utviklingspolitikk' Meld St.24. 2016–2017 ('Common Responsibility for our Common Future' White Paper 24). Available online.

GPRI (Global Phosphorus Research Initiative) (2010) 'Statement on global phosphorus scarcity' Available online.

Habermas J (1981) *Kleine Politische Schriften, I–IV*. Frankfurt am Main: Suhrkamp.

Halvorsen T (1992) *Parsons on Professions. A Post-Postivist Debate*. AHS Series B, University of Bergen, Norway.

Halvorsen T (2012a) 'University transformations: A crisis for the social sciences and the humanities' in T Halvorsen and P Vale (eds), *One World Many Knowledges: Regional Experiences and Cross-regional Links in Higher Education*. Cape Town: SANORD and African Minds. Available online.

Halvorsen T (2012b) 'Academic co-operation in a bi-polar world: Where does SANORD fit in?' in T Halvorsen and P Vale (eds), *One World Many Knowledges: Regional Experiences and Cross-regional Links in Higher Education*. Cape Town: SANORD and African Minds. Available online.

Halvorsen T (2017) 'Breaking the bond between knowledge and democracy?' in *Kagisano 11: Constituting Higher Education*. Pretoria: Council on Higher Education.

Halvorsen T and J Nossum (2016) *North–South Knowledge Networks: Towards Equitable Collaboration Between Academics, Donors and Universities*. Cape Town: African Minds. Available online.

Hamilton C (2013) *Earthmasters: The Dawn of the Age of Climate Engineering*. New Haven: Yale University Press.

Himanen P (2014) 'Dignity as development' in M Castells and P Himanen (eds), *Reconceptualizing Development in the Global Information Age*. Oxford: Oxford University Press.

Honneth A (2011) *Freedom's Right: The Social Foundations of Democratic Life*. Cambridge: Polity.

ICSU and ISSC (International Council for Science and International Social Science Council) (2015) *Review of targets for sustainable development goals: The science perspective*. Paris: Available online.

Jarausch KH (1990) *The Unfree Professions: German Lawyers, Teachers, and Engineers, 1900–1950*. Oxford: Oxford University Press.

Klein N (2015) *This Changes Everything*. New York: Penguin.

Koch S and P Weingart (2016) *The Delusion of Knowledge Transfer: The Impact of Foreign Aid Experts on Policy-Making in South Africa and Tanzania*. Cape Town: African Minds.

Kocka J (1987) *Interdisiplinarität*. Franfurt am Main: Suhrkamp.

Kocka J (2016) *Capitalism. A Short History*. Princeton: Princeton University Press.

Latour B (2013) *An Inquiry into Modes of Existence: An Anthropology of the Moderns.* Cambridge, MA: Harvard University Press.

Leonard TC (2016) *Illiberal Reformers. Race, Eugenics and American Economics in the Progressive Era*. Princeton, NJ: Princeton University Press.

Merkel W (2014) 'Is capitalism compatible with democracy?' *Zeitschrift für Vergleichende Politikwissenschaft* 8: 109–128.

Mirowski P (2013) *Never Let a Serious Crisis go to Waste: How Neoliberalism Survived the Financial Meltdown*. London: Verso.

Sachs J, G Schmidt-Traub, C Kroll, D Durand-Dalacre and K Teksoz (2016) *SDG Index and Dashboards: Global Report*. New York: Bertelsmann Stiftung and Sustainable Development Solutions Network. Available online.

Schmelzer M (2016) *The Hegemony of Growth: The OECD and the Making of the Economic Growth Paradigm*. Cambridge: Cambridge University Press.

UN (United Nations) (2015) *Global Sustainable Development Report: 2015 Edition* (Advance unedited edition). New York. Available online.

UN (2016) 'Experts, eminent scientists to draft report on sustainable development ahead of global review set for 2019' Press release ENV/DEV/1770, 3 January 2017. Available online.

UNDP and UNRISD (United Nations Development Programme and United Nations Research Institute for Social Development) (2017) *Global Trends: Challenges and Opportunities in the Implementation of the Sustainable Development Goals*. New York and Geneva.

UNRISD (2016) *Policy Innovation for Transformative Change: Implementing the 2030 Agenda for Sustainable Development*. Geneva.

Veblen T (1921/2012) *The Engineers and the Price System*. Eastford, CT: Martino Fine Books.

Chapter 2

The Sustainable Development Goals, the Paris Agreement and the Addis Agenda: Neo-liberalism, unequal development and the rise of a new imperialism

Henri-Count Evans and Rosemary Musvipwa

HUMANITARIAN PROBLEMS AFFECTING THE PLANET are increasing, with the world's lower-income countries worst affected. This is often attributed to budgetary constraints and inadequate access to expertise and technology. More people are exposed to widespread poverty, disease (especially HIV/ Aids and malaria), war, terrorism and climate change (see UNDP 2017). Climate change has the potential to add immeasurably to these problems – sparking further mass displacements, resource wars within and between nations, and challenging human viability on earth in the medium to long term.

Climate change and related global humanitarian and environmental problems have brought nations together under the auspices of the United Nations to promote climate-change adaptation and mitigation measures long touted as 'sustainable development'. In 2015 and 2016, through the United Nations, most of the world's governments sought to address some of the factors causing climate change and poverty by adopting the Paris Agreement and the 2030 Agenda for Sustainable Development, also known as the Sustainable Development Goals (SDGs). However, these measures remain anchored in neo-liberal economic policies that entrench the capitalist interests of the North, which are set to benefit from renewable energy businesses and technology transfer; and neo-liberalism, rather than being a panacea to global inequality and disintegration, has, in fact, always promoted both (Beck 1992; Cabello 2009).

It is important to note that the United Nations is arguably the key driver of global initiatives on sustainable development. To assess their position on sustainable development and climate-change governance, we analyse three key documents in this chapter – the Paris Agreement, the Addis Ababa Action Agenda (the financial policy on which the SDGs are based) and the

SDGs themselves. All developed under the auspices of the United Nations, the three documents detail how the signatories to these United Nations documents seek to achieve sustainable development, reduce carbon emissions and introduce measures that help communities both adapt to and mitigate the effects of climate change.

Our analysis revealed that three key themes or assumptions underpin and inform these documents; namely that humanity should adopt neo-liberal market policies, carbon trading, and technology transfer as primary strategies in addressing the challenges we face. In this chapter, we tackle each of these themes, and show that, essentially, the United Nations plans to advance neo-liberal capitalist interests through establishing carbon trading, devolving state power to the private sector when it comes to climate mitigation and poverty reduction, and facilitating the transfer of renewable energy and other technologies from North to South. The three documents are likely to be central to the ways in which future discourse on climate change and sustainable development emerges. All three place economic growth and development above all else, thus subjecting both poverty reduction and climate change mitigation to the principles of profit-making, market forces and market growth. As a response to this, we then focus on the role that higher education institutions could play in defining and encouraging understandings of climate change responses and that focus less on the interests of global elites and more on sustainability.

Debates about the environment and the neo-liberal approach

The twenty-first century has been inundated with buzzwords and catchphrases such as 'sustainable development', 'the information society' and 'globalisation'. Debates about sustainable development are often linked to discourses around the need for education information and knowledge-sharing. Global problems related to poverty and climate change have brought certain countries together – around various 'sustainable development initiatives' – to attempt to address these challenges. However, the sustainability discourse remains entrenched within neo-liberal economic principles that favour global capitalism by attempting to expand business initiatives to the South and promote the maximisation of profits in anticipation of the famous 'trickle-down effect' (Beck 1992; Kumi et al. 2014). As Cabello (2009) argues, climate change is the result of the capitalist system that continues to rely on the use of fossil fuels, and embodies the unequal distribution of impact, historical responsibility as well as economic, political and social injustice. We contend that the sustainable development discourse, as it is currently unfolding, is embedded within a capitalist agenda that reinforces and recycles the theoretically bankrupt but still often used modernist theory of linear development (Garnham 1993).

Newell and Paterson (2010: 1) supported neo-liberal environmental policies, arguing that these would take the world into a new political and economic paradigm shaped by what they called 'climate capitalism'. They saw this as having the potential to decarbonise the earth's atmosphere *and* maintain capitalist economic growth. Böhm et al. (2012) questioned the discourse around sustainable development and the green economy, asking if it was indeed the best way to transform capitalism, address climate change or reduce emissions. As Böhm et al. pointed out, the discourse on sustainable development gained traction after 1987, with the publication of the Brundtland Commission's Report (titled *Our Common Future*). This was before the 1992 Earth Summit in Rio de Janeiro, at which environmentalists expected capitalist countries to endorse a radical transformation towards a truly environmental sustainability that would also correct the global imbalances between the West and the rest. Instead, the Rio summit further institutionalised neo-liberal approaches to development (Böhm et al. 2012).

Since then, the United Nations has continued to embrace neo-liberal responses to climate change. The 1997 Kyoto Protocol introduced carbon trading as a means of reducing carbon emissions and dealing with global warming. At the 2012 Rio+20 summit, the 2014 Conference of Parties (COP20) in Lima, and the Paris Summit (COP21) in 2015, the United Nations Conference on Environment and Development (UNCED) and its Framework Convention on Climate Change (UNFCCC) have continued to advance carbon market strategies. As Bachman (2004, cited in Böhm et al. 2012) asserted, these market-led strategies reveal the neo-colonial dimensions of the United Nations' climate-change framework. Similarly, Heartfield (2008) and Sullivan (2010) have shown how carbon markets are part of a broader set of 'green economy' discourses and practices, which facilitate profit accumulation through the capture and monetisation of ecosystems and environmental 'resources'.

The promotion of neo-liberal policies, such as the Kyoto Protocol's Clean Development Mechanism for carbon trading, has enabled many of the higher-income countries to shift climate-change solutions into the hands of private industrial capital, thus 'devolving power to global market forces and non-state actors – establishing the emissions trading scheme "carbon markets" as the most efficient way of dealing with environmental and climate change problems' (Cabello 2009: 192). In this way, free-market environmentalism has been touted as the cure for massive environmental devastation. Kumi et al. (2014: 540, citing Benhin and Barbier 2004) supported this argument, noting that 'socio-economic development and environmental problems in the developing countries have been left to free-market mechanisms such as marketisation, deregulation, privatisation and the commodification of common property resources such as land, forest resources, etc'.

Félix Guattari has described these responses to climate change as exploitative. Arguing that capitalism is never symbiotic and always parasitic in nature, he concluded that a 'capitalism that does not exploit resources – be they natural or human – is yet unthinkable' (Guattari 2000: 15). Guattari posited that little immediate action to address climate change would be taken, noting that 'political action is unlikely when the worst polluting nations continue to insist that 'emissions trading' occurs under free-market principles' (2000: 15).

Similarly, Rodrigues (2003, cited in Kumi et al. 2014: 540) criticised neo-liberal systems, such as limited state regulation and privatisation, because of the negative impacts they have on the environment and social development. Meanwhile, Kumi et al. went on to define neo-liberalism as an economic and political ideology that aims to subject social and ecological affairs to capitalist market dynamics (2014).

Neo-liberal economics emphasise the supremacy of market forces, that is market self-regulation and rampant commodification, subordinating of all forms of activity to the economic logic of profit and loss. As Chang (2002 cited in Kumi et al. 2014) noted, neo-liberalism renders governments incapable of providing price stability and more prone to manipulation, forcing them to give markets the autonomy to self-regulate and reducing the role of the state in economic affairs. Within the discourses around climate change and environmental sustainability, proponents of neo-liberalism seek a limitation on state interventions and the deregulation of environmental governance, arguing that carbon trading and the sale of renewable energy technologies will be enough to stabilise the atmosphere. As Harvey (2005) observed, however, far from promoting economic efficiency or environmental accountability, the neo-liberal agenda has become a vehicle for the expansion of monopolies, and the privatisation of environmental goods by global capital.

The Clean Development Mechanism

The Clean Development Mechanism (CDM) outlined in the Kyoto Protocol suggests that the developed countries offset their ongoing carbon emissions within a carbon market that allows the buying and selling of carbon credits. This allows such countries to exceed their emission targets but offset the excess by buying carbon credits from poorer countries. The scheme allows companies in the industrialised countries to buy carbon credits from so-called 'clean development' projects located in less industrialised countries (Böhm et al. 2012). Initially suggested by the Brazilian delegation to the Kyoto meeting, which proposed the principle the polluter pays, the CDM was endorsed by the 7 (G77+China), and even the United States delegation to Kyoto backed the idea (Böhm et al. 2012).

In fact, what countries like Brazil wanted was the establishment of a Clean Development Fund, which would ensure that the industrialised countries paid penalties for exceeding their targets, and that income collected would be used to finance clean energy projects as well as mitigation and adaptation measures in less industrialised countries (Böhm et al. 2012).

As Cabello (2009) observed, the idea of the fund was transformed into the CDM. Lohmann (2009a: 15) concurred, noting that 'fines were transformed into prices; a judicial system was transformed into a market'. Cabello (2009: 195) went on to explain that

> ongoing marketization and privatization of climate governance has turned the negotiations into structures for legitimized accumulation – with corporate powers at the heart of it – that sustain and increase old relations and imbalances and relations of power between rich and poor, North and South, as well as the idea of maintaining continuous business-as-usual growth on a finite planet.

Through the CDM, emission-reduction projects in lower-income countries can earn certified credits, each of which is equivalent to a ton of carbon dioxide (UNFCCC 2010). These certificates can be traded, and if bought by industrialised countries, they can be used to offset part of their emissions targets under the Kyoto Protocol. This enables industrialised countries to offset rather than reduce their emissions at source (Dale 2008).

As Böhm et al. (2012) argued, the concept of carbon markets is ideally meant to decarbonise and green the economy while creating minimal disruption to the global economic status quo. Carbon trading was designed to help industrialised countries decrease their carbon emissions, by capping permissible emissions levels, and creating incentives for companies and entire industries to meet their caps in the cleanest possible ways. Effectively, this allows big companies to buy their way out of some of the pollution problems they create. In addition, if they reduce their carbon emissions they can also sell carbon credits on the open market and generate profits (UNFCCC 2010).

Lohmann (2009b: 510) contended that, rather than reducing emissions, the carbon market is creating additional profit opportunities for a range of existing investment and infrastructure projects. Böhm et al. (2012) and Cabello (2009: 191) observed that through emissions trading, 'industrialised countries distributed their initial allocation of credits or "rights to pollute" to their dirtiest industries…as [if pollution were] a market commodity'. Cabello then went on to criticise the CDM and the carbon market as key vehicles in the expansion of capitalism, arguing that this expansion is twofold. First, the schemes allow for the creation of new financial markets, securing the conditions for accumulation and capital reproduction while allowing polluters to avoid paying the real costs associated with structural change. Second, the schemes legitimise and reinforce the commoditisation of nature and green capitalism.

Instead of working towards reducing emissions, the CDM actually subsidises polluting industries in lower-income countries. As Smith (2008) explained, 'CDM financing has entrenched dirty development [in the South] by acting as a financial subsidy for big power stations and pulp and paper mills' (Smith 2008: 2). The commoditisation of the environment through carbon trading and technology transfers thus enables the extension and expansion of capitalist businesses, furthers the subordination of less industrialised countries to the highly industrialised ones, and sustains global inequalities. As Cabello (2009: 196) concluded:

> Planting trees, fertilizing oceans, burning methane from landfills to generate electricity, or setting up wind farms cannot be verified to be climatically equivalent to reducing fossil fuel consumption. Moreover, since these offset projects…allow emissions somewhere else, then there is no reduction happening at the global scale. On the contrary, they are creating new credits for Emissions Trading schemes, underestimating the already inadequate caps established in the [Kyoto] Protocol. Northern polluters can continue to pollute, and even increase pollution legitimately, with the help of the carbon market without being concerned about abatement actions.

In addition, large-scale renewable-energy projects (wind farms, solar stations, dams, biofuel plantations etc.) require vast tracts of land that have the potential to trigger land-grabbing, migration to cities, human- and indigenous-rights violations, the repression of social movements etc. (Cabello 2009). A key priority for many countries is to attract foreign investment. To do so, they are often willing to approve CDM-related projects even though these might undermine strict sustainability requirements. In this way, 'the CDM is legitimizing a type of sustainability whose definition is not contested at the governance decision-making tables and whose legitimization is more important than even its attempt to accomplish it' (Cabello 2009: 197). Cabello went on to argue that sustainable development is a 'false notion' that assigns 'primacy to capital, depending on capital, and substituting nature as capital' (2009: 198).

The principles behind the CDM and Certified Emission Reduction Certificates ensure that industrialised countries are allowed to emit and 'pay for' increased emissions, not by paying any penalties but by extending their businesses into the less industrialised countries. While the industrialised countries that agreed to the Kyoto Protocol were expected to reduce their emissions by 5.2 per cent below the 1990 levels, emissions continue to increase. Carbon trading has thus proven ineffective.

While the less industrialised countries seek funding for renewable energy plants, multinational corporations and Northern governments continue to develop using fossil fuels, secure in the knowledge that they will be able to buy carbon credits on the international carbon market, thus sacrificing nature on the altar of capitalism.

An analysis of the United Nations documents

The three documents analysed adopt a neo-liberal approach to sustainable development, which they define as balancing the economic developmental needs of societies with their social and environmental capacity. All three documents define sustainable development as resting on three main pillars: economic, social and environmental. Our analysis is that the economic aspect is given priority while the other two components feature only so far as they serve the interests of the former; that is, environmental and social concerns are subordinated to the logic of capital accumulation. In our view, truly sustainable development has three components, social justice, economic development and environmental protection, but, as shown in this section, the dominant discourse on sustainable development, as reflected in these three documents, has always worked to maintain the global economic status quo. The language of free trade, market supremacy and liberalisation underpins the capitalist system, seeking to reinforce the hegemony of Northern governments and corporations while maintaining relations of dominance and dependency with the South.

The Paris Agreement

The Paris Agreement has been praised as a historic achievement in terms of global climate-change responses. The agreement has three key objectives: limiting greenhouse gas emissions to prevent further rise in the earth's surface temperature; escalating climate-change adaptation and resilience measures; and increasing financial flows towards renewable energy technologies for the achievement of sustainable development.

However, under the agreement, the reduction in greenhouse gas emissions depends on individual countries developing their own nationally determined contributions. Article 4 states that countries are to 'communicate their successive nationally determined contributions they intend to achieve' every five years and pursue 'domestic mitigation measures'. This means that although climate change is widely understood to be a global problem, the future of environmental and climate issues has been left in the hands of individual countries. The agreement makes no provision for an international mechanism that could force countries to cap their carbon emissions. With no internationally binding mechanism to regulate emissions and police what countries actually do, as opposed to what they *say* they *hope* to do, the Paris Agreement can be seen as a 'toothless bulldog' that has little chance of success, a loud-sounding nothing, and a compromise with zero potential to save the planet.

Previous approaches to limiting greenhouse gas emissions have focused on market-related mechanisms such as carbon trading, but these have been strongly criticised, especially by countries in the South. Negotiations towards the Paris Agreement were closely linked to this debate, and countries from the South sought to avoid leaving the issue of climate change in the hands of private capital from the North. Their arguments tended to be strongly ideological, citing the problems of neo-liberalism and imperialism. Consequently, the Paris Agreement makes no mention of carbon markets or emissions trading. As Andrei Marcu, an advisor to the Centre for European Policy Studies and a negotiator on behalf of Panama observed (2016), the omission of these words was not accidental, and they do not appear in the Kyoto Protocol either.

Marcu (2016: 4) points out that a reference to carbon markets in Article 6 would have been contentious because of the 'ideological opposition of some Parties to include any provision that referred to markets or could be seen as facilitating markets'. Language is important in discourse, as negotiators from the South no doubt argued. However, in this instance, language was used to pacify and placate, while the spirit and substance of the Paris Agreement remains focused on market mechanisms albeit without using the words.

Whereas under the Kyoto Protocol the CDM made provision for *regulated* carbon trading schemes, Article 6 of the Paris Agreement gives countries permission to trade in carbon units and simply report on this rather than also requiring certification from the United Nations Framework Convention on Climate Change (UNFCCC). That is, signatories to the Paris Agreement may choose to co-operate in the implementation of their nationally determined contributions on a voluntary basis. The first paragraph of Article 6 recognises that 'Parties choose to pursue voluntary cooperation in the implementation of their nationally determined contributions'. The second paragraph states that, 'Parties shall, where engaging on a voluntary basis in cooperative approaches that involve the use of internationally transferred mitigation outcomes towards nationally determined contributions, promote sustainable development and ensure environmental integrity and transparency'. No definitions are provided for the terms 'sustainable development', 'environmental integrity' or 'transparency'.

As Marcu noted, the term 'cooperative approaches' can be taken to mean that 'all types of cooperation are allowed' and 'the implication is that the formation of the so-called "clubs", including carbon market clubs, is possible under this paragraph' (Marcu 2016: 4). Marcu goes on to say that 'the genesis of the discussion reinforces the understanding that the concept of "clubs" is in no way discouraged by the Paris Agreement, but on the contrary, is very much part of its intellectual heritage' (2016: 4). Thus, the absence of references to markets in the agreement is textual only, and the ideology of the market system is enshrined in the agreement. It seems that negotiators from the South over-focused on semantic issues, rather than on the spirit of the agreement. The removal of text about markets was strategically useful for the finalisation of the agreement. As Marcu (2016: 5) observed, 'no direct reference to markets or mechanisms was seen as possible', and the phrase 'cooperative approaches' became a 'safety hook in case everything else failed'.

To replace references to markets, the phrase 'internationally transferred mitigation outcomes' (ITMOs) is used instead. According to Marcu, the phrase is a product of informal UNFCCC discussions dating back to 2014, and was formally accepted into the Paris Agreement because 'there was resistance from the developing countries to the use of the word "markets"… The term ITMO was introduced and became an undefined, but accepted term' (2016: 7).

In essence, Article 6 provides for the establishment of a mechanism to enhance climate change mitigation. In our view, the mechanism will simply develop and reinforce the principles of the CDM. Addressing the CDM's executive, Christiana Figueres, head of the UNFCCC, suggested the same thing, observing that establishing the new mitigation mechanism would not be difficult as people could be expected to build on the strengths of the CDM rather than starting from nowhere (UNFCCC 2016). In addition, Article 6 'provides the ability to create an international market if Parties agree' and this may well 'lead to the convergence of domestic carbon prices over time' (Marcu 2016: 6).

The Paris Agreement thus gives supremacy to market forces in achieving emissions reductions and climate change adaptation. The document is written in the capitalist language of carbon pricing which supports the primacy of the carbon market system as set out in the Kyoto Protocol. As noted, the carbon market system has done little to reduce greenhouse gas emissions but has rather enabled industrialised countries to offset their emissions targets through purchasing carbon credits and export their emissions to the South.

Although acknowledging that ideally governments (public funding) should be the main source of climate-change-related finance, the Paris Agreement still encourages governments to engage private capital in the financing of mitigation measures. For example, many countries have created incentives for the renewable energy sector 'to promote universal access to sustainable energy in developing countries, in particular Africa, through the enhanced deployment of renewable energy'. The agreement recognises 'the urgent need to enhance the provision of finance, technology and capacity-building support by developed country Parties, in a predictable manner, to enable enhanced pre-2020 action by developing country Parties' (UNFCCC 2015: 2).

Financing mechanisms: the Addis Agenda

The Addis Agenda bases its sustainability funding on private capital to ensure what it calls 'equitable development'. Investments in energy and clean-energy infrastructure are seen as key drivers of economic growth, and the document highlights the need to increase investments in green technologies with a view to achieving this: 'We will promote both public and private investment in energy infrastructure and clean energy technologies including carbon capture and storage technologies' (UN 2015a: Para. 49).

The Addis Agenda also emphasises the need to adopt neo-liberal principles in response to poverty and climate change, and seeks to unlock the 'transformative potential of people and the private sector, and incentivizing changes in financing as well as consumption and production patterns to support sustainable development' (Para. 5). Similarly, it recognises the use of market activities in relation to mitigation commitments. The Addis Agenda also attaches key importance to foreign direct investment (FDI) and argues that this is crucial to achieving a sustainable future:

> We recognize the important contribution that direct investment, including FDI, can make to sustainable development, particularly when projects are aligned with national and regional sustainable development strategies. Government policies can strengthen positive spill overs from FDI, such as know-how and technology, including through establishing linkages with domestic suppliers, as well as encouraging the integration of local enterprises...Internationally, we will support these efforts through financial and technical support and capacity-building, and closer

collaboration between home and host country agencies. We will consider the use of insurance, investment guarantees, including through MIGA [the World Bank's Multilateral Investment Guarantee Agency], and new financial instruments to incentivize FDI to developing countries. (Para. 45)

The Addis Agenda states that 'private investment' is key to infrastructure financing and proposes that international private capital should be combined with local public investment through 'tools and mechanisms such as public–private partnerships, blended finance, which combines concessional public finance with non-concessional private finance'. The document goes on to state its position on public–private partnerships, arguing that they 'serve to lower investment specific risks and incentivize additional private sector finance across key development sectors' (Para. 48).

In its support for private-sector-led development financing, the Addis Agenda argues that 'international trade is an engine for inclusive economic growth and poverty reduction, and contributes to the promotion of sustainable development' (Para.79). The document also states that signatories will seek to enable trade liberalisation and foster multilateral trading through the World Trade Organization.

The Sustainable Development Goals

The 2030 Agenda, which contains the SDGs, also stresses the importance of the private sector and international private capital in facilitating economic development as follows:

We acknowledge the role of the diverse private sector, ranging from micro-enterprises to cooperatives to multinationals...the mobilization of financial resources as well as capacity-building and the transfer of environmentally sound technologies to developing countries on favourable terms, including on concessional and preferential terms, as mutually agreed. (UN 2015b: Para. 41)

The agenda further recognises multinational corporations and financial institutions as central to achieving poverty reduction and climate-change mitigation. The agenda advocates for stronger international trade as this is viewed 'as an engine for development, debt and debt sustainability, addressing systemic issues and science, technology, innovation and capacity-building, and data, monitoring and follow-up' (Para. 62). The document also states that:

Private business activity, investment and innovation are major drivers of productivity, inclusive economic growth and job creation...We call on all businesses to apply their creativity and innovation to solving sustainable development challenges. (Para. 67)

In allocating such a central role to the private sector, not one of the documents analysed either questions or seeks to change the prevailing structural economic imbalances. In fact, while they might mark a strategic migration from coal-based capitalism to a form that promotes itself using the rhetoric of sustainable development, all three documents clearly perpetuate domination by the global elite. As noted, multinational companies stand to benefit from the sale of renewable-energy technologies. The dominance of private capital in green energy initiatives opens lower-income countries up to further manipulation and the extremes of structural adjustment policies. Meanwhile, so-called 'free-trade' agreements weaken their capacities to nurture their own economies, much less compete in the global economic sphere. Capitalism is exploitative and the movement towards a green form of capitalism will do little to help the already poor sections of the world. Instead it is likely to simply perpetuate their poverty through further exploitation, displacements and economic exclusion.

Technology transfer

All three documents discuss technology transfer and (without explaining how, of course) argue that this will see to economic transformation and a reduction in global greenhouse emissions. The SDGs seek to facilitate development through 'infrastructure development...enhanced financial, technological and technical support to African countries' (UN 2015b: SDG 9a). Similarly, the Paris Agreement also reinforces the United Nations' position on technology transfer stating that:

> Support, including financial support, shall be provided to developing country Parties for the implementation of this Article, including for strengthening cooperative action on technology development and transfer at different stages of the technology cycle, with a view to achieving a balance between support for mitigation and adaptation. (UNFCCC 2015: Article 10.6)

The Paris Agreement encourages countries to remove any barriers to the smooth transfer of technology and to accelerate technology development and transfer, again seeing the private sector as the vehicle through which maximum value from technological development and transfer can be achieved. The agreement envisages a 'technology framework' as providing 'overarching guidance for the work of the Technology Mechanism in promoting and facilitating enhanced action on technology development and transfer in order to support the implementation of this Agreement' (Article 10.4).

Likewise, the Addis Agenda encourages the 'creation, development and diffusion of new innovations and technologies and associated know-how, including the transfer of technology on mutually agreed terms,' describing these transfers as 'powerful drivers of economic growth and sustainable development' (UN 2015a: Para 114). As a way of achieving sustainable development, the Addis Agenda argues that parties to it 'will encourage the development, dissemination and diffusion and transfer of environmentally sound technologies to developing countries on favourable terms, including on concessional and preferential terms, as mutually agreed' (UN 2015a: Para 120). The SDGs echo this call for private-sector technology development and transfer, with signatories undertaking to,

> by 2030, enhance international cooperation to facilitate access to clean energy research and technology, including renewable energy, energy efficiency and advanced and cleaner fossil-fuel technology, and promote investment in energy infrastructure and clean energy technology. (Goal 7a)

The SDGs also seek to foster technologies that have the potential to widen access to information. Its signatories have agreed to 'significantly increase access to information and communications technology and strive to provide universal and affordable access to the Internet in least-developed countries by 2020' (Goal 9c) in order to 'enhance North–South, South–South and triangular regional and international cooperation on and access to science, technology and innovation' and 'enhance the use of enabling technology, in particular information and communications technology' (Goal 17.6).

Neo-liberalism and its non-solutions

While poverty alleviation as well as adaptation to and mitigation of climate change are crucial, it must be remembered that the environmental problems affecting the planet today are a product of capitalism's risk culture (Beck 1992). The three-poverty alleviation and climate-change response frameworks discussed simply promote the ideologies and interests of those countries most responsible for creating these problems in the first place. Any responses to poverty and environmental problems that hinge on further entrenching and spreading neo-liberal capitalism will surely deepen rather than close the global inequality gaps, and yet, the rhetoric of sustainability and global development so loved by the United Nations and the North seems set to dictate its agenda to the South once more.

As Beck (1992) argues, it is not possible to cure the planet using the same principles that are destroying it now. What is needed instead is a change in our understanding of the relationship between the economy and nature. Views that dominate in the contemporary era are based on principles that hold nature captive to shareholder profits, so much so that most multinational conglomerates and even governments in the North seem to see climate change less as a problem and more as another opportunity for profit making.

Bauman (1992) noted that, so far, all attempts at dealing with the risks created by industrial societies have produced further problems. Fighting against the risks of unrestrained business activity has itself become a 'major business, offering a new lease of life to scientific/technological dreams of unlimited expansions'. In the contemporary Western-dominated view, risk-fighting literally means business; and the bigger the risks, the more politicians seem to see business-led solutions as impressive and reassuring. Thus, the politics of fear lubricates the wheels of consumerism, and helps to 'keep the economy going', apparently steering countries away from the 'bane of recession'. Apparently ever more resources have to be consumed to repair the gruesome effects of yesterday's resource consumption. Individual fears, beefed up by exposure to the hazards created by yesterday's risks, are deployed in the service of collectively producing even higher risks for tomorrow (Bauman 1992).

Beck (1992) noted that environmental risks and hazards affect some communities more than others. As a result, 'social risk positions spring up' that mirror the inequalities of class and other social divisions. According to Beck (1992: 23), these have the potential to reinforce structural international inequalities, 'firstly between the Third World and the industrial states, secondly among the industrial states themselves'. He argued that the 'diffusion and commercialisation' of risks is entirely in line with the logic of capitalism.

Essentially, Beck showed that the environmental crisis not only follows the tenets of capitalism but strengthens them, with wealth accumulating at the top and risks at the bottom (or wealth at the centre and risk at the periphery). Samir Amin (1997) concurred with this view, and noted that capitalism is strengthened by the relaxation of economic policies linked to privatisation and the deregulation of markets. Such relaxation, Amin argued, enables the spread of multinational corporations across the world and sees them assuming an almost institutionalised character.

In elaborating on the contradictions within climate-change responses, Amin (1997) noted that an 'awareness' of environmental interdependence has become part and parcel of global politics but the principles of capital have not been of any use. The ideologies that have legitimised the uneven spread of control over the world's resources also spawned a linear model of economic development (Amin 1997). This same linearity is evident in the design of the UN's climate-change response mechanisms – only those approaches that favour the political and economic interests of the North are implemented.

Drawing on Amin's work, we suggest that the rhetoric around technology transfer should also be understood as emanating from the spirit and principles of neo-liberalism. We also agree with Boumashoul (2009: 73) who, grounding his stance in the Sartrean concept of 'bad faith', argued that 'technology is the pretext whereby capitalism extends its power over new territories'. With few exceptions, the flow of technologies has been linear (from North to South), primarily benefitting multinational companies whose profits flow steadily from South to North. Similarly, the global discourse on 'sustainable development' is not value-neutral but deeply embedded in the principles of neo-liberalism. The discourse is promoted, not to advance the livelihoods of the globally disadvantaged, but rather to create a new marketplace in which multinational corporations can sell their renewable energy and forecasting technologies to the South. The terms 'sustainable development' and 'technology transfer' are one-dimensional in that they both see 'development' from a Northern perspective.

Massive inequalities remain embedded in the production, distribution and consumption of these technologies. They are generally designed and produced in the North for consumption in the South. The technologies carry with them the ideologies and preferences of their producers. These include a preference for high-tech digital solutions that employ minimal amounts of local labour and require highly skilled (read Northern) experts to install and maintain. Built-in obsolescence means that new and costly installations need to be repurchased frequently thus ensuring an ongoing flow of profits to the manufacturers. Thus, the technologies transferred from the North are not value neutral but speak the same language of profit as their manufacturers. Amin (1997: 172) criticised their passive acceptance asking,

> Transfer of what? Transfer to whom? If it is a question of modern technologies, we will have to bear in mind that these are capitalist technologies, and that they are, moreover, controlled by monopolies. Hence, we will be transferring, at the same time as the technology itself, the underlying capitalist relations of production. Moreover, by this transfer we will not be escaping the domination of imperialist capitalism; rather on the contrary we will be extending its scope by integrating the periphery more firmly into the imperialist system.

Alhassan (2004: 98) concurred with Amin, noting that 'the new conjuncture of global digital capitalism has produced a new form of illusion that equates development with the connection of major postcolonial capitals to the global digital hub while their rural communities are left out.' Boumashoul noted that what he called the 'Internet Order' has created 'an urgent need' for the North to

> transfer more technology to the developing countries, for technology and information play a vital role in the new information order. The basic contributions of information are: first, the integration of the transnational corporate system, and second, the deepening of the 'dependency' of the peripheral world on hardware, software, training, management, administration, software, and maintenance which are mainly borrowed from the advanced post-industrial countries. (2009: 112)

In addition, Boumashoul (2009: 112) observed that the 'developed' countries 'provide the consumption patterns, technology, skills, capital etc. for the 'developing' countries, which then establish production facilities to serve the markets of the North'. This, he suggested, explains why the United Nations is so keen on technology transfer.

Higher education institutions and sustainable development

Debates pertaining to neo-liberal policies on climate change and poverty alleviation are often critical of the system, but fall short of providing answers about another way forward. We, too, do not offer a new alternative here. Rather, we attempt to highlight opportunities that are open to higher and tertiary education institutions to contribute to redefining sustainability that would benefit all, and help formulate effective climate-change mitigation and adaptation mechanisms that do not require subjecting nature to the logic of capitalist exploitation.

Our argument was shaped by relevant and critical discussions that occurred during the 2015 SANORD conference in Windhoek. Through several presentations, speakers noted the need to redefine knowledge and encourage the sharing of alternative knowledge practices. A call was made at the conference for a framework that views knowledge, not only from a 'formal' Northern perspective but shifts towards including the often undocumented but equally useful knowledge, including knowledge systems and practices, of the South. This line of thinking advances the notions of delinking and decoloniality advanced by Amin and Mignolo. As Amin said:

> The response to the challenge of our age that we propose is called 'delinking'. The concept is to some extent half of an equation: adjustment

or delinking!...In more precise terms, delinking is the refusal to submit to the demands of the worldview law of value, or the supposed 'rationality' of the system of world prices that embody the demands of reproduction of worldwide capital. It, therefore, presupposes the society's capacity to define for itself an alternative range of criteria of rationality of internal economic options, in short a 'law of value of national application'. (1990: 109–110)

Whereas Amin argued for delinking especially in terms of the economy, Mignolo was more interested in first delinking knowledge systems. He called for delinking 'that leads to decolonial epistemic shift and brings to the foreground other epistemologies, other principles of knowledge and understanding and, consequently, other economy, other politics, other ethics' (2007: 453). Mignolo also saw delinking as a 'move toward a geo- and body politics of knowledge that on the one hand denounces the pretended universality of a particular ethnicity (body politics), located in a specific part of the planet (geo-politics)...Delinking then shall be understood as a de-colonial epistemic shift leading to other-universality, that is, to pluri-versality' (2007: 453).

We see institutions of higher learning as having a leading role in delinking in two ways. First, by transforming knowledge systems or 'decolonising the mind' as Ngūgī wa Thiong'o famously put it. Second, by developing and formalising indigenous forms of knowledge so as to be able to share what we call 'alternative knowledge'. This transformation should not be undertaken as an add-on or an 'adjustment' to the knowledge practices of the North, but rather as a process of developing indigenous knowledge as a sufficient and viable form of knowledge in itself.

Such transformations would allow universities to develop and embrace locally developed technologies that respond to indigenous circumstances and are relevant to communities. There is a clear need for *local* research and technology development to be prioritised (through increased funding) in ways that free that higher education funding in the South from its dependence on Northern donors.

At the same time, however, epistemic delinking cannot be blind to the glaring need for global collaboration. For this reason, we see SANORD, and projects like it, as a great step towards co-operation and partnership based on the equal participation of southern African and northern European universities. Such platforms are excellent conduits for the formalisation as well as enhanced knowledge-sharing and dissemination of alternative knowledge.

In line with this, we note that, thus far, the sustainability discourse has largely expressed the economic language of neo-liberalism, subjecting developmental issues globally to the narrow issue of capital accumulation. The South, more generally, needs to consider delinking as a viable option, thereby subjecting not only the demands of global capital to local dynamics but also developing knowledge systems and technology infrastructures that have the potential to properly address poverty alleviation and climate change without further entrenching or deepening existing inequalities. Mignolo's (2007) concepts of other knowledge systems and pluriversality are useful here (see also Maistry and Eidsvik, this volume). To be effective, delinking must be pursued with a clear understanding of how capitalism exerts power via technology transfers as well as the flow of trade and information.

Conclusion

The humanitarian problems affecting the planet will increase exponentially as the effects of climate change compound poverty, diseases (such as HIV/Aids and malaria), conflict and terrorism. While climate change and related global environmental problems brought nations together to promote climate change adaptation and mitigation through 'sustainable development', the United Nations has sought to mainstream sustainability using neo-liberal market principles. Sustainable development and climate governance have been placed in the hands of the private sector, thus subordinating the social and environmental aspects of sustainability to the interests of private capital. As shown in this chapter, the three United Nations documents analysed all prioritise economic considerations and favour the concentration of climate adaptation and mitigation measures in the hands of global private capital.

Despite wild promises being made about how new technologies will solve humanity's problems, the flow of these technologies has largely been unidirectional (from North to South), with the key beneficiaries being multinational companies headquartered in the industrialised countries. The global discourse on 'sustainable development' is not value neutral but deeply embedded in the principles of old capitalism. Accordingly, while sustainable development is promoted as a means to advance the livelihoods of the disadvantaged populations worldwide, it is, in fact, being used to create a new marketplace in which multinational corporations can market and sell their renewable energy products and weather forecasting technologies to the entire planet.

We ended the chapter by highlighting the theory of delinking, and stressing the need for higher education institutions to pursue alternative knowledge systems and practices as a starting point for developing technologies that are relevant and responsive to local needs. The need for collaboration between and among universities remains key, and platforms like SANORD that have the potential to achieve international collaboration based on equal partnerships that exchange, share and disseminate all knowledge are crucial.

References

Alhassan A (2004) Development Communication Policy and Economic Fundamentalism in Ghana. Academic dissertation, University of Tampere, Finland. Available online.

Amin S (1990) *Delinking: Towards a Polycentric World*. London: Zed.

Amin S (1997) *Capitalism in the Age of Globalization: The Management of Contemporary Society*. London: Zed.

Bauman Z (1992) 'The solution as problem' *Times Higher Education Supplement*, 13 November, 1045: 25.

Beck U (1992) *Risk Society: Towards a New Modernity*. London: Sage.

Benhin JA and E Barbier (2004) 'Structural adjustment programme, deforestation and bio-diversity loss in Ghana' *Environmental and Resource Economics* 27: 337–366.

Böhm S, MC Misoczky and S Moog (2012) 'Greening capitalism? A Marxist critique of carbon markets' *Journal of Organisation Studies*, 33 (11): 1–22.

Boumashoul R (2009) Re-articulating Information Society Discourse(s): A Cultural Studies Approach to Postcolonial Locales. PhD thesis, University of Tampere, Finland.

Cabello J (2009) 'The politics of the Clean Development Mechanism: Hiding capitalism under the green rug' in S Böhm and S Dabhi (eds), *Upsetting the Offset: The Political Economy of Carbon Markets*. London: Mayfly. Available online.

Dale G (2008) '"Green shift": An analysis of corporate responses to climate change' *International Journal of Management Concepts and Philosophy* 3 (2): 134–155.

Garnham N (1993) 'The mass media, cultural identity, and the public sphere in the modern world' *Public Culture* 5: 251–265.

Guattari F (2000) *The Three Ecologies* (translated by Paul Sutton). London: Athlone.

Harvey D (2005) *The New Imperialism*. Oxford: Oxford University Press.

Heartfield J (2008) *Green Capitalism: Manufacturing Scarcity in an Age of Abundance*. London: Mute.

Kumi E, AA Arhin and T Yeboah (2014) 'Can post-2015 sustainable development goals survive neoliberalism? A critical examination of the sustainable development-neoliberalism nexus in developing countries' *Environment, Development and Sustainability* 16 (3): 539–554.

Lohmann L (2009a) 'Neoliberalism and the calculable world: The rise of carbon trading' in S Böhm and S Dabhi (eds), *Upsetting the Offset: The Political Economy of Carbon Markets*. London: Mayfly. Available online.

Lohmann L (2009b) 'Toward a different debate in environmental accounting: The cases of carbon and cost– benefit' *Accounting, Organizations and Society* 34: 499–534.

Marcu A (2016) *Carbon Market Provisions in the Paris Agreement (Article 6)*. CEPS Special Report No. 128. Centre for European Policy Studies, Brussels. Available online.

Mignolo WD (2007) 'Delinking' *Cultural Studies* 21 (2–3): 449–514. Available online.

Newell P and M Paterson (2010) *Climate Capitalism: Global Warming and the Transformation of the Global Economy*. Cambridge: Cambridge University Press.

Smith K (2008) 'Offset standard is off target' *Red Pepper*, April. Available online.

Sullivan S (2010) '"Ecosystem service commodities": A new imperial ecology? Implications for animist immanent ecologies with Deleuze and Guattari' *New Formations* 69: 111–128.

UN (United Nations) (2015a) *Addis Ababa Action Agenda* (Final text adopted at the Third International Conference on Financing for Development, Addis Ababa, 13–16 July, and endorsed by UN General Assembly Resolution 69/313 of 27 July) Available online.

UN (2015b) *Transforming our world: The 2030 agenda for sustainable development*. Resolution 70/1 adopted by the UN General Assembly, 25 September 2015. Available online.

UNDP (United Nations Development Programme) (2017) Human Development Report 2016: Human Development for Everyone. New York.

UNFCCC (United Nations Framework Convention on Climate Change) (2010) *About CDM*. Available online.

UNFCCC (2015) *Paris Agreement*. Adopted by consensus at the 21st Conference of the Parties of the UNFCCC, Paris, 21 December. Available online.

UNFCCC (2016) 'Lessons from the Clean Development Mechanism critical to implementation of Paris Agreement'. Online article, 13 May 2016. Available online.

Chapter 3

Academic freedom and its enemies: Lessons from Sweden

Jens Stilhoff Sörensen and Erik J Olsson

FOR SCIENTISTS AND RESEARCHERS TO FULFIL their purpose of understanding and explaining the world, they have to be free to work without concern for short-term political, ideological and economic interests. Situations in which political or economic interests dictate research priorities, findings or conclusions are not only contrary to the fundamental principles of science, but also to those of open and democratic societies. That such conditions lead to stagnation is one of the historical lessons to be learned from the Soviet Union, where scientists had to work under a state-imposed ideological straightjacket.

To prevent such conditions from arising again, organisations such as UNESCO and the Council of Europe have set down some basic recommendations with regard to governance of the higher education sector (see Council of Europe 2006; UNESCO 1997). Accordingly, member states and their universities committed themselves to upholding academic principles, including that universities should enjoy a high degree of autonomy and collegial governance. This is based on the idea that the science and research community is best placed to assess and determine: what constitutes good science; which researchers are best qualified and most suited for particular positions; which research questions are most pressing and prominent; which methodologies are most suited to exploring those questions, and so on. Besides the freedom of inquiry, academic freedom also includes freedom of speech, and the freedom to disseminate research findings, as well as institutional autonomy, collegial governance and security of tenure. In essence, academic freedom is both a vaccine against totalitarianism and unwarranted political influence; at the same time, it helps to guarantee the quality of educational provision and research practice.

While the struggle for academic freedom is undoubtedly linked to development and emancipation in lower-income countries and in authoritarian or semi-authoritarian states such as Turkey, it remains highly pertinent in the liberal democracies of Europe and North America. In fact, academic freedom is arguably under more pressure today than at any time in the last 150 years. Paradoxically, much of this pressure, and even direct threat, emanates from within the liberal democracies and is exerted precisely via their apparently liberal governing practices. Indeed, it can be argued that the current form of liberalism and its advocates constitute the major threat facing academic freedom and freedom of speech within the academy. In addition, forces across the political spectrum – that is, from both the left and the right, are behind this threat.[1] The academy – and especially the humanities and social sciences – has few friends these days.

In this chapter, we discuss major trends and threats facing academic freedom. While we are aware that these trends are applicable to many countries, we mainly cite empirical evidence from Sweden as the basis of our study because we both monitor and promote academic freedom through Sweden's Academic Rights Watch (ARW).[2] We begin by outlining the pressures exerted by neo-liberal ideology to create a research and education market, and show how this is the undercurrent steering specific reforms and policies that are both attacking academic freedom and undermining quality in education and research. We then identify and comment briefly on some of the reforms and changes that we see as the major threats to academic freedom, using some examples from ARW's detailed database of cases, rulings and policies. For reasons of space, we have limited ourselves to outlining the trends and threats and summarising their effects, and we refer readers to the ARW website and database for further documentation and richer analyses of cited cases and principles.[3]

The demise of academic freedom: major threats

The gradual demise of academic freedom in the West has been ongoing for some time and is related to the broader trend of neo-liberal influence on public policy and 'public management', as well as on reforms that have targeted the higher education and research sectors. Even a cursory glance reveals that academics are held captive by three major discourses. The first is the general trend of neo-liberal reforms implemented in the public sector since the early 1980s often labelled 'new public management' (NPM). This has been a major factor reshaping the governing mentality within the public sector, which has a direct and strong impact on universities. The second is the Bologna Process in Europe, which set out to streamline all fields of education and research using the natural and health sciences as models. The result has been the replacement of the ideals of the classical Western university and the notion of *Bildung* that have informed the liberal arts and humanities for centuries[4] with specific chunks of knowledge and packages of skills that are more measureable and interchangeable within what is conceptualised as a global education *market*. The third discourse includes a set of country-specific reforms related to university governance and higher education, which, as shown later in the chapter, are directly linked to neo-liberal ideology. In Sweden, the Autonomy Reform, implemented in 2011, is the primary document (Sveriges regering 2010); in Norway, for example, it is the University Reform, also effective from 2011.

New public management: neo-liberal ideology and the public sector

Christopher Hood (1991) coined the term 'new public management' to describe an array of reforms introduced across the public sectors in liberal democracies from the early 1980s. While individual reforms vary across countries and sectors, sometimes with contradictory effects, NPM can denote an underlying philosophy that aims to 'remake' public administration and the public sector 'in the image of the market' (see also Hood and Dixon 2015). As such, the reforms provide a recipe for a neo-liberal redesign of the public sector and a neo-liberal governing mechanism for those parts of the public sector that cannot be privatised. The whole NMP package is sometimes summed up with reference to the 'three M's': markets, managers and measures.

The idea is simple. The public sector produces services which are consumed by citizens and, in this sense, the public sector can be thought of as a producer and citizens as consumers. Although compelling, this conceptual shift away from a model of state and citizen to a market-based model brings with it new associations and a rationality shaped by market-led thinking that is fundamentally opposed to notions of public interest, shared goods and common property (or 'the commons'). The concepts of public interest and the public good have a long history in political thought, dating back to Aristotle, Thomas Aquinas and John Locke, but they have all fallen out of favour in recent decades (Bozeman 2007). This philosophical shift can, as Michael Sandel suggested, be conceptualised as a move away from a market *economy* and towards a market *society*. In the former, the state embraces a market economy but reserves important spheres for other forms of collective governance; in the latter, the principle of competition inherent in the market colonises all spheres of society (Sandel 2013).

The results and ramifications of NPM

With citizens construed as 'customers' or 'users' (the actual customer may be a municipal agency, etc. that provides services to 'users'), even the language we use reflects this market-based philosophy or ideology, signifying the break made with the classical model of public administration. The classical model was founded on rule-governance and public funding. Based on a conviction that the public sector had a special and unique role in serving citizens, and ultimately democracy, each service or agency received an estimated budget lump sum. This combination of a legislative foundation and public spending formed the very architecture of the democratic state, enabling it to be governed by its own principles and rationality that is quite different from those of the market (Lundquist 1998, 2012; see also Rothstein 2014).

A further result of NPM is that all public-sector activity must now be measurable in economic and numerical terms. To make this work, measurements have to be developed and introduced into all kinds of activities, and managers have to be employed to design these measures and then monitor progress made in relation to them. In general, this leads to an expansion rather than a reduction of the administrative sector.

A related problem is that measurements, evaluations and administrative controls tend to take precedence over professional assessments and judgements, with teachers, medical professionals, police officers and civil engineers often being discouraged from using their professional initiative. The need to tick boxes and fill in forms leads to both an increase in bureaucratic red tape and the de-professionalisation of individuals. To the extent that managers and administrators are, directly or indirectly, politically appointed, there is also more or less room for political goal scoring via the setting of specific targets within a variety of areas. For example, staff at a particular institution might be expected to achieve certain political goals while carrying out their tasks. These could include achieving 'gender parity' or quotas related to 'diversity' of staff, or the directing of an institutions' services at a particular demographic or geographical area. Certification relating to 'sustainability' or other forms of 'environmental certification' might be added to the existing work of hospitals, museums or universities. Paradoxically, even left-wing parties hail neo-liberal governance reform as an instrument to implement their own agendas through increased political control over academia. This paradoxical alignment of the new left identity politics and neo-liberalism is central to what Nancy Fraser has called 'progressive neo-liberalism' (see Fraser 2017). From a democratic perspective, the most problematic aspect of all this is that public institutions and agencies gradually begin to emulate private companies. This includes focusing on issues such as profitability and 'brand identity', while allowing these to form the rationales against which they develop and implement policy.

At a more specific level, an academic career in many countries now includes having to divide work time into detailed and continuously supervised points or hours that are pre-allocated to specific tasks such as teaching, student supervision, research, and so on. For academics in universities across Europe and many other parts of the world, this is a new and unwelcome feature of the scholarly life.

Possibly the most ominous shift attributable to NPM is the emergence of what can be called shadow management. On the one hand, the public sector is governed by laws and regulations, while, on the other hand, governments issue directives, often on an annual basis. (In Sweden, these annual directives are known as *Regleringsbrev* or letters of regulation.) During the twentieth century, the core legislation governing the public sector, such as administrative law, developed alongside the democratisation of the state. Across liberal states, in countries such as Sweden, such legislation emphasises values associated with the 'rational state model' as outlined by Max Weber. These include notions of equal opportunity and equal treatment, meritocracy, accountability and transparency. In Sweden, this rational model actually predates democratisation and wider popular participation, with meritocratic recruitment formalised in the 1809 Constitution. When NPM adds market values, such as competition, profit making and economic individualism into this context, the two value systems come into conflict with one another.

What happens when they clash? Where an NPM-inspired government directive clashes with the more traditional principles set out in a country's laws or its national constitution, the managers of public agencies have to choose whether to follow the old values (i.e. the law) or the new (i.e. the directive). If they follow the more traditional values, they risk being seen as obstructing government policy, which could have a negative effect on their careers. If they follow the NPM model, they risk violating state law and facing exposure by political rivals, whistle-blowers, lobby groups or the media.

In response to this dilemma, a third option has emerged. This involves removing sensitive issues from the usual formal channels and introducing a 'shadow management' process. By this we mean administrative practices that allow for issues that might be sensitive in relation to laws and regulations to be managed in parallel to the usual measures that ensure accountability but in ways that are neither transparent nor subject to the standard levels of scrutiny. This parallel structure or set of practices is rendered invisible to outsiders, and deals with all errands and projects that do not fit the relevant legal requirements, or which are in direct or possible violation of the law, especially constitutional and administrative law. By dealing with such cases internally, external auditors rarely become aware of them and the systems can operate without being subject to independent scrutiny. In this way, a range of informal practices, networks and routines are cultivated but not recorded or regulated; the public sector ceases to be transparent or to conform to the rule of law despite giving the outward impression that it is doing things 'by the book'.

In Sweden, all the major political parties represented in parliament have been enthusiastic proponents of NPM,[5] and Sweden ranks among the countries in which NPM reforms have been most diligently pursued (Hood and Dixon 2015). One aggressive advocate of NPM and the marketisation of Sweden's university and higher education sector is the neo-liberal lobby group Svenskt Näringsliv (the Confederation of Swedish Enterprises).

The Bologna Process

The Bologna Process is the label given to a series of reforms and initiatives to streamline course content and course credits and make them more transferrable between European universities and countries. Like NPM, the general idea appears sensible, in that it promises to promote student mobility and streamline qualifications. However, just like NPM, such streamlining has created major problems by forcing universities to squeeze many dimensions of their work that are specific and particular to education and its disciplines, into a model that does not fit all, or even most, course programmes. For example, the Bologna Process, and its policy on research, is modelled primarily on the natural and medical sciences. This is highly problematic for the humanities and many of the social sciences. The strong focus on instrumentality and measurable skills, as demonstrable via examination processes, has left little room for the encouragement of knowledge-seeking in its broader sense or for the humanist and classical ideal of higher education as *Bildung*.

Increasingly, the role of the university is being challenged by narrow and short-term political, economic and administrative interests typical of NPM. The free exploration and testing of ideas, and the open search for knowledge guided by professional teachers and researchers, is being replaced by chunks of predetermined and assessable 'skills' and 'competencies'. These are articulated as 'learning goals' and 'outcomes', which students are expected to attain so that they can be ticked off in a strictly behaviourist fashion. An integral part of the problem is the introduction of a continuous auditing process that uses these same preset criteria and thus encourages the de-professionalisation of academic staff. In the words of Inger Enkvist, a Spanish language professor who is highly critical of the demonstrable regress in the Swedish education sector, the system is now more concerned with economy and politics than the search for knowledge. For teachers and researchers, the changes are about bureaucratisation and control, and for students, they are about standardisation, learning through technology and declining standards of education. (Enkvist 2013, our translation)

The tragedy of the Bologna Process is that the result of European states coming together around a set of principles and reforms for the higher education and research sector turned out to have very little connection to the ideals of free enquiry, independent knowledge and *Bildung* that have shaped the idea of university education in Europe for the last two centuries. For those working in the humanities and the social sciences, these reforms have been particularly disruptive and troubling.

Autonomy reform: transforming university governance

In line with NPM's managerial philosophy, major reforms were introduced in Sweden and Norway in 2011, with classical forms of university governance being transformed to resemble those used in the private sector. Sweden's reform process has been instructive in terms of how immediately it acted against the core principles of academic freedom.

The central feature of the reform process is that university governing structures introduced a so-called 'line of command' that concentrates power in the hands of the (essentially politically) appointed vice-chancellor, who, in turn, appoints all deans and heads of departments. The principle of collegial governance – whereby faculty members elected the best person to lead a department, normally on a rotating basis, and the various disciplines elected the deans of their faculties – has either been completely abolished or reduced to a merely advisory role. In effect, Swedish universities are now governed much like its army.

In addition, university boards, as the top management structures in Swedish universities are called, are dominated by non-academics who are selected primarily to ensure the correct levels of political and private-sector representation. Ironically, the term given to Sweden's university reform directive was the Autonomy Reform, as if to denote an increased level of autonomy for universities, but this was pure spin doctoring. Its effect has been to consolidate the 'rule by rectorate' system while considerably decreasing academic freedom for university staff and students. Historically, similar university governance systems operated in the former Soviet Union, and in Germany between 1933 and 1945 where the so-called Führer principle came into effect (Seier 1964).

A further irony is that, in the private sector, this form of governance is being phased out of knowledge-driven organisations. The more prescient and cutting edge-companies, such as Google, are beginning to emulate the forms of academic governance practised at Stanford University in the US. According to Schmidt and Rosenberg (2017), Google's management team have realised that knowledge-driven enterprises require decentralised decision-making processes that enable professionals to play key roles in their respective fields.

The centralisation of research funding

In addition to exerting increased political control over the universities and utilising them to promote the interests of regional businesses and meet the needs of the job market, the Swedish government – like those of many other countries – has not only reduced the influence of academics within university governing bodies but also the autonomy they have in relation to their own research. Allocated research time and funding that used to be guaranteed as part of every academic appointment has been reduced at nearly every level – especially for lecturers, but also for professors. The expectations of academics to conduct research has not decreased, however, thus pressurising them to apply for external funding and research grants. Here, national research councils play a significant role, designing budgets for particular research areas or themes as selected by policy-makers. Just one effect of this is that researchers are spending much more of their limited time assessing research grants, and then writing grant proposals and research reports.

While it is difficult to calculate the waste of research time and energy this engenders, Agneta Stark, an economist and former vice-chancellor of Dalarna University in Sweden, made a rough assessment for the application year 2003. She estimated that the time and cost to Sweden alone was equivalent to 417 years and SEK230 million (equivalent to approximately US$34 million) (Stark 2004; see also Songur 2015). Given a decrease in the research projects actually funded, the relative costs may well have increased since then (Songur 2015).

While having less time and resources to direct towards research, academics are now expected to focus more on anticipating the assessments done by research councils, and be prepared to adapt or conform to whatever the councils might find attractive. Arguably, this promotes conformity over exploration and streamlining over diversity. In essence, the centralisation of funding, combined with the hollowing out of academics' research function is both a threat to academic freedom and, more generally, to the quality and diversity of research.

Algorithmification

Another threat to academic freedom is the general shift in how knowledge and knowledge production are viewed. Arguably, the focus on measurable and quantifiable results and outputs, as well as the bibliometric system, with its pressure to publish in peer-reviewed journals, rather than write monographs or contribute to edited volumes, is having a negative impact on academic freedom. While publishing in peer-reviewed journals is highly suited to the health and natural sciences, it is arguably less useful for disciplines such as history or literature. For the latter, the broad and deep reading, combined with extended reflection on a theme, that tends to be a signifier of quality is often more appropriately encompassed in a monograph or an edited collection. Thus, in a field such as literature, short articles on a single idea, in the style of one variable per article, can contribute to shallowness and cluttering of discourse.[6]

Further, the systems that are used to rank universities and journals, while driving quality in some respects, are creating a similar pressure towards conformity. A key challenge implicit in the focus on these measurable units is that the rankings can take on a life of their own. Rather than being seen as useful albeit limited indicators of quality, they are mistakenly viewed as defining it. The result is a kind of pseudo-quantification of qualitative values. Citation cartels, strategic referencing for political purposes and excessive self-citations are other distorting consequences of these systems.

Monitoring academic freedom in Sweden

In 2012, a group of Swedish academics formed Academic Rights Watch (ARW). By mid-2017, using UNESCO's (1997) recommendations for higher education as a 'gold standard', some 120 violations of academic freedom, involving most of the universities and higher education institutions in Sweden had been documented. In 2013 alone, 25 violations at 15 universities were documented. For example, several scholars have been dismissed or silenced after criticising university management. This violates Article 31 of UNESCO's recommendations, which states that 'higher education teaching personnel should have the right and opportunity…to criticize the functioning of higher education institutions, including their own' (UNESCO 1997). In addition, in contravention of Article 32 of the recommendations, several higher education institutions have reduced or abolished collegial governance. These violations have been consistently accompanied by a reduction in quality as evaluated by the Swedish Higher Education Authority and various international accreditation agencies.

ARW's findings are consistent with other studies conducted elsewhere in Europe. For example, a study by Terrence Karran (2009) found that compliance with UNESCO's recommendations is generally low in the EU, and particularly so in Sweden and the UK.

However, by 2016, the situation in both countries had deteriorated even further. In the perhaps largest comparative study of academic freedom in Europe to date, Karran et al. (2017) rated 28 countries according to 37 parameters. Sweden and the UK rank near the bottom along with Hungary, Malta, Denmark and the Netherlands. Several of the former communist countries including Bulgaria and Croatia are rated most highly, perhaps indicating that they have drawn some lessons from their authoritarian pasts. The 2017 study by Karran et al. confirms the trend evident in ARW's documented cases, and the European University Association (EUA) arrived at similar results in a study updated to 2016.[7] However, the EUA study assessed university autonomy in relation to organisational, financial, staffing and academic criteria. It does not include legal protection, collegial forms of governance or security of tenure for academic staff.

The character of violations

In ARW's documenting of cases since 2013, some clear trends have emerged. The most frequent violations of academic freedom relate to:

- Reprisals against staff and students who critique the university.
- Internal regulations that infringe academics' civil liberties or freedom of speech.
- Irregular recruitment and other discriminatory practices.
- A lack of institutional autonomy, collegiality (dismantled collegial governance) and transparency.

Cases of direct censorship have also occurred, including the removal of documents from databases and academics being pressured to present certain findings rather than others at conferences.[8] Almost all cases directly violate one or more Swedish laws, including the national constitution, as well as UNESCO's (1997) and the Council of Europe's (2006) recommendations.

While these violations and infringements have been fairly evenly distributed and continuous since monitoring began, some patterns have been identified. In 2013, the first full year of documentation, a malpractice evident in many cases was the introduction of restrictions on freedom of expression. It was common for university leaders to punish academics for any criticisms they raised against management, including when professors attempted to defend their research areas against cutbacks. Another common practice was the introduction of communication policies at various universities; 10 out of 18 of these policies violated the Swedish constitution. The silencing of critics and the enforcing of communication regulations have since continued, with little or no judicial intervention, even though complaints were filed with the Chancellor of Justice.[9]

Another trend that emerged after the Autonomy Reform took effect in 2011, was the rapid dismantling of collegial governance across most universities. By 2014, two kinds of violations were common to many of the cases documented by ARW. The first is that internal policies (or guidelines) violate freedom of speech and the second is a form of discrimination directed against male academics.[10] The latter involves particular regulations and restrictions that effectively block the careers of male academics with the expressed purpose of favouring female academics. This violates Swedish law, yet it remains a common practice. This is in fact in line with NPM which, as we noted, leads to increased political control through a line-of-command style governance in combination with the political appointments of vice chancellors. NPM facilitates the flourishing of short-term political interests, whether these originate from the left or the right.

In 2017, clear cases of recruitment and employment on essentially political and ideological grounds were documented, at both Stockholm University and Stockholm University of the Arts.

Through reprisals, declining collegiality, discriminatory employment practices, silencing, and censorship, a strong trend that threatens academic freedom and university autonomy has become established in Sweden.

Conclusion

Academic freedom and university autonomy are in as dire a state in Sweden as they are in many other European countries that have long been perceived as core liberal democracies. The major threat is marketisation and its neo-liberal governing philosophy that has become hegemonic in many European governments, institutions and mainstream political parties. The liberal values that once lay at the core of the concept of academic freedom are now being threatened by liberalism itself. In terms of policy, this ideology is expressed in the wide array of public sector reforms subsumable under the NPM label. In Sweden, as elsewhere, heavy lobbying from private enterprises and professional bodies is a major driver of these reforms.

The undermining of academic freedom is clear and well-documented. Freedom of expression, probably the most fundamental aspect of academic freedom, is directly threatened as retaliation against internal critics becomes commonplace, and locally formulated codes of conduct are introduced to regulate and restrict communication. Diminished or dismantled collegial governance, and increasing line-of-command-type management, is widening the gap between core academic activities and the work of managerial leaders who are appointed rather than elected. Lack of transparency, discriminatory recruitment and employment practices, other forms of discrimination or promotion based on political and ideological grounds, and sometimes direct censorship, are well-documented. Although many of the principles of academic freedom are protected in fundamental Swedish and European law, these are often contravened while a form of shadow management gives the impression that all laws are being scrupulously followed. In addition, Sweden is blatantly violating the recommendations issued by both UNESCO and the Council of Europe, while auditing institutions, such as the Swedish Chancellor of Justice, are largely failing to exercise effective control and act as a corrective force.

Amid these trends, academics must stand together to defend the fundamental conditions of our working environment that are essential to our professional activity and to the survival of an open and democratic society. We must combine our efforts and energies to promote open and creative universities, where independent and critical intellectuals are seen not as a threat to universities freely invented 'brands', but treasured and rewarded for their ability to ensure quality in intellectual inquiry and the democratic function of higher education.

Notes

1   It may seem paradoxical, but both the Social Democrats and the Green Left have embraced new public management (NPM) in the public sector as it provides direct instruments and space for policy development on a range of identity-related political programmes that these groups wish to pursue. Moreover, in Sweden, many neo-liberal reforms were first introduced by the Social Democrats, unlike in Britain, for example, where they were implemented by the Conservative Party under Margaret Thatcher.

2   For similar problems in Europe more generally see Karran et al (2017); for the United States, see, for example, Mirowski (2011).

3   The url is www.academicrightswatch.se; note that most of the detailed documentation is in Swedish.

4   For more on the concept of *Bildung* and its influence in European and North American educational traditions, see Horlacher (2015), Luth (1998), Wulf (2003) and Humboldt (1792/2000).

5   At the time of writing, in mid-2017, this comprised four opposition parties in a centre-conservative alliance, and a ruling coalition made up of the Social Democrats and the Green Party. The, hitherto marginalised, Sweden Democrats have been critical of NPM.

6   Inger Enkvist, pers. com, Lund University, 26 June 2017.
7   The EUA's 2016 ranking of university autonomy is available at http://www.
    university-autonomy.eu/ (accessed 8 August 2017).
8   See the case at the Swedish University of Agricultural Science (SLU), published
    on the ARW database on 1 July 2013 and on the SLU website on 7 Feb 2015.
9   See, for example, the Chancellor of Justice's decision regarding Uppsala
    University, documented on the ARW website on 31 July 2017: 'Justitiekanslerns
    beslut i Haverling-affären: chefer vid Uppsala universitet missförstod
    yttrandefriheten'. Other cases involving the Chancellor of Justice are
    documented on the ARW website.
10 For an overview of cases in 2014, see the ARW's 2014 annual report,
    Årsberättelse 2014 (ARW 2014).

References

ARW (Academic Rights Watch) (2013) *Academic Freedom in Sweden, Annual Report
    2013*. Available online.

ARW (2014) *Årsberättelse 2014*. Available online.

Bozeman B (2007) *Public Values and Public Interest: Counterbalancing Economic
    Individualism*. Washington, DC: Georgetown University Press.

Council of Europe (2006) *Recommendations on Academic Freedom and University
    Autonomy*, Document 10943. Available online.

Enkvist I (2013) 'Moralisk förvirring på universiteten' *Svenska Dagbladet* 27 August.

Fraser N (2017) 'The end of progressive neoliberalism' *Dissent* 2 January 2017.
    Available online.

Hood C (1991) 'A public management for all seasons' *Public Administration* 69 (2):
    3–19.

Hood C and R. Dixon (2015) *A Government that Worked Better and Costed Less?*
    Oxford: Oxford University Press.

Horlacher R (2015) *The Educated Subject and the German Concept of Bildung: A
    Comparative Cultural History*. London: Routledge.

Humboldt WV (1792/2000) 'Theory of Bildung' in I Westbury, S Hopmann and
    K Riquarts (eds), *Teaching as Reflective Practice: The German Didaktik Tradition*.
    Mahwah: Lawrence Erlbaum.

Karran T (2009) 'Academic freedom in Europe: Reviewing UNESCO's
    recommendation', *British Journal of Educational Studies* 57 (2): 191–215.

Karran T, K Beiter and K Appiagyei-Atua (2017) 'Measuring academic freedom in
    Europe: A criterion referenced approach' *Policy Reviews in Higher Education*
    1 (2): 209–239.

Lundquist L (1998) *Demokratins Väktare: Ämbetsmännen och vårt offentliga etos*. Lund:
    Studentlitteratur.

Lundquist L (2012) *Slutet på Yttrandefriheten (och demokratin?)*. Lund:
    Studentlitteratur.

Luth C (1998) 'On Wilhelm von Humboldt's theory of Bildung (Dedicated to Wolfgang Klafki for his 70th Birthday)' *Journal of Curriculum Studies* 30 (1): 43–60.

Mirowski P (2011) *Science-Mart: Privatizing American Science.* Harvard University Press.

Rothstein B (2014) Politik som Organisation: Förvaltningspolitikens grundproblem. Lund: Studentlitteratur.

Sandel M (2013) *What Money Can't Buy: The Moral Limits of Markets.* Farrar: Strauss and Giroux.

Schmidt E and J Rosenberg (2017) *How Google Works.* New York: Grand Central.

Seier H (1964) 'Der Rektor als Führer. Zur Hochschulpolitik der Reichserziehungsministeriums 1934–1945', *Vierteljahrshefte für Zeitgeschichte* 12 (2) 105–146.

Songur W (2015) 'Lägg ner Vetenskapsrådet' (Close the research council), *Universitetsläraren,* 24 April, Swedish Association of University Teachers and Researchers (SULF).

Stark A (2004) Debatt (otherwise untitled), *Universitetsläraren,* 16 December 2004, SULF.

Sveriges regering (2009) En akademi i tiden - ökad frihet för universitet och högskolor. (Autonomy reform policy) Regeringens proposition 2009/10:149, Stockholm. Available online.

UNESCO (1997) *Recommendation Concerning the Status of Higher Education Teaching Personnel,* 11 November. Available online.

Wulf C (2003) 'Perfecting the individual: Wilhelm von Humboldt's concept of anthropology, Bildung, and Mimesis' *Educational Philosophy and Theory* 35 (2) 241–249.

Chapter 4

New public management as a mechanism
of accumulation by dispossession: The case of a public
bulk water provider in South Africa

Carina van Rooyen

SINCE THE 1980S, mainly due to perceptions of state failures, economic crises and fiscal deficits, we have seen changes in the role of the state in many societies. Both the welfare state and the traditional Weberian model of bureaucracy have been the focus of such changes (Batley and Larbi 2004). In the initial phase, or first-generation reforms of rolling-back the state (Peck and Tickell 2002), the reforms included liberalisation, 'deregulation' and privatisation, and, in the later phase, since the 1990s, it involved state re-regulation (Brenner and Theodore 2007; Peck and Tickell 2002) through the introduction of measures such as private-sector management approaches, cost-recovery, efficiency and public–private partnerships (PPPs) (Batley and Larbi 2004). Nickson (2006: 82) has described these second-generation state reforms as focused on the four E's: effectiveness, economic efficiency, equity, and an enabling environment for private-sector development. These do not involve a diminished role for the state as much as a new role in terms of *what* the state does and *how* it does it (Batley and Larbi 2004: 2) – what Bakker (2003) has called re-regulation.

The increased use of private-sector principles and the actual participation of the private-sector in what is 'public' have meant that the boundaries between private and public-sector domains have become somewhat blurred, although distinctions remain (Larbi 2006). Various structural, organisational and managerial changes in the public sector – with national and sectoral differences – have become 'necessary', including the separation of policy making and management functions, the corporatisation of public utilities, the ring-fencing of so-called non-core activities, the outsourcing of non-core services, the introduction of an 'entrepreneurial ethos', etc. (Batley and Larbi 2004). The notion of new public management (NPM) has come to capture much of this shift from government to governance, in which – in the language of the post-Washington Consensus – 'getting institutions right' is obligatory.

In the last few years, however, NPM's hegemony has weakened somewhat, especially in developing countries, through anomalies and paradoxes between theory and practice (Brinkerhoff and Brinkerhoff 2015). Nevertheless, it continues, albeit in new, less one-size-fits-all forms. The tinkering, tweaking, sedimentation and layering of so-called post-NPM goes by an array of names, such as new public governance, joined-up government, network governance or strategic government (Brinkerhoff and Brinkerhoff 2015). However, I concur with Lodge and Gill (2011: 141) who refer to 'the myth of post-NPM' and argue that there is no evidence that post-NPM entails any significant shift away from NPM.

In this chapter, I consider the implementation of NPM within a particular public institution in South Africa (Rand Water), to show why moving 'beyond NPM' is necessary. My research question is: how has NPM been implemented in Rand Water, and what can we learn from this about the nature of 'publicness'? I show how NPM acts as a mechanism for David Harvey's notion of 'accumulation by dispossession', so that through NPM, private-sector interests penetrate and commodify the state and its services (Bakker and Hemson 2000: 10). Consequent changes to the nature of publicness, and the tensions created when public services providers act like private-sector actors hint at what the key foundations for 'beyond NPM' could be.

I draw on data gathered during nine months of fieldwork conducted in 2005 and 2006 at Rand Water. In addition to reading various Rand Water documents, I conducted in-depth formal interviews with senior managers of Rand Water on changes in the organisation since 1994, and had many informal discussions with middle-range managers within Rand Water on this topic. I also conducted formal interviews with local government officials responsible for water services who regularly interacted with Rand Water. Various informal discussions took place with other local government officials and councillors at monthly Water Services Forums arranged by Rand Water. All these interviews and discussions were conducted on condition of anonymity, and I thus use pseudonyms when referring to individuals I interviewed.

In the sections that follow, I first indicate two broad strands of NPM and then turn to the case of Rand Water to show how NPM-type reforms were implemented. I draw on Harvey's (2003, 2004) notion of 'accumulation by dispossession' to argue that NPM acts as a mechanism to enhance accumulation by dispossession. I conclude the chapter with a look at what publicness 'beyond NPM' could possibly mean, given the case of Rand Water.

New public management

In the 1980s to early 1990s, NPM came to the fore, especially in the United Kingdom, New Zealand and Australia, as an approach to public-sector reform (Larbi 1999; Pollitt and Bouckaert 2004; Uneca 2003). It replaced 'public administration', with its hierarchies in a unified bureaucracy, as a form of public governance. Pollitt (in Larbi 1999: 12) defined NPM as a vision, an ideology or a bundle of managerial approaches and techniques imported from the private sector for application in the public sector. NPM approaches advocate a variety of structural, organisational and managerial reforms in the public sector that mirror critical aspects of private for-profit sector modes. The belief is that by cutting costs, efficiency can be enhanced, government's response to public concerns improved, and better quality and cheaper services provided (Uneca 2003).

NPM then provides room for actors other than government to provide public services. However, when other actors become involved, partnerships and relational contracting are expected. These then require the state to play an active role in selective deregulation and re-regulation to create a 'competitive' environment for service delivery (Bakker 2003; McDonald and Ruiters 2005b). As a result, private interests penetrate right into the heart of state bureaucracy (Bakker and Hemson 2000: 10). Much more than a set of new techniques, NPM is about values, and specifically the values of market economics instead of democratic governance (Stoker in Ewalt 2001: 8).

While generic elements exist, this does not mean that there is convergence in how NPM is practised globally. Rather, NPM is implemented in different ways in different states and sectors for diverse reasons and with a variety of impacts (Haque 2007: 181; Larbi 2006: 26). As Manning (2001: 298) puts it, NPM offers 'a menu of choices, rather than a single option'. For the purposes of this chapter, I discuss two broad 'but not mutually exclusive strands' of NPM: one focuses on horizontal managerial improvement and organisational restructuring, and the other on techniques and practices that give prominence to markets and competition in vertical restructuring (Batley and Larbi 2004; Larbi 1999).

Managerial and organisational restructuring

Managerial restructuring includes: a focus on organisational and managerial performance; decentralising the management of public services through devolving financial and human resources management; the professionalisation of staff and more entrepreneurial styles of performance; and the development of new forms of corporate governance (or 'a board of directors' model) for the public sector (Batley and Larbi 2004: 15, 41, 46; Osborne and Gaebler 1992). Bangura and Larbi (2006: 8) found decentralised management to be a key trend in NPM reforms in lower-income countries. They noted that this could take various organisational forms including unbundling, downsizing, corporatisation, and the formation of arm's-length executive agencies (see also Larbi 1999: 17–21). Given the corporatisation that happened at Rand Water, I briefly discuss this type of decentralised management in the public sector.

Corporatisation is a process of *institutional* change whereby management institutions (that is, rules, norms and customs) change to allow for the introduction of commercial principles (such as full cost-recovery and competition), commercial methods (such as cost-benefit analysis, ring-fencing and performance contracts) and commercial objectives (such as achieving short-term financial bottom-lines and profit-making) (Bakker 2007; McDonald and Ruiters 2005b). As McDonald and Ruiters (2005a) explain, corporatisation is about running a public service like a business, without necessarily involving any private-sector actors. To enable corporatisation to take place, a re-regulation of public services has to occur through two organisational shifts, namely financial ring-fencing and managerial ring-fencing (McDonald and Ruiters 2006; Smith 2005).

Financial ring-fencing involves a process of separating all resources *directly* involved in the delivery of a service from all other service functions (McDonald and Ruiters 2006: 12). Ultimately it means that a department making use of a shared resource within a public entity (such as information technology) has to pay the unit providing that resource a full-cost fee for access to that resource. The aim of such financial ring-fencing is to clearly identify all costs and revenues related to the delivery of a specific service to allow managers to identify areas of financial loss/gain (McDonald 2002: 3; McDonald and Ruiters 2005b: 18).

Managerial ring-fencing ensures that these separate business units and entities are managed by appointed officials who work at arm's length from the public authority (McDonald and Ruiters 2006: 12). While elected officials still set service delivery goals and standards, and monitor and evaluate these, day-to-day management and long-term planning is left to the management of the ring-fenced entity (McDonald 2002: 3; McDonald and Ruiters 2005b: 18). This entity has a separate legal status from other public service providers, and its corporate structure mimics that of private-sector companies (McDonald 2014: 1). Further, corporatisation fundamentally alters the underlying managerial ethos of services provision by ensuring that a private-sector ethos is internalised within the public sector (Smith 2005: 168). When economic maximisation (meaning efficiency) becomes the goal, social and political values such as equity, social justice, subsidisation, universal access, integrated and long-term planning, and democracy tend to receive less attention; service delivery becomes increasingly technocratic (McDonald and Ruiters 2005a: 3, 2005b: 17).

Mechanisms for markets and competition

The second broad strand of NPM, closely related to the first, is the introduction of mechanisms for markets and competition in the public sector, supposedly to ensure more 'choice' and 'voice' to users, and to promote efficiency and value-for-money in public service delivery (1999: 16, 2006: 30). The argument is that replacing the hierarchy of the 'old' public administration with markets and contractual relationships (Haque 2007: 180) will help to minimise so-called dysfunctions (Batley and Larbi 2004: 40). Thus, the goal of introducing these mechanisms is to improve efficiency (Uneca 2003: 7), and not to improve services or equity per se (Taylor 2002: 115), although the belief is that improved efficiency will lead to improved services.

Markets and quasi-markets can be introduced in various ways. First, to create markets in the public sector requires a separation of policy from operation, meaning ring-fencing, as discussed above. Then market-type mechanisms can include: contracting out services and other forms of private-sector participation (such as PPPs); the introduction of user charges for public services; an increasing focus on 'the customer'; an emphasis on quality; the widespread use of contracts or contract-like relationships; and performance-based management and benchmarking (Batley and Larbi 2004: 44–49; McDonald 2014: 11).

I now provide some brief background on Rand Water, before illustrating how, in the case of this public utility, NPM became a mechanism for accumulation by dispossession.

Background on Rand Water

Rand Water is the oldest public utility, and the first water board (a bulk potable water provider), in South Africa, having been formed in May 1903 when the state took over private concessions to provide water to Johannesburg and the Witwatersrand area (Rand Water Board 1978). Today Rand Water is the biggest water board in South Africa, providing 62 per cent of all bulk water in the country (Diedricks 2015), and the largest public water utility in Africa (Rand Water 2006: 4). Over the years, it has expanded its area of supply to 18 000 km², covering an area that produces more than 40 per cent of South Africa's gross domestic product (Rand Water 2016: 187).

Rand Water's primary function is the abstraction, purification and distribution of bulk potable water. For abstraction, Rand Water withdraws 99 per cent of the raw water it uses from the Vaal Dam (some 70 km away from its headquarters) (Rand Water 2005a: 15). The water is then elevated by about 380 metres as it is sent to two purification stations. Once treated, water is pumped to four booster stations at a head of about 190 metres above the Vaal River, creating high pumping costs. From the booster stations, 90 per cent of the water is elevated a further 200 metres to 58 reservoirs through a network of 3 500 km of large diameter pipelines (Rand Water 2016: 82). A further 13 tertiary pump stations and five tertiary chemical dosing plants clean the water before it gravitates to Rand Water's consumers.

Rand Water distributes bulk water to three metropolitan municipalities (Johannesburg, Ekurhuleni and Tshwane), 24 local municipalities, just under 50 mines, and around 330 industries; it also provides potable water directly to about 600 households. About 92 per cent of its water sales are to municipalities (Rand Water 2016: 82–83). In 2016, the organisation, with its 3 500 employees, indirectly served 19 million people (Rand Water 2016: 187) – this amounts to nearly a quarter of South African's population. Its capacity to supply bulk potable water is 5 300 megalitres per day (Ml/d), of which an average of about 4 684 Ml/d is used (Rand Water 2016: 17). In terms of quality, the water supplied compares with the best in the world. In the 1990s, the World Health Organization rated Rand Water's water quality among the top three in the world (Rand Water 2002), and Rand Water's own quality standard is higher than the South African Bureau of Standards' national standard for drinking water (Rand Water Board December 2004: 701; Rand Water 2016: 96).

Rand Water is a public utility and the South African government is its sole shareholder. In terms of the Water Services Act of 1997 it is accountable to the national Department of Water and Sanitation. Rand Water (1996: 4) defines itself as a not-for-profit public utility, run on strict business lines. It has a non-executive board that is appointed by the Minister of Water and Sanitation (Rand Water 2005a: 3). The board delegates day-to-day management of the utility to a portfolio integrating committee, since October 2005 comprised of the chief executive officer (CEO) and six portfolio heads. This managerial structure is aligned with various portfolios, based on process integration and key organisational outputs, and is supposed to ensure improved organisational performance and facilitate growth in full water services provision (Rand Water 2005b: 32–33; 2016: 20–21).

Rand Water's latest vision statement, formulated in 2012, is 'to be a provider of sustainable, universally competitive water and sanitation solutions for Africa' (Rand Water 2016: 62). The key strategic objectives guiding its activities, budget and business focus are: 'to achieve operational integrity and use best fit technology; achieve growth [in infrastructure, through new areas of supply and through new product streams]; achieve a high-performance culture; positively engage stakeholder base; [and] maintain financial health and sustainability' (Rand Water 2016: 63). For the purposes of this discussion, it is important to note that the word 'water supply' (or 'water' for that matter), the reason for Rand Water's existence, does not appear once in its strategic objectives.

NPM as accumulation by dispossession: the case of Rand Water

Since apartheid was abolished in 1994, Rand Water's organisational activities have become more complex and diverse, as have its structure and staffing. Changes related to policies, structures and activities sped up after the appointment of Simo Lushaba as CEO in 2002. Drawing on Batley and Larbi (2004: 81), the organisational changes that have taken place can be categorised as internal management reforms (related to the increasing corporatisation of the core activity of bulk water provision) and externally oriented market-type reforms (focusing on activities outside of this core role). In the rest of this section I use this categorisation to indicate how NPM acted as a mechanism to enhance opportunities for 'accumulation by dispossession'.

The intensification of corporatisation at Rand Water

Since the 1980s, Rand Water has been transformed from being primarily a public engineering organisation providing bulk water (Laburn 1979: 93) to a state enterprise in which financial sustainability and efficiencies have become prominent. In the 1980s and early 1990s, an early process of corporatisation took place, under Vincent Bath as the first CEO.

The implementation of the Water Services Act of 1997 meant that corporatisation deepened between 1997 and 2001 (see Van Rooyen 2012). A third phase of corporatisation began in 2002, with the appointment of Simo Lushaba, Rand Water's first black CEO, and first CEO with a managerial rather than an engineering background. Lushaba was brought into Rand Water to drive business and social transformation within the organisation. Under him, the key business drivers were identified as customer focus, high product and service quality, business growth through partnerships, effective transformation, and creating a high-performance organisation (Rand Water 2005b: 1). Lushaba was expected to create a customer-driven organisation that could take advantage of new business opportunities in South Africa and Africa (Dube 2002: 55).

The key features of the corporatisation of Rand Water are evident in its organisational structure, its focus on efficiency, its customer and business orientation, as well as its prices and profits. In this chapter, I focus only on efficiency, and pricing and profits. Whilst I show that the economic transformations within Rand Water largely followed the model of NPM, I also show how some contestations – both within and outside of the utility – have led to its transformation from a bureaucratic public body to a business-like publicly owned company that is enhancing enclosure of water and dispossession of 'publicness'.

Efficiency drive

Rand Water's corporate business plan of 2005 identified efficiency, effectiveness and innovation (Rand Water 2005c: 21) as the key business drivers around which its activities were planned and conducted. In terms of the water sector, efficiency can take several forms: technical efficiency (maximising throughput and reuse in water production); economic/operational efficiency (the optimal use of resources in the production of water); social efficiency (maximising public benefit and welfare); and environmental efficiency (maximising production of ecological services) (Bakker 2001: 144; Chesnutt 2005; Spronk 2010: 161). During the time of my fieldwork at Rand Water, efficiency essentially referred to operational efficiencies only. The mechanisms used to achieve such efficiencies were to enhance productivity using the accounting logic (Broadbent and Laughlin 2002) of performance management and performance contracts (with financial rewards for staff), reducing costs (for example, reducing staff), technology utilisation and benchmarking (see Van Rooyen 2012 for detailed discussions of each of these).

The reactions from a number of senior managers within Rand Water to this focus on operational efficiencies are captured for me in a quote from one of the senior managers who said: 'We have forgotten that we are actually here to provide water. If you look at our Balanced Performance Management Framework, you probably won't even see anything about producing water.' The idea of attention being diverted away from the core activities of Rand Water was expressed by one of the executive managers as:

> My supposition is that when Simo [Lushaba] came into the organisation, he embarked on a regime of attempting to get Rand Water competitive in a commercial sense...which I think is a bit inclined to divert us from this non-profit making organisation sort of notion.

In this context, a useful distinction can be made between efficiency and effectiveness. As Therkildsen (2001: 3) argues, 'increased efficiency (maximising outcomes for given inputs) does not always fall in with increased effectiveness (the extent to which the objectives of a policy or programme are achieved)'. An organisation can thus be inefficient (in terms of low ratio of output to input, meaning high cost), but still be effective in achieving the right objectives. And an organisation can be efficient (in terms of high ratio of output to input), but be pursuing the wrong objectives, 'often with more damaging results', argues Israel (1987: 12). One of the executive managers of Rand Water expressed this as:

> I suspect that one of the areas that we haven't really looked at that require a bit of focus would be the notion of over-engineering. Because of the situation that we are in, we could be efficient, but we could be efficient in building a Rolls Royce to do the job of a Mini.

Added to such over-specification is the over-sizing of capacity (Pearson et al. 1998: 1). Figure 4.1 shows Rand Water's installed raw water capacity versus actual water use (measured in average annual daily demand) since its formation. As shown, since the 1970s the gap between surplus capacity and daily demand has been growing steadily. By the mid-2000s only 59 per cent of Rand Water's raw water installed capacity was used, 70 per cent of its treatment capacity, 66 per cent of its primary pumping capacity and 64 per cent of its booster pumping capacity (Rand Water 2006: 17). Rand Water's infrastructure was thus kept well ahead of consumption, leading to large and growing surplus capacity in Rand Water's bulk water supply system.

FIGURE 4.1   Rand Water's installed raw water capacity versus actual water demand

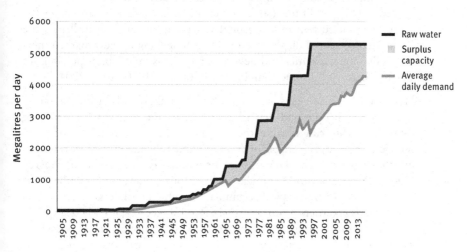

Source: Adapted from Els (2006).

In the context of climate change and the likelihood of increased water scarcity in Rand Water's supply area, priority must be given to reducing water usage. Arguably, this will enable Rand Water to serve the public good far more than its over-specification and over-sizing of supply capacity. Not encouraging a radical reduction in water use in this water-scarce region will enhance enclosure of this common even further in the long run, through inevitable exorbitant cost of water or water cuts/rationing.

Why would Rand Water have continuously invested in infrastructure that led to such over-capacity? Harvey's (2003, 2004) idea of accumulation by dispossession offers one explanation.[1] Harvey showed how capitalism has dealt with its inherent tendency towards crises of over-accumulation and uneven development since the 1970s. The theory of over-accumulation of capital through expanded reproduction states that, due to over-exploitation of labour, surplus capital and commodities are available but cannot be bought or used. Unless ways are found to absorb such surpluses, system-wide devaluations and destructions of capital and labour will occur (Harvey 2004). To avoid the devaluation of surpluses, Harvey (2003) argues that late-twentieth-century capitalism makes use of spatio-temporal fixes. That is,

> surpluses may be absorbed by (a) temporal displacement through investment in long-term capital projects [such as water infrastructure] or social expenditures (such as education and research) that defer the re-entry of current excess capital values into circulation well into the future; (b) spatial displacements through opening up new markets, new production capacities and new resources, social and labour possibilities elsewhere; or (c) some combination of (a) and (b). (Harvey 2004: 2)

Harvey (2003, 2004) goes on to show how capital expands by incorporating those goods, people and activities that have not hitherto been part of capitalism. This can include the commodification of public goods and services, and the conversion of common and collective property rights to private property rights. Drawing on the work of Rosa Luxemburg, Harvey (2003, 2004) calls this 'accumulation by dispossession', and describes it as the dominant form of capital accumulation in the neo-liberal era.

Harvey's arguments seem to explain Rand Water's apparently unrequired 'over'-investment in infrastructure. In the case of a public provider, where would the surplus capital come from that needs investing before it devalues? For this, I turn to pricing and profitmaking in Rand Water.

Pricing and profits

Since its formation in 1903, Rand Water has not been subsidised nor received money from government for its core operations (Rand Water 2005a: 3). Traditionally, its revenue has come from the sale of bulk water, and capital raised in financial markets through bonds and loans, none of which have been government guaranteed. Throughout its history, Rand Water has operated on (at least) a full cost-recovery basis, as well as (they claim) a not-for-profit basis as required by its then statutes (Rand Water Board 1978; Rand Water 2005a: 3). Rand Water's definition of full cost-recovery is noteworthy though; it includes all working costs (including maintenance costs), management costs, costs related to the repayment of loans (so far cost-reflective), *and* an appropriation for surplus (Rand Water Board 1978). Thus, built into its bulk water tariff is a portion for surplus/profit, which in the 2000s was targeted at 15 per cent (Rand Water Board June 2003: 580; personal interviews). This is what I refer to as 'cost-reflective plus' tariff.

A further element of this tariff is that Rand Water receives 886 Ml/d of the raw water it withdraws from the Vaal Dam for free from the Department of Water and Sanitation. This is due to a longstanding agreement dating back to 1938, when Rand Water contributed £1.1 million (of the total cost of £1.7 million) towards the building of the Vaal Dam (Laburn 1979: 23). Thus, by including the cost of this water in its budgets, Rand Water is over-calculating its costs and increasing its profits, which counters its claim of cost-reflectivity. This 'over-pricing' effectively dispossesses citizens by them having to pay more for water.

These kind of predatory practices, as well as the efficiency measures implemented by Rand Water since the early 2000s, combined with continuous growth in water sales and a higher bulk water tariff that has been above inflation since 2003, have led Rand Water to experience many years of net surpluses since 1994. Figure 4.2 shows the utility's potable water sales, annual revenue and surplus from 1995 to 2015. Over this time, revenue has increased, based mainly on increased sales of potable water due to the expansion of Rand Water's supply area and increased water demand from consumers.

Figure 4.2 also reveals that Rand Water has seen increased surpluses (or profits) over the period, and since 2001, surplus growth per year for most of the period has consistently been over 30 per cent. As a public entity, Rand Water is not supposed to make a profit, so the surplus is justified and used as capital for new infrastructure and to pay off debt. The utility refers to such surpluses as 'not profiteering but recovering cost of capital' (Rand Water 2004). But as indicated above, such profits are being used to build a Rolls Royce, where a Mini would do.

FIGURE 4.2   Rand Water's key business performance, 1995–2015

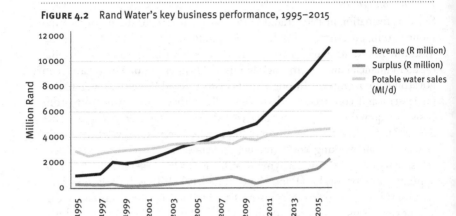

Source: Rand Water (1996, 2005a, 2006, 2014, 2016).

To sum up, in the case of Rand Water NPM led to the intensification of corporatisation, opening up water provision to capital accumulation by the state, and ultimately being a tool for accumulation by dispossession. While transformations in Rand Water's core services in the late 1990s and the 2000s were extensive, I now describe changes in Rand Water's 'other activities', including extending its scope to new services and to new areas, which have perhaps been more controversial, especially for water activists.

Expansion into other activities

The second category of NPM-led organisational reform that Rand Water underwent relates to externally oriented market-type reforms that led the utility into activities beyond its core role of bulk water provision. Since the mid-1990s the organisation has been slowly expanding these activities. The signing into law of the Water Services Act in 1997, enabled Rand Water to became involved in the full cycle of water services, including bulk and retail water supply, bulk and retail sanitation, and resource protection (Rand Water 2005a: 2; 2005c: 1). In pursuit of expanding its involvement in all water services, and becoming a source-to-tap utility company, Rand Water has both expanded the geographical area of its bulk water supply, and begun supplying a range of other services in South Africa and in other countries. These 'other activities' include corporate social investment, capacity building and commercial activities in retail water services, as well as bulk and retail sanitation services.

In the 1990s, these other activities mainly involved corporate social responsibility activities that were directed through community-based projects in support of the government's Reconstruction and Development Programme. In the 2000s, the focus changed to full cost-recovery and profit-making. Alongside this, a shift occurred which entailed a move away from dealing with these activities in an ad hoc manner through cost centres, to consolidating them via the establishment of a set of ring-fenced subsidiary companies.

Thus, in 2004, as part of Rand Water's corporate social investment, the Rand Water Foundation was founded as a section 21 company,[2] to support communities with water-related projects (Rand Water 2005b: 6). In 2005, another subsidiary, Rand Water Services (Pty) Ltd, started operating to drive commercial engagement in other activities both within South Africa and outside of its borders, in the rest of Africa, the Indian Ocean islands and the Middle East (Rand Water 2005b: 31). In 2010, due to reasons related to not making profits and allegations of corruption (see *NoseWeek* January 2011), the Rand Water Board decided to reintegrate the operations of Rand Water Services back into the utility itself. In 2012, a third entity was formed, the Rand Water Academy, to enhance skills within Rand Water and the broader South African water sector, but especially at local government level (Rand Water 2014: 26).

For the rest of the section, I focus on how Rand Water has used 'public–public partnerships' (PUPs) in carrying out its retail water and sanitation activities,[3] and show how these are enhancing accumulation by dispossession. My engagement with this is a response to the appeal by Boag and McDonald (2010: 2) to counter the 'tendency to uncritically celebrate PUP initiatives'. PUPs have been celebrated by some as an alternative to PPPs and privatisation, as partnerships between public utilities that can enhance access to services and support capacity building, especially for the poor, as well as democratise public utilities and publicness (Boag and McDonald 2010: 2; Xhafa 2013: 4). While I agree that PUPs can achieve these things, they do not necessarily do so, and in fact, they can just as easily enhance the corporatisation of public utilities, and in this case, the commodification of water and the enclosure of the water commons. Rand Water, seen by some as a 'leading exponent' of PUPs in the water sector (Kriel et al. 2003), demonstrates this well.

In their PUPs, Rand Water not only aimed to transfer the business model of running water services to local municipalities both within South Africa and elsewhere in Africa, but also to make a profit in the process of 'support' (Rand Water 2005b: 23). In its own words, the aim was to promote a shift 'from municipal public to corporatised public' (Rand Water 2003: 3). For example, Rand Water defined one characteristic of PUPs as allowing 'for full cost recovery (*including a mark-up*) [cost-plus] or in certain instances for a sharing of profit' (Rand Water 2000: 12, emphasis added). When involved in 'capacity building' through these PUPs, Rand Water also promoted principles such as efficiency and competition to help entrench its corporatised model. It was especially in its contracts outside of South Africa, signed during the 2000s via its commercial arm (Rand Water Services), that Rand Water was being particularly deceptive when highlighting its nature as a public utility and describing these contracts as being in the public interest. Such actions led people such as Al-Hassen Adam (2005) to proclaim that, in Africa, Rand Water runs in the name of the public, but acts in the interest of the private, and uses its 'public' ownership as a smokescreen to hide its profit-making intentions. For some in Rand Water, the PUPs also aimed to ensure that, should any of the public utilities involved in the PUPs be privatised, they would have 'value' for the private sector. As one manager involved in Rand Water's expansion attempts in Africa said:

> It is...generally accepted that in order for a utility to run efficiency, it needs to privatise. Rand Water has proven that this is not the case. There is a role for private sector but we don't believe that it lies in improving efficiency. Utilities should work on increasing their own efficiencies and profitability prior to considering privatisation so as to raise their value to investors... There is no reason why a public-sector entity cannot run on business principles and be efficient – this is the message we plan to take throughout the continent, and we have our own successful track record to back up what we say. Rand Water wants to assist utilities get to this point so that what is on offer to the private sector has value.

The language of PUPs was thus appropriated to legitimate enclosure and dispossession.

The intensification of corporatisation and expansionary activities within Rand Water has not happened without difficulties, however. In fact, these activities highlighted contradictions, tensions, resistances and failures, as can be expected in what Polanyi (1944) described as a 'double movement'.[4] For example, some staff members did not want to manage divisions that were out to make a profit, others were not interested in pursuing projects outside of South Africa, or in working for a company that was 'making a profit out of the problems of local government', as one senior manager put it. In response to a question about how Rand Water Services fits into Rand Water, another senior manager who had been involved in other activities before 2005, responded:

> Well it doesn't. It doesn't help us; in fact it has been a distraction. Again, it has taken our focus off from what we are supposed to be doing. But

why do we need it? Why do we need to earn profits? We were formed a hundred years ago now. For 95 years, we supplied water; and the money it cost us to supply that water is what we set our tariff at. Now why do we need to have ten million extra coming in? I think we have lost the plot.

Yet another senior manager captured the cynicism felt by several of his peers:

At the moment, we are heading straight for the iceberg. And if we don't re-plot that course, we are going to hit the iceberg; there's no doubt in my mind.

How do such failures and resistances lead us beyond NPM to publicness?

Publicness beyond NPM

The case of Rand Water warns against uncritical support for PUPs as part of a 'beyond NPM' strategy, and shows that PUPs might actually simply involve a refinement of NPM. In this regard, it is useful to consider what publicness might mean in a 'beyond NPM' context.

For one, we need to unpack what kinds of capacity (types of knowledge and skills) PUPs are supposed to build in what areas, and in whose interests. Unless capacity building extends the capacity of the public sector to act in the interest of the public good, fulfilling both equity and efficiency goals in a transparent and democratic manner, it is not public-sector capacity building but private-sector promotion. In other words, simply having one public-sector entity engaged in building the capacity of another public-sector entity, is no guarantee of the kind of PUP that progressive-minded people should support. The muddied waters surrounding PUPs need to be cleared away and the various guises of 'public' need to be unveiled (so that it is clear to everyone whether the term 'public' is being used to cover up the interests of private capital, and/or nationalist, gendered, or any other kind of interest).

A typology of PUPs that identifies various kinds of partners (who are non-private sector) that can be involved in a PUP might be helpful here. Brennan and colleagues (2004) suggested one that includes public–popular, public–community, public–workers, public–cooperatives and public–public. The typology provided by Hall, Lethbridge and Lobina (2005: 2) builds on this, by adding the objectives of the partnership, such as building capacity, improving services, defending against privatisation, building stronger community support and accountability. Lobina and Hall (2006: 16, emphasis added) advocate PUPs as 'a peer relationship forged around common values and objectives, which *excludes profit-seeking*'.

Swyngedouw (2006: 64) warns against the common fault of equating public ownership with a non-commodified form of service delivery. The case of Rand Water demonstrated this well. In fact, Rand Water asserted its public entity status – partly due to the contestations it faced both inside and outside of its own ranks – to access more easily the many opportunities for money making in capacity building, support activities and management contracts. That is, in many cases, Rand Water used its 'publicness' to promote its commercial interests. Such Janus-faced seemingly contradictory behaviours are part of the hybrid, schizophrenic nature that tends to beset public institutions that implement NPM. 'Publicness' then has to be much more than public ownership; it has to be about public entities – including non-state ones – acting in the interests of the public, performing activities for the benefit of public good in a transparent and democratic manner.

What then should initiatives that aim to look 'beyond NPM' to enhance publicness look like? Some of the efforts at re-municipalisation and re-nationalisation in the water sector since 2000 are certain to be useful as part of this unpacking (McDonald 2015: 1). Other names given to such efforts are new public service (Denhardt and Denhardt 2003), public value management (Stoker 2006), managing publicness (Bozeman 2007), new civic politics (Boyte 2011) and capable government (Brinkerhoff and Brinkerhoff 2015: 223). In these initiatives, the focus is on the principles underlying the delivery of public services such as water supply. Criteria for practices particular to the public domain include service (rather than accumulating profit), equity and co-operation (rather than competition) (Ranson and Stewart 1994), as well as universal provision, accountability, transparency and democracy. Haque (cited in Martin 2003: 3) usefully identified five criteria of publicness:

- The extent of the public sector's distinction from the private sector (such as the public characteristics of openness, equity and representation).
- The scope and composition of service recipients (a higher degree of publicness is necessary if there is a greater number and broader scope of service recipients).
- The magnitude and intensity of its socio-economic role (with wider societal impact a greater degree of publicness is required).
- The degree of public accountability.
- The level of public trust.

Similarly, Cumbers (2017: 216–217) suggested five principles to keep in mind when constructing public democratic ownership:
- Commitment to a 'fuzzy' but still egalitarian notion of the common good.
- The importance of ownership and its use to the benefit of the whole.
- Commitment to dispersed decision-making.

- The importance of diversity, pluralism and tolerance.
- Developing forms of ownership that allow for public discourse and collective learning.

To these McDonald (2014: 5) added that we should anticipate 'publicness... being disassembled and reassembled'.

Conclusion

My starting point in writing this chapter is to acknowledge the crucial role of the public provision of water for achieving SDG 6 (clean water and sanitation). However, I caution that NPM is not the best tool for public utilities to adopt as they attempt to fulfil this goal. Using the case of Rand Water, I showed how an engineering-dominated public utility was transformed into a corporate public entity dominated by professional managers and for-profit approaches, practices and values. Through various NPM-type reforms, such as the prioritisation of efficiency over effectiveness, and profit-making through pricing as well as other (albeit less successful) activities, Rand Water is enclosing the provision of affordable quality water for all in its primary supply area. The story of this public utility offers a clear example of NPM and PUPs working as mechanisms of 'accumulation by dispossession'.

In this process, the ideas, practices and interests of the private sector have invaded thinking about the public sector, raising questions about what is 'public'. In many of its activities Rand Water appears schizophrenic: is it a public utility that acts in the public good or is it a profit-making company? Should a public utility be making profit, as Rand Water does? Can a privatised public utility act in the interest of the public? Not so, I argue.

The case of Rand Water is a good example of the role of the state in accumulation by dispossession as outlined by Harvey (2004). This is not just an economic process in which over-accumulated capital seizes non-market entities and assets, but rather a political process in which the state wields its power to overcome barriers to continued accumulation (Levien 2012: 940). In this process, the expropriation, or 'enclosure of the commons', imposes new social relations of power. Unease about and resistance to the changes occurring in Rand Water as expressed by staff and management during my fieldwork highlight the nature of contestations within state organisations undergoing NPM, and possibly indicate what might be possible with regard to moving 'beyond NPM'.

Crucially, given that public ownership does not guarantee non-commodified forms of service delivery, the notion of 'publicness' beyond NPM must be further explored. How can the principles of equity, inclusivity, collaborative dialogue, efficiency, affordability, quality, social justice, solidarity, sustainability, democracy, citizenship and public accountability be practised? And what is the role of non-state public role players in constructing such 'publicness'?

Notes

1 In a context of growing demand, it is, of course, prudent to have spare capacity; Ramsey and Mobbs (2001:29) indicate recommended 'headroom' of 5–10 per cent. But numerous respondents within Rand Water implied that the surplus capacity was continuously and rapidly expanded in ways that they saw as questionable and unnecessary.
2 In terms of South Africa's Companies Act, Section 21 companies provide services with the intention not to make a profit.
3 For a detailed description of Rand Water's other activities, see Van Rooyen and Hall (2007), and Van Rooyen (2012).
4 Karl Polanyi (1944) predicted that efforts to extend the market economy would be countered by society.

References

Adam A (2005) Radio-debate about Rand Water in Ghana, *The Vuyo Mbuli Show*, SAfm, 8 July 2005.
Bakker KJ (2001) 'Paying for water: Water pricing and equity in England and Wales' *Transnational Institute of British Geographers* 26: 143–164.
Bakker KJ (2003) *An Uncooperative Commodity: Privatising Water in England and Wales.* Oxford: Oxford University Press.
Bakker K (2007) 'The "commons" versus the "commodity": Alter-globalization, anti-privatization and the human right to water in the global South' *Antipode* 39 (3): 430–455.
Bakker KJ and D Hemson (2000) 'Privatising water: BoTT and hydropolitics in the new South Africa' *South African Geographical Journal* 82 (1): 3–12.
Bangura Y and GA Larbi (2006) 'Introduction: Globalisation and public sector reform' in Y Bangura and GA Larbi (eds), *Public Sector Reform in Developing Countries: Capacity Challenges to Improve Services.* Basingstoke: Palgrave Macmillan.
Batley R and G Larbi (2004) *The Changing Role of Government: The Reform of Public Services in Developing Countries.* Basingstoke: Palgrave Macmillan.
Boag G and DA McDonald (2010) 'A critical review of public-public partnerships in water services' *Water Alternatives* 3 (1): 1–25.
Boyte H (2011) 'Constrictive politics as public work: Organising the literature' *Political Theory* 39 (5): 630–660.
Bozeman B (2007) *Public Values and Public Interest: Counterbalancing Economic Individualism.* Washington, DC: Georgetown University Press.

Brennan B, B Hack, O Hoedeman, S Kishimato and P Terhast (2004) *Reclaiming Public Water! Participatory Alternatives to Privatisation*, TNI Briefing series 7, Transnational Institute, Amsterdam.

Brenner N and N Theodore (2007) 'Neoliberalism and the regulation of "environment"' in N Heynen, J McCarthy, S Prudham and P Robbins (eds), *Neoliberal Environments: False Promises and Unnatural Consequences*. New York: Routledge.

Brinkerhoff DW and JM Brinkerhoff (2015) 'Public sector management reform in developing countries: Perspectives beyond NPM orthodoxy' *Public Administration and Development* 35: 222–237.

Broadbent J and R Laughlin (2002) 'Public service professionals and the new public management: Control of the professionals in the public services' in K McLaughlin, SP Osborne and E Ferlie (eds), *New Public Management: Current Trends and Future Prospects*. London: Routledge.

Chesnutt T (2005) 'Direct utility avoided cost estimation for integrated water management', paper presented at the third IWA conference on efficient use and management of water, Santiago, Chile, 15–17 March 2005.

Cumbers A (2017) 'Rethinking public ownership as economic democracy' in B Jones and M O'Donnell (eds), *Alternatives to Neoliberalism: Towards Equality and Democracy*. Bristol: Policy.

Denhardt JV and RB Denhardt (2003) *The New Public Service: Serving, Not Steering*. New York: Sharpe.

Diedricks M (2015) Briefing on the provision of bulk potable water services by the water boards. Presentation to the Parliamentary Select Committee on Social Services, 9 May 2015, Department of Water and Sanitation, Pretoria.

Dube MG (September 2002) 'New look Rand Water' *Enterprise*: 52–55.

Els G (2006) 'Bulk water services', presentation at Rand Water, Johannesburg.

Ewalt JG (2001) 'Theories of governance and new public management: Links to understanding welfare policy implementation', paper presented at the annual conference of the American Society for Public Administration, Newark, NJ, 12 March 2001.

Hall D, J Lethbridge and E Lobina (2005) *Public-Public Partnerships in Health and Essential Services*, Equinet and MSP Discussion Paper 23. Available online.

Haque MS (2007) 'Revisiting the new public management' *Public Administration Review* 67 (1): 179–182.

Harvey D (2003) *The New Imperialism*. Oxford: Oxford University Press.

Harvey D (2004) 'The "new imperialism": On spatio-temporal fixes and accumulation by dispossession' in L Panitch and C Leys (eds), *The Socialist Register 2004* 40: 63–87. Available online.

Israel A (1987) *Institutional Development: Incentives to Performance*. Baltimore: Johns Hopkins University Press.

Kriel R, M Monadjem and J Ferreira (2003) *When Public Partnerships Work: A Case Study by the MIIU and Emfuleni Local Municipality of Government Policy in the Proposed Partnership between Emfuleni and Metsi-a-Lekoa (Pty) Ltd*. Johannesburg: Ashira Consulting.

Laburn RJ (1979) *The Rand Water Board – 1903 to 1978: A Treatise on the Rand Water Board with Specific Reference to its Responsibilities, Achievements and Policies during 75 Years of Operation*. Johannesburg: Rand Water.

Larbi GA (1999) *The New Public Management Approach and Crisis States*, Discussion Paper 112. UNRISD, Geneva.

Larbi GA (2006) 'Applying the New Public Management in developing countries' in Y Bangura and GA Larbi (eds), *Public Sector Reform in Developing Countries: Capacity Challenges to Improve Services*. Basingstoke: Palgrave Macmillan.

Levien M (2012) 'The land question: Special economic zones and the political economy of dispossession in India' *Journal of Peasant Studies* 39: 933–969.

Lobina E and D Hall (2006) *Public-Public Partnerships as a Catalyst for Capacity Building and Institutional Development: Lessons from Stockholm Vatten's Experience in the Baltic Region*. London: Public Services International Research Unit. Available online.

Lodge M and D Gill (2011) 'Toward a new era of administrative reform: The myth of post-NPM in New Zealand' *Governance* 24 (1): 141–166.

Manning N (2001) 'The legacy of the new public management in developing countries' *International Review of Administrative Sciences* 67 (2): 297–312.

Martin B (2003) *What is Public About Public Services?* Background Paper for the World Development Report 2004. Available online.

McDonald DA (2002) 'You get what you can pay for: Cost recovery and the crisis of service delivery in South Africa', Harold Wolpe Memorial Lecture, University of KwaZulu-Natal, Durban, 28 August.

McDonald DA (2014) 'Public ambiguity and the multiple meanings of corporatization', in DA McDonald (ed.), *Rethinking Corporatization and Public services in the Global South*. London: Zed.

McDonald DA (2015) 'Back to the future? The curious case of "public" services', paper prepared for the UIC Urban Forum, Chicago, 17 September 2015.

McDonald DA and G Ruiters (2005a) 'Introduction: From public to private (to public again?)' in DA McDonald and G Ruiters (eds), *The Age of Commodity: Water Privatisation in Southern Africa*. London: Earthscan.

McDonald DA and G Ruiters (2005b) 'Theorising water privatisation in Southern Africa' in DA McDonald and G Ruiters (eds), *The Age of Commodity: Water Privatisation in Southern Africa*. London: Earthscan.

McDonald DA and G Ruiters (2006) 'Rethinking privatisation: Towards a critical theoretical perspective' in *Public Services Yearbook 2005/6*. Amsterdam: Transnational Institute.

Nickson A (2006) 'Public sector management reform in Latin America' in Y Bangura and GA Larbi (eds), *Public Sector Reform in Developing Countries: Capacity Challenges to Improve Services*. Basingstoke: Palgrave Macmillan.

NoseWeek (January 2011) 'Same old bull' *NoseWeek Online* 135. Available online.

Osborne D and T Gaebler (1992) *Reinventing Government: How the Entrepreneurial Spirit is Transforming the Public Sector*. Reading, MA: Addison-Wesley.

Pearson G, W Coxon, R Thomson, J Britt, M Mkize, W Warrior and H Ott (1998) 'Infrastructure design to operational efficiencies', paper prepared for Rand Water's first strategic workshop review, 17–18 November 1998.

Peck J and A Tickell (2002) 'Neoliberalising space' *Antipode* 34 (3): 380–404.

Polanyi K (1944) *The Great Transformation: The Political and Economic Origins of Our Time*. Boston: Beacon.

Pollitt C and G Bouckaert (2004) *Public Management Reform: A Comparative Analysis – New Public Management, Governance and the Neo-Weberian State* (second edition). Oxford: Oxford University Press.

Ramsey S and P Mobbs (2001) *Report of Performance Indicators: African Water Supply and Sanitation Utilities 2001*. Abidjan: Water Utility Partnership.

Rand Water (1996) *Rand Water Annual Report 1996*. Rietvlei: Rand Water.

Rand Water (2000) 'Corporate Policy of Rand Water', an unpublished policy document adopted by the board, 24 February 2000.

Rand Water (2002) 'Rand Water position paper on the public–public partnership position and the role of public water utilities in service delivery', paper prepared for a South African Allied Workers Union 'declaration' at the World Summit on Sustainable Development, Johannesburg, 26 August–2 September 2002.

Rand Water (2003) Submission by Rand Water to the Parliamentary Portfolio Committee on Water Affairs and Forestry (Proposed amendments to the *Water Services Act*).

Rand Water (2004) Submission by Rand Water to a parliamentary portfolio committee on the proposed amendment to the Water Services Act. 6 October.

Rand Water (2005a) *Annual Report 2004/5*. Johannesburg: Rand Water.

Rand Water (2005b) Corporate business plan 2005–2010 (Unpublished document).

Rand Water (2005c) *Rand Water Policy Statement*. Johannesburg: Rand Water.

Rand Water (2006) *Annual Report 2005/6*. Johannesburg: Rand Water.

Rand Water (2014) *Annual Report 2014/5*. Johannesburg: Rand Water.

Rand Water (2016) *2015/16 Integrated Annual Report*. Johannesburg: Rand Water.

Rand Water Board (1978) *Rand Water Board* (Informational brochure.) Johannesburg: Rand Water.

Rand Water Board (2003) Minutes of the 1218th ordinary meeting of the board on 5 June 2003. (Unpublished document).

Rand Water Board (2004) Minutes of the 1227th ordinary meeting of the board on 2 December 2004 (Unpublished document).

Ranson S and J Stewart (1994) *Management for the Public Domain: Enabling the Learning Society*. Basingstoke: Macmillan.

Smith L (2005) 'The murky waters of second wave neoliberalism: Corporatisation as a service delivery model in Cape Town' in DA McDonald and G Ruiters (eds), *The Age of Commodity: Water Privatisation in Southern Africa*. London: Earthscan.

Spronk S (2010) 'Water and sanitation utilities in the Global South: Re-centering the debate on "efficiency"' *Review of Radical Political Economics* 42 (2): 156–174.

Stoker G (2006) 'Public value management: A new narrative for networked governance?' *American Review of Public Administration* 36 (1): 41–57.

Swyngedouw E (2006) *Power, Water and Money: Exploring the Nexus*, Occasional Paper 14, Human Development Report Office, UNDP.

Taylor M (2002) 'The new public management and social exclusion: Cause or response?' in K McLaughlin, SP Osborne and E Ferlie (eds), *New Public Management: Current Trends and Future Prospects*. London: Routledge.

Therkildsen O (2001) *Efficiency, Accountability and Implementation: Public Sector Reform in East and Southern Africa*, Paper 3, Democracy Governance and Human Rights Programme, UNRISD, Geneva.

Uneca (United Nations Economic Commission for Africa) (2003) *Public Sector Management Reforms in Africa: Lessons Learned*. Addis Ababa: Uneca.

Van Rooyen C (2012) Articulated Transformations and Accumulation by Dispossession: Rand Water in South Africa, PhD thesis, University of London.

Van Rooyen C and D Hall (2007) *Public is as Private Does: The Confused Case of Rand Water in South Africa*, MSP Occasional Paper 15, Municipal Services Project, Cape Town.

Xhafa E (2013) *Alternative Ways of Organising Public Services and Work in the Public Sector: What Role for Public–Public Partnerships?* Working Paper 9, Postwachstumsgesellschaften Kolleg, Friedrich-Schiller University, Jena, Germany.

Chapter 5

To fit or not to fit, is that the question? Global goals, basic education and theories of knowledge in South Africa and Sweden

Hilde Ibsen, Sharon Penderis and Karin Bengtsson

IN 2015, THE UNITED NATIONS ADOPTED sustainable development as the 'best path forward for improving the lives of people everywhere' (UN 2015). That is, following on from the Millennium Development Goals (MDGs), which committed nations to reducing extreme poverty through eight time-bound targets by 2015, the United Nations introduced the Sustainable Development Goals (SDGs), which set out a global agenda beyond 2015. The MDGs were acknowledged to have focused insufficiently on the world's most excluded people, and to have failed to address aspects of development related to democracy and inclusive growth. The SDGs reflect a stronger focus on ending extreme poverty and ensuring that no one is denied universal human rights.

However, despite this new global agenda, much of the world's underlying political economy remains driven by the competitive world of market accumulation (Halvorsen 2015). Even knowledge production and reproduction has, according to Halvorsen, been drawn into a growth process, based on the values and interests of global multilateral organisations, such as the World Trade Organisation, the OECD (Organisation for Economic Cooperation and Development) and BRICS (the alliance between Brazil, Russia, India, China and South Africa). Halvorsen argues that change is necessary and asks how the academic community might help shape and promote alternatives to the prevailing neo-liberal approach to politics and economics.

In the SDGs, higher education institutions are allocated a prominent role in shaping sustainable development. However, there is reason to question the knowledge and knowledge-systems underlying the new global agenda. Our argument is that higher education institutions must critically interrogate the dominant knowledge systems and question the neo-liberal logic underlying accepted notions of development, economic growth and the politics of education. In this chapter, we attempt to address these issues through the lens of a North-South research partnership that investigates theories of knowledge as reflected in curriculum documents at the level of basic education (schooling) in South Africa and Sweden. High level documentation is just one way in which a comparison between the two education systems might be carried out, and educational practice and pupil learning cannot be read off policy documents in any simple way. However, despite vast differences in historical background and contemporary contexts, what can be read from curriculum documents and previous studies of the curricula of both countries, is how areas of overlap point to the power of neo-liberal ideas and the prevalence of their policy templates.

A number of scholars, including Le Blanc (2015) and Sarabhai (2016), have argued that education lies at the core of the SDGs and is key to their achievement As Sterling put it:

> The role of education is more profound and comprehensive than is recognized in the text of the SDGs as regards its potential to address their implementation. Education requires a re-invention, and re-purposing so that it can assume the responsibility these challenges require, and develop the agency that is needed for transformative progress to be made. (2016: 208)

Much of the international discourse refers to enhancing the quality of education. However, we are reminded that 'quality education is modified according to the social, economic and environmental contexts. Because quality education must be locally relevant and culturally appropriate, quality education will take many forms around the world' (UNESCO 2005: 1). In this context, Laurie et al. (2016: 229) discuss the different models of quality education. They note that, besides the 'economic model' (that uses quantitative measurable outputs) and the 'humanist tradition' (that places students at the centre of the learning process and embraces social goals of human rights, social justice and democracy), the 'learner as connection model', which emerged in sub-Saharan Africa, emphasises the importance of applying learners' existing knowledge of the local contexts to the process of learning abstract concepts. Laurie et al. argue that this model promotes the incorporation of everyday knowledge into academic concepts 'so that both can grow together' (2016: 229). As the SDGs increasingly focus our attention on sustainability at the global level, education-research alliances between North and South are becoming paramount in achieving quality education that reflects the contextual and cultural environments of all communities.

The effectiveness of SDG17, with its focus on multi-stakeholder partnerships, will be determined by the ability of stakeholders to work together to share knowledge and expertise as well as to create innovative intersectoral and interdisciplinary approaches to development issues (Prescott and Stibbe 2016). Cross-sectoral North–South partnerships, collaborations and information-sharing forums enable a more holistic understanding of local contexts, which is essential for global transformation.

Our main research questions are: how are global ideas about education and knowledge expressed in South African and Swedish curricula; and what are the main challenges for higher education institutions in enhancing quality basic education? Our focus is not only to explore the role of education, which we see as the key to achieving all the SDGs, but also to highlight the value of our own experience of learning through collaboration, and to show how joint projects have the potential to deepen our knowledge of our own contexts and cultures as much as they extend our knowledge of other environments and perspectives.

Methods and theories

The design of this chapter is inspired by a genre referred to as 'occasioned writing', which is deliberately reflexive. The central task of this genre 'is to try to disturb the easy flow and circulation of received ideas' (Higgins 2013: 2).[1] Working in higher education at this time, when academic freedom and autonomy is under severe pressure from neo-liberal hegemony, we see universities and scholars as having a particular responsibility to pay attention to how ideas of development and knowledge emerge and are presented, as well as to unveil the social imaginary behind which texts are written. More than ever, we believe that higher education institutions should participate in global debates on the role and dominance of contemporary Western theories of knowledge, while seeking alternatives that are more inclusive and emancipatory.

A critique of so-called 'global knowledge', and its ignorance of other cultures' knowledges, guided our research questions. In the first section, we outline the international educational policy context and contemporary basic education systems, since it is at this level that ideologies are first spelled out before they trickle up to higher education. We use a narrative method to analyse core international and national documents on education. As Catherine Riessman (2008) noted, narrative analysis refers to interpretations of texts as they unfold for specific actors in specific places and times. The aim is to understand the basic content of a story by asking questions such as:

> For whom was this story constructed, and for what purpose? Why is the succession of events configured that way? What cultural resources does the story draw on, or take for granted? What storehouse of plots

does it call upon? What does the story accomplish? Are there gaps and inconsistencies that might suggest preferred, alternative, or counter-narratives? (Riessman 2008: 11)

This choice of approach is based on the fact that, as scholars working in higher education institutions in South Africa and Sweden, we are, according to the UN, responsible for providing knowledge that supports and points out the 'best' path for sustainable development. We are, therefore, part of the grand neo-liberal narrative that has been the leading ideological basis for knowledge and development since the late 1980s. However, like any received wisdom, this narrative must be questioned. What is knowledge? What kind of knowledge and whose knowledge is included? Who is knowledge for and who decides this? As story tellers, we have to acknowledge that we are not only free to angle the story and impact the narrative (Goffman 1959/1990), we cannot help but do so. A mode of enquiry developed by Paulo Freire (1970/2017) and referred to as critical literacy is helpful here, and comprises three dimensions of interpretation: textual, historical and theoretical (Higgins 2013).

In this chapter we focus on the textual and theoretical interpretation of curriculum changes that occurred in both countries between 1994 and 2011 under the influence of neo-liberal trends in education.[2]

Critical theory guides the theoretical underpinning of our narrative. According to Razmig Keucheyan (2010), critical theories 'more or less comprehensively challenge the existing social order...and the contemporary social world' (Keucheyan 2010: 2–3). Radical social transformation is at stake. To borrow another expression from Higgins (2013), scholars must challenge the 'template fever' dominating higher education policy globally. Because of this global template, knowledge is increasingly being reproduced within a context of managerialism where the ultimate goal is to serve the free market system (Biesta 2011). Education policy takes a top-down approach and adopts a one-size-fits-all format that is hierarchical and dominated by the interests of the political and economic elite (Li 2007).

In *Two Cheers for Anarchism* (2012), political scientist and anthropologist James C Scott demonstrates that neo-liberal policies have created an 'imbalance of life chances in the world...the point is simply that huge disparities in wealth, property, and status make a mockery of freedom' (Scott 2012: xv). This imbalance influences theories of knowledge as well as development initiatives, enabling experts to devise interventions that simply write people and the planet out of the story (Li 2007). In his condemnation of the role of the state, Scott invites us to look at the world using an 'anarchist squint' as a means of gaining insights that are obscured from view by more conventional perspectives. He uses the term anarchism as Pierre-Joseph Proudhon did, to mean 'mutuality, or co-operation without hierarchy or state rule' (2012: xii). He also reminds us of Rosa Luxemburg's support for 'the anarchist tolerance for confusion and improvisation that accompanies social learning, and confidence in spontaneous cooperation and reciprocity' (2012: xii). Donning anarchist glasses requires us to look for narratives that reveal the independent, creative and emancipatory power of individuals to challenge contemporary truisms of growth, efficiency and elitism.

Competing knowledge systems

All people are equipped with knowledge and all societies build upon different knowledge systems. Throughout history, ideas about knowledge have changed as have understandings of how knowledge should be stored and shared. But knowledge is a sticky concept. In the West, knowledge is dominated by the rational scientific paradigm, while experiential vernacular knowledge, or phronesis, is seldom regarded as knowledge at all. Knowledge based on experience (vernacular knowledge) tends to break with more expert ways of knowing that are often based on systems of hierarchy, supervision and control. Instead, it is based on everyday practices, transmitted though social networks and shared experience. Tacit knowledge is similar in some ways, in that it is mostly transmitted without explicit statements, and is seldom even formulated in linguistic form (Johannessen 2002; Polanyi 1966/1983). Tacit knowledge can be very difficult to document, but usually refers to 'know-how' as opposed to knowing facts.

Both experiential and tacit knowledge resonate with the concept of indigenous knowledge. However, indigenous knowledge has been presented and interpreted in many ways. Bharati Sen sees it as embedded in 'community practices, institutions, relationships and rituals. It is essentially tacit knowledge that is not easily codifiable' (Sen 2005: 376). For many, the concept is reserved for those who study indigenous peoples, and has little or no relevance for mainstream education or development paradigms. Seen as belonging to 'other knowledge systems', indigenous knowledge tends to be dismissed by scholars trained in the rational scientific method (Karbo 2005). Often transmitted orally and expressed in practical ways, it is perceived as existing outside of the logic of science and abstract thinking. This has, to a large extent, led Western thinkers to relegate indigenous knowledge to the category of folklore and superstition. In fact, indigenous knowledge practices are often deeply adapted to local biospheres, culture and history, and are both meaningful and 'as precise as (they) need to be for the purposes on hand' (Scott 2012: 33; see also the chapters by Danbolt et al. and Erkkilä and Endongo in this volume).

In 1998, the World Bank launched a programme on Indigenous Knowledge for Development after being persuaded to do so by governments and civil-society organisations at the 1997 Global Knowledge Conference in Toronto. A critical reading of this programme gives rise to several epistemological concerns. Although the World Bank used various strategies to incorporate indigenous knowledge into its programmes, this knowledge remained 'othered' –an exotic element to be integrated into the dominant Western paradigm, provided it continued to frame development as economic growth and efficient delivery of services. In one of their own working papers, Nicolas Gorjestani (2000) gives several examples of how indigenous knowledge was seen as interesting or useful primarily when it served this agenda.

Catherine Odora Hoppers explains why a deeper understanding of indigenous knowledge has the potential to offer scholars so much more than this. Using the southern African concept of ubuntu as an example, she notes that in southern African cultures, self-knowledge begins with the notion 'I am because I belong' rather than 'I think therefore I am'. She then shows how this turns Western rationality and its 'eternal truths' upside down (Odora Hoppers 2013: 70). Instead of upholding a dog-eat-dog world of ruthless competition for survival, the concept of ubuntu affirms the values of human dignity, mutuality, reconciliation, compassion and restorative justice, while stressing the importance of community and identity (Odora Hoppers 2013). Of course this challenges the received wisdom of Western knowledge and Eurocentric development discourse, explicitly putting communities at the centre of development processes. Interestingly, the 1981 African Charter of Human and Peoples' Rights (also known as the Banjul Charter), accords people the right to education, as well as social and cultural development, *within* the framework of their own traditional values.

Education and development

In the late 1890s, Emile Durkheim presented the idea that a nation's education system 'is only the image and reflection of society. It imitates and reproduces the latter…it does not create it' (Durkheim, 1897/1951: 372–373). Durkheim reasoned that education systems, as social constructs, are dependent on and reflect the structural features of society and therefore 'can be reformed only if society itself is reformed' (quoted in Thompson 1982/2002: 116). Building on this idea, Filloux (1993: 306) argued that, like any other social system, the educational sub-system or 'classroom micro-society' is simultaneously subject 'to forces of permanence and forces of change – forces of permanence that are derived from the system as a whole, and forces of change that respond to emerging needs and are specific to it'.

In our globalised world, the development path proposed by international giants such as the United Nations (including its specialised agencies such as UNESCO), the European Union and the OECD have a considerable impact on the development of educational principles worldwide. One principle agreed upon at the historic Jomtien Conference in Thailand in 1990s by delegates from more than 155 countries, was the principle of basic education for all. The result of the conference, the 1990 World Declaration on Education for All and its associated Framework for Action to Meet Basic Learning Needs set out to make primary education accessible to all children and to massively reduce illiteracy before 2000. Targets and strategies were defined that signatories undertook to put in place. Views of education that had previously focused on individuals in school, expanded to include life outside of school, and education was increasingly seen as a basis for escaping poverty and overcoming inequality (UNESCO 1990).

Further, with the 1994 Salamanca Statement and Framework for Action on Special Needs Education, the United Nations affirmed the need for the equalisation of educational opportunities. The statement recognised the principle of 'schools for all' that 'celebrate differences, support learning, and respond to individual needs' thereby making 'schools educationally more effective' (UNESCO 1994: iii).

In 1998, at UNESCO's World Conference on Higher Education in Mumbai, a shift took place within the discourse of lifelong learning, highlighting the importance of democratic citizenship, the right to education, and paying attention to the demands of the less privileged sectors of society (UNESCO 1997, 1998).

A next step towards Education for All was taken in 2000, when the World Education Forum in Dakar reaffirmed the Jomtien statement that 'all children…have the human right to benefit from an education…that includes learning to know, to do, to live together and to be' (UNESCO 2000: 8). Seeing education as a fundamental human right is part of an egalitarian ethic that includes 'all' – every citizen in every society. However, the rationale given for promoting education as a right was also linked to efficiency and progress: education was seen as

> the key to sustainable development and peace…and thus an indispensable means for effective participation in the societies and economies of the twenty-first century, which are affected by rapid globalization…The basic learning needs of all can and must be met as a matter of urgency. (UNESCO 2000: 8)

Alongside the strong focus on basic education, the framework acknowledged that since education reflects the nature and development of the society of which it is part, 'the scope of basic learning needs and how they should be met varies with individual countries and cultures, and inevitably, changes with the passage of time' (UNESCO 2000: 65). What this meant was that core activities should be decided at country level, but within regional frameworks so that practices and experiences in 'the management…of basic education could be facilitated' (UNESCO 2000: 67). Accordingly, the World Education Forum identified six goals to be met in different regions of the world by 2015. For sub-Saharan Africa, the goal was *equality of educational opportunity*, while for Europe and Northern America the goal was to *contribute to the world's progress*.

Clearly, the perspectives of key players and academics in the North dominated the framing of these goals. Sustainability was considered purely in the light of the skills required to advance economic prosperity, such as maths, science, communication and leadership. Strategies devised for the countries in the South apportion scant attention to the role of social capital, people's participation, peace building, human rights issues and sustainable development. As Julia Preece argues in her book, *Lifelong Learning and Development: A Southern Perspective* (2009), there is a dearth of theoretical and conceptual analyses focusing on the views of countries in the South. She notes that formerly colonised nations are hardly represented in the literature,

> partly because their voices are not heard or their texts are made invisible, and partly because such nations are already constrained by conditional aid agendas; unequal power relationships with former colonial masters means that country policies which depend on external financial support are heavily compromised. (2009: 17)

South Africa: visions of equality

When taking office in 1994, South Africa's first democratically elected government saw the reformation of the education system, including the substantive revision of all education curricula, as a key priority. The Department of Education set out the foundations of a new national qualifications framework in 1996 (DoE 1996), which together with several other documents laid the foundations for the revision of South Africa's national basic education curriculum, and resulted in the Revised National Curriculum Statement, widely known as Curriculum 2005 or simply C2005.

A core objective of the 1996 framework was to create 'a prosperous, truly united, democratic internationally competitive country with literate, creative and critical citizens leading productive, self-fulfilling lives in a country free of violence, discrimination and prejudice' (DoE 1996: 1). While Breidlid (2009) questioned the meaning of the values and knowledge systems underpinning the statement, Msila (2007) highlighted the focus on democracy and equality, and emphasised that the revisions were rooted in the values of South Africa's new constitution, which are listed as: 'social justice; equality; non-racism and non-sexism; ubuntu; an open society; accountability; rule of law; respect; and reconciliation' (Msila 2007: 152). Msila also noted that the revised curriculum strives to create a South African identity (Msila 2007). A major obstacle to the implementation of the new curriculum was the legacy of the colonial and apartheid education system which left many schools in historically black townships and rural settlements chronically under-rescourced and over-crowded, leaving teachers ill-equipped to change their teaching in terms of process or content.

At the same time, the sweeping changes embedded in the new curriculum laid bare struggles over values, interests and knowledge systems (Breidlid 2009; Chisholm 2005;Vandeyar and Killen 2003). Even the vocabulary used in C2005 was different: the word teacher was changed to educator, student to learner, syllabus to learning programme and textbooks to learning support materials. In addition, following the example of the United States and Australia, a set of assessment criteria were introduced that reflected the ideals of new public management. This meant that the curriculum centred more on standardised outcomes than on the learning process. This is captured in phrases that reflect how learners were expected to behave rather than what they should be expected to know; for example learners were expected to 'organise and manage themselves', 'contribute to their own success' and 'use science and technology effectively' (DoE 1996: 10). A powerful vocational-education lobby group fully embraced this imported assessment-driven terminology, as it aligned to their primary focus of raising national skills levels in mathematics and science. In thrall to neo-liberal ideals of globalisation, the government, too, deemed this important as they thought it would assist them in their aspirations of integrating certain sectors of the population into the global economy (Chisholm 2005). Another small, but strong, indigenous-knowledge lobby was driven by Catherine Odora Hoppers, a researcher and social scientist who led a task team to draft national policy on indigenous knowledge systems in South Africa (see Odora Hoppers 2007, 2013).

An analysis of different learning areas in C2005 reveals that some attempts were made to bridge these competing knowledge systems. For example, the C2005 history curriculum noted that 'pedagogy should promote the relationship between universal and local knowledge and worldviews' but also that curricula should be 'designed to give space to the silent voices of history and to marginalized communities' (DoE 2002: 5, 6). It seems to have been envisaged that this could be done by bringing family and local histories into the learning process (Chisholm 2005).

In terms of learning outcomes, questions arose about what 'advancing both universal and local knowledge' really meant? To give just two examples, the curriculum documents relating to the humanities and natural sciences show that indigenous knowledge was included in rather general terms. In the arts and culture curriculum, learning outcomes focused on culture, heritage and music, and aimed at investigating and explaining 'the purpose, function and role of different instruments used in indigenous, traditional or Western forms of music in South Africa' (DoE 2002). What was seen as important was the ability to classify African traditional instruments and compare them with Western instruments, to discuss the construction of instruments, and to sing or play South African songs from various cultures. Similarly, in the natural science curriculum for Grade 9, children were expected to learn to recognise different explanatory systems. This involved identifying the sources and nature of authority in explanations of an event from two differing worldviews. Children were also expected to be able to compare the ways in which knowledge is held in an oral versus a written culture. These kinds of outcomes reveal a fairly superficial and standardised understanding of indigenous knowledge systems. Ironically though, learning to 'recognise' and 'identify' has everything to do with Western empiricism and very little to do with learning to value, understand or engage with traditional practices.

C2005 was simultaneously vague and ambitious. As Breidlid (2009) explained, in terms of its epistemological basis, it is difficult to know what is included and what is excluded from this curriculum. Breidlid went on to conclude that indigenous knowledge systems had been accorded no prominence.

Sweden: 'Everyone is equal, but some are more equal than others'
In 1962, Sweden introduced a modern, comprehensive and compulsory schooling system for all 'normal' children between seven and sixteen years old. Based on a knowledge system that favours Western scientific rationality, it focused on schooling as preparing children for a 'changing society' (Englund 1994: 7). The system was considered equitable in that it was free and intended to provide citizens with 'equal access to education and to a certain standard of schooling irrespective of social background or place of residence' (Ahlin and Mörk 2007: 4). Children with mild or moderate intellectual

disabilities, deemed 'educable', could attend special schools, while those with severe intellectual disabilities were not entitled to any education until 1967 (Berthén 2007).

The Sami people (traditionally known in English as Lapps or Laplanders) are the only indigenous people recognised and protected in the Scandinavian countries under international conventions of indigenous peoples. For Sami children, the 1962 reforms meant they had the right to learn their own Sami language at school, but for only two hours a week. They learned to read and write in Swedish. Sami parents were also allowed to choose between sending their children to a Swedish school or a special Sami boarding school.

Since the early 1960s, the schooling system in Sweden has been divided into i) compulsory for 'normal children'; ii) compulsory schooling for pupils with mild intellectual disability; iii) special schools for children with physical disability such as hearing impairments; and iv) special schools for Sami children. In curricula and official documents, the latter three categories are always referred to together, often in the same sentence, and as separate from 'normal' schools.

Following the radicalisation and spirit of collectivism that arose in the 1960s and 1970s, the Swedish schooling system underwent reforms that mirror those of other modern and mature welfare states. A new curriculum was prepared and established in 1980. Its main focus was to prepare children to become conscientious and well-functioning citizens who would later take responsibility for the further democratic development of their country. Schools were expected to 'actively and consciously seek to influence and encourage children and young people to be willing to embrace the fundamental values of our democracy' (Curriculum 1980, quoted in Englund 1994: 7). Knowledge was understood as a cumulative process, and the focus of teaching was on input not output.

During the 1980s, Swedish society changed rapidly, hit by a severe national economic crisis and accelerating globalisation. Highly influenced by the restructuring of the public sector in the United Kingdom, and the new public management model, notions of marketisation, efficiency and individualisation quickly infiltrated the Swedish system. The goals of democracy and equality were called into question, and the 1980 Curriculum suffered a crisis of legitimacy (Lindblad and Wallin 1993). Social Democrats as well as the Conservative Party advocated an increase in steering and control as means to 'attain greater efficiency and improved quality in schools' (Ministry of Education and Research 2014: 14).

In 1994, extensive school reforms paved the way for fundamental change. Responsibility for schools was transferred from the state to local providers.

This meant the decentralisation and municipalisation of schools, the opening of private or independent schools, and the possibility for parents and caregivers to choose between schools (Ahlin and Mörk 2007). A dual model combining apparently strong steering from the state with local implementation and interpretation was launched, giving each individual teacher a new kind of responsibility. While the state set goals, and conducted evaluations and inspections, providers were given responsibility for ensuring that the goals were met.

The 1994 Curriculum reflects a society embracing neo-liberalism in the political arena, and the new public management philosophy in the public sector. It was a response to globalisation, and possible EU membership, which both placed stricter emphasis on foreign languages, maths and science. Knowledge in the 1994 Curriculum was taught in relation to target- and results-based management models – so called 'performance management' (SOU 2014: 4). Knowledge was understood as measurable and obtainable within a certain time period.

Education scholars have subsequently described the 1994 Curriculum as still typical of competency-based education, albeit with pupils having some autonomy and schools able to adapt to local conditions (Sundberg and Wahlström 2016). However, nothing was said about the meaning of local knowledge and since the curriculum was open for interpretation, individual teachers had to decide about whether or not to include any elements of this.

Sweden became a member of the European Union in 1994, and debates over education and schooling from then until 2011, when the new Education Act was passed and the 2011 Curriculum was introduced, must be understood as having occurred within a transnational context (Sundberg and Wahlström 2016). Step-by-step, and particularly after the signing of the Lisbon Strategy in 2000, Sweden adapted to European perspectives on education quality. The concept of the knowledge economy was introduced, creating a shift in focus from competence to performance, from teaching to learning. Soon schools were no longer being viewed as institutions for facilitating knowledge acquisition and nurturing responsible citizenship, but as agencies for the delivery of education services to students (Wahlström 2016). The European Union prescribed stricter indicators for evaluation, based on a view of knowledge as objective and evidence based (as formulated in its Schools for the 21st Century educational policy). In this programme, surveillance and quantitative targets achieved prominence, as did the so-called STEM subjects (science, technology, economics and management). In 2008, the government responded to all this by establishing a new agency, the Swedish Schools Inspectorate, and by initiating a revision of the 1994 Curriculum.

When it was launched in 2011, the new curriculum was said to be a revision of the previous one, but scholars critical of the new public management model as applied to education policy in Sweden argue that it was, in fact, a significant departure from what preceded it (Sundberg and Wahlström 2016). Most importantly, what was understood as knowledge changed to conform to a performance-based pedagogic model based on evaluation, positional control and performance. In practice, this meant substantial changes in how knowledge should be measured. Under the banner of clearer and more concrete goals for teachers and pupils, a detailed grading system was introduced from Year 6. In an article published in the Swedish newspaper, *Svenska Dagbladet*, on 15 March 2011, the then-minister of education admitted that municipalisation had created too much scope for choice, leaving Sweden with decreasing international ratings in key learning areas, and argued that the standardisation of knowledge was therefore crucial.

'Knowledge requirements' became the new mantra, with knowledge to be controlled and evaluated at specific times during the year. Pupils' autonomy was limited by the new policy but, according to the government, the results-based model and instrumental knowledge would prepare individuals for professional life in a complex and globalised world. The emphasis is on individualism and entrepreneurship, with the Curriculum document explicitly stating that it is important for pupils to 'discover their own uniqueness as individuals' and to develop attitudes that 'promote entrepreneurship' (Skolverket 2011a: 9, 11).

The document also indicates a strong orientation towards Christianity, as well as Western and Swedish values, among the education authortities. Thus, the curriculum emphasises that the values schools should represent and impart are, 'the inviolability of human life, individual freedom and integrity, the equal value of all people, equality between women and men, and solidarity with the weak and vulnerable'. However, the document goes on to claim these values as being 'in accordance with the ethics borne by *Christian* tradition and *Western* humanism' (Skolverket 2011a: 9, emphasis added).[3]

The pressures of globalisation and cross-border mobility were countered with reference to Swedish cultural heritage as a means of providing 'a secure identity'. When this was in place, pupils would understand the values of 'others' (Skolverket 2011a: 9). The Curriculum states that it is crucial for schools to be non-discriminatory, but attitudes towards 'other' values are not specified. The document states only that schools should help pupils to establish 'well-balanced perspectives' (Skolverket 2011a: 11).

Establishing balance and harmony are mentioned several times as tasks for schools, and there is an emphasis on shared experiences building 'different forms of knowledge' that make up a 'meaningful whole' (Skolverket 2011a:12).

A critical reading of the Curriculum reveals its contradictions. Its values are rooted in Christianity, but teaching is expected to be 'objective' (2011a: 10); the pupils should be creative and familiar with critical thinking, but within a framework of 'harmonious development' (2011a: 12).

To be sure, being 'familiar with critical thinking' is not the same as challenging received wisdoms, and critique does not always resonate with 'harmonious development'. The descriptions of knowledge that permeate Curriculum 2011 are vague at best.

In the 2011 Curriculum for Sami schools, however, Sami culture is at least included.

> The teaching in the Sami subject will be aimed at students developing knowledge in and about the Sami language and knowledge of the Sami culture. Through teaching, students are given the opportunity to develop a functional bilingualism, their understanding of the world and their identity. (Skolverket 2011b: 213)

However, the term functional is vague, and functional for whom? It is hard to read the text without seeing the 'otherness' that is described as being important to preserve, although not for anyone outside of the Sami communities themselves. The idea that pupils in Swedish schools might benefit from, or be inspired by, Sami knowledge and culture is not even imagined.

Curriculum reforms in Sweden in 1994 and 2011 were also implemented partly to help ensure that Sweden conforms to the statement in the Education for All Declaration that nations should guarantee an equal education to all citizens.[4] In Sweden, this is provided for by the state by giving all children free access to education and through 'equal and fair assessment and grading' (Ministry of Education and Research 2014: 15).

However, these visions and intentions have not trickled down into the everyday realities of Swedish schools. Scholars in higher education institutions were critical of the 1994 curriculum even before this was formalised (Englund 1994). Subsequent reports and research articles show that instead of equality and adaption of the school to local knowledge and needs, segregation and difference came to the fore (IFAU 2014; Kornhall 2013). In addition, a general trend during the 1990s was a lowering of pass rates among Swedish pupils, particularly in the STEM subjects.

Alarmingly, by 2014, children from disadvantaged environments were being left behind in a system committed to benchmarking and standardisation of knowledge. These are mainly children from poorer families, who tend to obtain weaker results. The winners are pupils who fit into the system, who come from families that have an academic background, grow up in a metropolitan area, and/or attend a private school (IFAU 2014). Equal education in this context tends to fit George Orwell's description of equality in *Animal Farm* where 'everyone is equal, but some are more equal than others'.

The Swedish education system seems to have been unable to address issues of diversity among children, and its basic education system is less equal today than it was two decades ago. As political-science professor Leif Lewin argued (SOU 2014), the government has abdicated responsibility for the Swedish school system; thus providing neither good nor equitable schooling to its citizens.

Challenges and ways forward for higher education

Our analysis of curriculum documents related to basic education in South Africa and Sweden reveals that policy-makers' underlying understandings of knowledge have shifted towards an increasingly limited and limiting neo-liberal paradigm. This has had a demonstrably negative impact on teaching and learning in both countries. Managerial ideals of efficiency, measurement, assessment and grading were emphasised in the pursuit of a standardised Western paradigm that masquerades as universal knowledge. This paradigm is largely free-market oriented and reflects knowledge as received ideas, rather than as intellectual inquiry or as a basis for engaged and responsible citizenship.

In South Africa, as Breidlid (2009) argues, it is difficult to know exactly what is included or excluded from the knowledge system, but it is clear that neither indigenous knowledge systems nor local cultural practices have a prominent place, and there is an urgent need to address this. In Sweden, a one-dimensional view of knowledge dominates, and reforms introduced since 2011 have toned down opportunities for educators to adapt the school curriculum to local conditions.

In both countries, higher education institutions are seeing the effects of the basic education system on their students. Students enter university with great fears of being 'wrong', and experience real difficulties with logical, critical or nuanced thinking. While there might be many reasons for this, and further research is needed, the experience of having their learning measured primarily in quantitative ways, and of having little need to consider or present a critical argument, is very likely to be a strong factor.

Educational alternatives that are more inclusive and integrative than the hegemonic neo-liberal model do exist. To bring about change, higher education institutions need to stop playing the roles they play in the global education market. Universities must regain the freedom to challenge received wisdoms and the linear version of human development that legitimises ongoing exploitation and domination of people, nations and regions that are perceived as 'less developed'.

Since the 1960s and 1970s, numerous scholars have outlined the multifaceted nature of the term 'development' and the wide range of disciplinary lenses through which it can be viewed; (see for example, Devkota 2000; Peet and Hartwick 2009; Penderis 2012; Sen 2000; Ucilli and O'Neill 1992). They have suggested the adoption of more inclusive educational systems that can provide valuable insights into local conditions and the reality of the world that people live in (Gupta et al. 2004). In this context, participation becomes a transformative process and proactive 'learning by doing' exercise with people playing a pivotal role in shaping their future (Burkey 1993; Nelson and Wright 1995; Oakley 1991). Situated and local knowledge emerges between people through praxis and is built on a common understanding of concepts and also of actions that includes language. Praxis (Wittgenstein, cited in Johannessen 2002) gives meaning to words. It is knowledge that opens up for new praxis in new situations. Hammarén (2002) argues that knowledge that is not situated within this particular context excludes knowledge that is related to the lived experiences of people. Present knowledge regimes, however, are expressed in explicit rules which propose a high degree of measurement and control, and the system reproduces itself by the introduction of more rules independent of culture and situation. Thus, for higher education institutions to take responsibility for quality education that is inclusive and locally relevant, a shift from the dominant knowledge paradigm, which is universal and not situated, is needed. Local knowledge should be given a natural position in curricula and syllabi from basic education up to university level.

Conclusion

How are global ideas about education and knowledge expressed in South African and Swedish curricula? What are the main challenges for higher education institutions for contributing to quality education? These questions have been addressed through a North-South research partnership, which investigates the knowledge systems within basic education using South Africa and Sweden as a case study area. Addressing this issue according to the occasioned writing genre (Higgins 2013) and critical theory underpinning the narrative (Keucheyan 2010), we have challenged accepted wisdoms and truisms. Critical reading of core international documents and global goals related to education reveal good intentions. Slogans such as 'Education for All', 'Leave no one behind', 'global solidarity' and 'shared knowledge' might have rhetorical impact, but in practice they don't challenge the structural inequality embedded in the political economy of neo-liberal capitalism. The present universal knowledge regime gives prominence to notions of them and us, and further, universal knowledge fails to support otherness. Universal knowledge is not situated in peoples' local everyday life and does not consider the day-to-day lived experiences or indigenous knowledge, thus effectively excluding a large number of citizens. This is obvious from studies of basic education systems in both South Africa and Sweden.

During the 1990s, basic education in both countries underwent substantial transformation, following the dominant neo-liberal logic prevalent in the US, BRICS and OECD countries. Curricula in South Africa and Sweden have become blueprints of new public management, giving prominence to a universal knowledge system (Breidlid 2009) resembling what George Orwell called 'new speak' in his dystopic novel *1984*. This is captured in assessment-driven practices and empty phrases, terminology without definitions and many conceptual contradictions. Basic education curricula, driven by universal knowledge and standardised outcomes, can logically fulfil neither the ambition of providing education for all as a means to equality nor the goal of leaving no one behind. Schooling has become an enterprise and schools 'one-product' factories (Scott 2012). In South Africa, indigenous knowledge is acknowledged, but it is bound up within a universal knowledge system and a Western modernist development paradigm (Breidlid 2009). For Sweden, historically a more homogenous society than South Africa, indigenous knowledge has not been an issue in educational curricula. Indigenous knowledge has been 'othered', reserved for the Sami people who are seen as somehow exotic and as requiring something different from the system. Ideally, indigenous knowledge should challenge curricular, developmental and educational pathways, emphasising the importance of a knowledge system based on *phronesis*.

To educate for real change is a huge challenge for universities. 'By real change', Yusef Waghid, a professor of education at Stellenbosch University, South Africa, emphasises the values of tolerance, diversity and the desire to understand others. For Waghid, engaging students should be the first priority. He argues that encouraging 'autonomy, dissonance and reflective openness in relation to curriculum discourses are but a few ways in which we can ensure that our pedagogic encounters remain responsible, relevant and progressive' (Waghid 2017). This echoes Biesta (2011), who claims that societies should highlight good education rather than effective education. He argues that good is includes a questioning of current aims of education and to reject the framing of education as merely effective education. In Biesta's educational universe, three practices are presented as pillars: 'qualification, socialisation, and subjectification' (Biesta 2011: 19). That is, students need skills to participate in society, they need to be able to transmit values and traditions and most importantly, they must emerge as independent actors. According to Biesta, the purpose of education is to provide knowledge that opens us up for uniqueness to come into the world. This is ultimately a 'pedagogy of interruption' (Biesta 2011: 91).

Following Durkheim (1887/1951), who argued that education can be reformed 'only if society itself is reformed', we have shown that, by having lost autonomy and becoming market driven, higher education institutions face huge challenges. From basic education to university level, pupils and students are being measured according to quantitative and standardised principles with employability as the ultimate goal. This is contrary to Higgins's demand that education institutions should create a 'critically literate citizenry' (2013: xii). For changes to occur in basic education, higher education institutions that are responsible for educating not only teachers, but new generations of planners, scholars and bureaucrats, must interrogate current theories of knowledge, both in teaching and research, and call for reforms that challenge the notion of one-size-fits-all in a universal education system.

Notes

1 Higgins himself was inspired by Edward Said who, in his work *Humanism and Democratic Criticism*, suggested that academics should be responsible for inducing reflection and inquiring arguments, and for breaking 'the hold on us of the short, headline sound-bite format' (2004: 74).

2 In South Africa, the basic education curriculum was revised again after 2011, with the introduction of the Curriculum and Assessment Policy Statement (CAPS). For more on the integration of indigenous knowledge into this new curriculum, see Jacobs (2015).

3 An overt bias towards Christianity evident in the curriculum document has been the topic of much academic and public debate in Sweden but further discussion of this is beyond the scope of this chapter.

4 This is asserted on the website of the Swedish Schools Inspectorate at https://www.skolinspektionen (accessed September 2015).

References

Abel G, B Barakat and W Lutz (2016) 'Meeting the Sustainable Development Goals leads to lower population growth' *Proceedings of the National Academy of Sciences* 113 (50): 14294–14299.

Ahlin Å and E Mörk (2007) *Effects of Decentralization on School Resources: Sweden 1989–2002*. Working Paper 9, Department of Economics, Uppsala University, Sweden.

Berthén D (2007) *Förberedelse för särskildhet: Särskolans pedagogiska arbete i ett verksamhetsteoretiskt perspektiv.* Karlstad: Karlstads Universitet.

Biesta G (2011) *Good Education in an Age of Measurement: Ethics, Politics, Democracy.* Boulder, CO: Paradigm.

Breidlid A (2009) 'Culture, indigenous knowledge systems and sustainable development: A critical view of education in an African context' *International Journal of Educational Development* 29: 140–148.

Burkey S (1993) *People First: A Guide to Self-Reliant, Participatory Rural Development.* London: Zed.

Chisholm L (2005) 'The making of South Africa's National Curriculum Statement' *Journal of Curriculum Studies* 37 (2): 193–208.

DoE (Department of Education, South Africa) (1996) *Lifelong Learning Through a National Qualifications Framework: Report of the Ministerial Committee for Development Work on the National Qualifications Framework.* Pretoria.

DoE (2002) *Revised National Curriculum. Statement: Grades R–9 (Schools).* Pretoria. Available online.

Devkota PL (2000) *People-Centred Development in Nepal: An Innovative Approach.* An Occasional Paper. Available online.

Durkheim E (1897/1951) *Suicide: A Study in Sociology.* New York: The Free Press.

Englund T (1994) 'Communities, markets and traditional values: Swedish schooling in the 1990s' *Curriculum Studies* 2 (1): 5–29.

Filloux JC (1993) 'Emil Durkheim, 1858–1917' *Prospects: Quarterly Review of Comparative Education* 23 (1/2): 303–320.

Freire P (1970/2017) *Pedagogy of the Oppressed.* London: Penguin.

Goffman E (1959/1990) *The Presentation of Self in Everyday Life.* London: Penguin.

Gorjestani N (2000) *Indigenous Knowledge for Development. Opportunities and Challenges.* World Bank Working Paper 24869, Washington DC. Available online.

Gupta D, H Grandvoinnet and M Romani (2004) 'State-community synergies in community-driven development' *Journal of Development Studies* 40 (3): 27–32.

Halvorsen H (2015) Knowledge for Sustainable Democratic Development: Towards a New Political Economy. Unpublished.

Hammarén M (2002) 'Lyssnande är hårt arbete' i P Tillberg (red) *Dialoger – om yrkeskunnande och teknologi.* Stockholm: Föreningen Dialoger.

Higgins J (2013) *Academic Freedom in a Democratic South Africa. Essays and Interviews on Higher Education and the Humanities.* Johannesburg: Wits University Press.

IFAU (Institute for Evaluation of Labour Market and Education Policy, Ministry of Employment, Sweden) (2014) *Decentralisation, School Choice and Independent Schools: Results and Equivalence in the Swedish School System,* Report 25, IFAU, Upsalla. Available online.

Jacobs KR (2015) The Classroom Implementation of Indigenous Knowledge in the Science Curriculum by Science Teachers in the Western Cape Province, South Africa. PhD thesis, University of Cape Town. Available online.

Johannessen KS (2002) 'Tankar om tyst kunskap' i P Tillberg (red) *Dialoger – om yrkeskunnande och teknologi*. Stockholm: Föreningen Dialoger.

Karbo JA (2005) 'Managing indigenous knowledge: What role for public librarians in Sierra Leone?' *International Information and Library Review* 37: 199–207.

Keucheyan R (2010) *The Left Hemisphere: Mapping Critical Theory Today*. London and New York: Verso.

Kornhall P (2013) *Barnexperimentet: svensk skola i fritt fall*. Stockholm: Leopard Förlag.

Langenhoven K (2014) The Effectiveness of an Argumentation Instructional Model in Enhancing Pre-service Science Teacher's Efficacy to Implement a Relevant Science-indigenous Knowledge Curriculum in Western Cape Classrooms, PhD thesis, University of the Western Cape, South Africa.

Laurie, R, Y Nonoyama-Tarumi, R McKeoun and C Hopkins (2016) 'Contribution of education for sustainable development to quality education': A synthesis of research. *Journal of Education for Sustainable Development* 10 (2): 226–242.

Le Blanc D (2015) *Towards Integration At Last? The Sustainable Development Goals as a Network of Targets*. Working Paper 141. United Nations Department of Economic and Social Affairs.

Li TM (2007) *The Will to Improve: Governmentality, Development, and the Practice of Politics*. Durham/London: Duke University Press.

Lindblad S and Wallin E (1993) 'On transition of power, democracy and education in Sweden' *Journal of Curriculum Studies* 25: 77–88.

Ministry of Education and Research, Sweden (2014) *Sweden: Education for All 2015 National Review*. Stockholm: Regeringskansliet. Available online.

Msila V (2007) 'From apartheid education to the Revised National Curriculum Statement: Pedagogy for identity formation and nation building in South Africa' *Nordic Journal of African Studies* 16 (2): 146–160.

Nelson N and S Wright (1995) *Power and Participatory Development: Theory and Practice*. London: ITDG.

Oakley P (1991) *Project with People: The Practice of Participation in Rural Development*. Geneva: ILO.

Odora Hoppers CA (2007) 'Knowledge, democracy and justice in a globalizing world' *Nordisk Pedagogik* 27: 3–53.

Odora Hoppers CA (2013) 'Beyond human rights: Confronting atrocity with healing and reconciliation, merging African perspectives in a globalising world' *International Journal of African Renaissance Studies* 8:1: 59–77.

Peet R and E Hartwick (2009) *Theories of Development: Contentions, Arguments, Alternatives*. New York: Guilford.

Penderis S (2012) 'Theorizing participation: From tyranny to emancipation' *Journal of African and Asian Local Government Studies* 1 (3): 1–28.

Polanyi M (1966/1983). *The Tacit Dimension*. Gloucester, MA: Peter Smith.

Preece J (2009) *Lifelong Learning and Development: A Southern Perspective*. London: Continuum.

Prescott D and D Stibbe (2016) *Partnering for the SDGs: Building up the System of Support to Help Mainstream Collaboration for Sustainable Development*. Oxford: Partnering Initiative.

Riessman CK (2008) *Narrative Methods for the Human Sciences*. Thousand Oaks, CA: Sage.

Said E (2004) *Humanism and Democratic Criticism*. New York: Columbia.

Sarabhai K (2016) Editorial: Sustainable Development Goals. *Journal of Education for Sustainable Development* 10 (2): 205–207.

Scott JC (2012) *Two Cheers for Anarchism*. Princeton and Oxford: Princeton University Press.

Sen A (2000) *Development as Freedom*. Oxford: Oxford University Press.

Sen B (2005) 'Indigenous knowledge for development: Bringing research and practice together' *International Information and Library Review* 37: 375–382.

Skolverket (Swedish National Agency for Education) (2011a) *Curriculum for the Compulsory School, Preschool Class and the Recreation Centre, 2011*. Stockholm. Available online.

Skolverket (2011b) *Läroplan för sameskolan, förskoleklassen och fritidshemmet*. Stockholm.

SOU (Official Reports of the Swedish Government) (2014) *The Government Must Not Abdicate*. Stockholm.

Sterling S (2016) 'A commentary on education and Sustainable Development Goals' *Journal of Education for Sustainable Development* 10 (2): 208–213.

Sundberg D and N Wahlström (2016) *Den svenska läroplansutvecklingen: Begrepp och tendenser*. Available online.

Thompson K (1982/2002) *Emil Durkheim*. London: Routledge.

Ucilli J and D O'Neill (1992) 'Challenging Eurocentrism' *Forward Motion* 1: 34–45.

UN (United Nations) (2013) *A New Global Partnership: Eradicate Poverty and Transform Economies Through Sustainable Development*. Report of the High-Level Panel of Eminent Persons on the Post-2015 Development Agenda. Available online.

UN (2015) *Transforming our world: The 2030 agenda for sustainable development*. Resolution 70/1 adopted by the UN General Assembly, 25 September 2015. Available online.

UNESCO (1990) *World Declaration on Education for All. The Framework for Action: Meeting Basic Learning Needs*. Available online.

UNESCO (1994) *The Salamanca Statement and Framework for Action on Special Needs Education*. Salamanca, Spain. Available online.

UNESCO (1997) *Education for a Sustainable Future: A Transdisciplinary Vision for Concerted Action*. Available online.

UNESCO (1998) *The World Conference on Higher Education in the Twenty-first Century: Vision and Action*. Available online.

UNESCO (2000) *The Dakar Framework for Action. Education for All: Meeting our Collective Commitments*. Available online.

UNESCO (2005) *The Convention on the Protection and Promotion of the Diversity of Cultural Expression*. Available online.

Vandeyar S and Killen R (2003) 'Has curriculum reform in South Africa really changed assessment practices, and what promise does the revised National Curriuculum Statement hold?' *Perspectives in Education* 21 (1): 119–133.

Waghid Y (2017) 'Educate for real change' *Mail & Guardian*, 9 June. Available online.

Wahlström N (2016) 'A third wave of European education policy: Transnational and national conceptions of knowledge in Swedish curricula' *European Educational Research Journal* 15 (3): 298–313.

Chapter 6

Academia in the context of constraint and a performative SDG agenda: A perspective on South Africa

Suriamurthee Maistry and Erlend Eidsvik

IN THIS CHAPTER, we first examine the context within which academics, operating in a globalised academic space, have to give effect to their work. In the rapidly altering world of educational globalisation and the emerging global knowledge economy, we argue that there is a need to examine afresh what it means to function as an academic in an environment that is increasingly shaped by rightist neo-liberal ideology. The June 2017 withdrawal of the United States from the Paris Agreement on climate change indicates the resurgence of the neo-conservatism and neo-liberalism of the Reagan and Thatcher regimes. Although this resurgence has received some resistance from the left in the UK and the US, the extent to which this will be sustained remains uncertain. Significantly, the rightist movement (and new nationalism) necessarily traverses a 'slippery slope' as it attempts to augment the dominant neo-liberal agenda, and the inherent contradictions involved in this are likely to play out in unpredictable ways (Harvey 2007). Although individual freedom (including economic freedom) marks a defining (and appealing) feature of neo-liberalism, an increasingly dominant role for government might constrain this freedom.

As the neo-liberal agenda strengthens its hegemony over how society 'measures' development, it may pave the way for even narrower measurement regimes. Thus, our second focus highlights our concern for the performativity infused ideological subtext of the Sustainable Development Goals (SDGs), especially as the goals relate to educational 'performance'. We draw implications for what this could mean for academics in the SDG era. We also offer a critical perspective on SDG 4 (quality education) through a post-political lens, and explore what it means to engage the socially inclusive concept of the 'pluriverse' within the SDG debate.[1]

As a third area, we raise a few issues around mentoring and building capacity in higher education with a particular focus on South Africa and the role it plays (and doesn't play) in Africa's economic and educational development. In this section, we touch on the potential for North–South collaborative initiatives in relation to academic mentorship and development.

Finally, we consider the likely impact of the SDGs on the development of academics working in a global space. We depart from a critique that the targets and indicators related to SDG 4 are linked into a universalistic apparatus that obstructs 'pluriversal knowledge' within education. We begin, however, by reflecting on some of the contextual factors influencing and shaping higher education.

The academic space as a smouldering milieu

The transformation of higher education systems often happens in a somewhat contradictory space, especially in contexts where democratic and social justice priorities clash with market-driven imperatives for economic growth (Singh 2012). In South Africa, for example, following the abandonment of the Reconstruction and Development Programme, the adoption of the Growth, Employment and Redistribution policy failed dismally to alleviate poverty, create employment or fairly distribute economic gains (Habib 2013). Instead, neo-liberal and 'business friendly' policies favour corporations at the expense of poor citizens, allowing the upper-classes across all races to thrive while offering only marginal gains for the poor majority. Žižek's (2011) notion of 'inclusive exclusion' has relevance here as it speaks to a condition in which the majority of South Africans enjoy superficial political inclusion but are excluded economically. The promised post-apartheid dividends have not accrued. So, while democratic participation occurs, the values of equality, participation, redistribution, access to information and transparency, and gender parity remain merely at the level of political rhetoric.

Like in many other parts of the world, the South African education system has also failed to respond efficiently to market imperatives (ASSAF 2010), although this is one of its declared intentions in the National Development Plan (National Planning Commission 2012). This failure appears congruent with Stronach's (2010) critical assessment of the higher education system's inability to respond effectively to the needs of global capital. Stronach argued that while some claim that market responsiveness is the objective, in reality, such attempts have remained at the level of mimicry.

The global swing towards self-preservation, renewed nationalism, the securing of the physical boundaries of the nation-state (for example, Brexit), the election of a neo-conservative leadership in the United States, and the rise of right-wing political parties in Europe (for example, in Austria, Hungary and Denmark) present particular challenges for higher education globally. New patterns and modus operandi in international terrorism as well as in retaliatory measures adopted by global superpowers have begun to impact on the previously 'open' international movement of students and academics.

The tension between insularity and globalisation, and what this might mean for education and academic work in an evolving space, requires investigation. This, coupled with a dramatic change in the ways in which the world conceives of education's purpose, renders the international higher education project even more complex. That is, as Nussbaum (2010) and Sen (2009) point out, a distinct shift has occurred away from the concept of education as serving a social good to a performativity-driven and instrumentalist conception of education for economic profit.

That higher education should play a role in advancing world peace, international camaraderie and social cohesion is beyond question. How such an agenda can be realised is, however, worthy of careful thought. How might the curricula and pedagogy of higher education institutions embrace such a role? One possibility is to integrate this value orientation across the curriculum, as opposed to retaining it in its current location in certain social science programmes. However, it is likely that higher education institutions that offer programmes that are out of sync with international developments could lose currency and favour among students. This applies especially to students seeking relevant intellectual competencies applicable in the rapidly changing international context. The SDGs could perhaps serve as a globally 'approved' point of departure in the development of new higher education curricula. The higher education field certainly offers a fertile space for robust engagement with the SDGs, in which pressing issues, such as poverty alleviation and the creation of meaningful employment, could receive the strategic political and economic consideration they deserve.

In a context where higher education institutions market their courses in terms of the 'abundant' lifestyles that students might derive from success in such programmes, rather than as offering a space for high-level intellectual activity, the tension between 'hedonism and utility' (Haywood et al. 2011) plays out in particular ways. Of concern is the absence of dissent that might disrupt the status quo. While sporadic dissent is common among academics and students in many parts of the world, in our view, this is not widespread or consistent enough to trigger substantive disruption of the current value system. Also of concern is the lack of awareness about the current system's nefarious undertones and how these shape conceptualisations of the work of academics in a global space.

It is thus reasonable to presume that the development and delivery of robust, contemporary and cutting-edge higher education programmes, and research agendas underpinned by social justice imperatives, will depend on the availability of highly skilled academics with a global consciousness and social sensitivity. However, it is unrealistic to imagine that many senior academics, who often find themselves trapped in neo-liberal performativity, will prioritise the development of a 'radicalised' research and teaching agenda for young academics working in a global space. For this development to gain traction, it might have to follow the traditional manner through which knowledge is vetted in academia, that is, via platforms such as research conferences, colloquiums, seminars and publications.

The frailties of South Africa's higher education sector

Historically, South Africa has played a significant role in Africa's economic, political and educational development (Gelb 2001). However, there is uncertainty and scepticism among higher education professionals in many African countries as to exactly what this role should be. The country's status as hegemon in the African region also deserves interrogation. In our view, South Africa occupies a precarious and conflicted position in Africa as it grapples with the frailties arising from its past.

A major factor limiting South Africa's influence in Africa has been its inability to address its own debilitating structural problems, including its dual economy, persistently high rates of unemployment (30 per cent) and its inability to grow its GDP beyond 2 per cent per annum for the last two decades (Statistics South Africa 2017). Ineffectual political leadership has compounded these problems (Habib 2013; Jansen 2017), making the need for mentorship among South African and African academics all the more compelling.

Certainly, South African higher education is in a vexed position in terms of its own capacity to conduct, promote and supervise research. This is a fault line that has a profound impact on the country's ability to promote and sustain high-level knowledge production (Teferra 2015). For example, less than 35 per cent of tenured professors in South Africa hold a PhD (ASSAF 2010), and a sizeable proportion of these are close to retirement. This represents a significant challenge for South Africa's ability to maintain a core group of high-calibre academics.

Damtew Teferra (2015) rightly cautions that South Africa's limited research capacity has similarly significant implications for the country's neighbours whose future intellectuals consume its 'knowledge commodities'. He posits that while South Africa remains the foremost knowledge producer on the African continent, it is naive and even perilous to overstate this position, as inherent frailties threaten the ability of the system to continue to deliver high-quality post-graduate education.

This kind of precariousness makes the need for debate about academic training increasingly urgent. For example, the political imperatives to fast-track young academics from previously disadvantaged communities could well result in PhDs being seen as outcomes or commodities as opposed to a process of deep, rich, independent and high-level conceptual development. To add insult to injury, fast-tracked PhD graduates are often quickly burdened with high numbers of research students whom they are expected to mentor, despite having received very little meaningful mentoring themselves.

The negative legacy of apartheid on South Africa's education system is well documented (see, for example, Jansen 2009, 2017), and the contemporary crises make it clear that apartheid continues to haunt the country two decades into democracy. In fact, it can be argued that both democracy and the equitable provision of education are under threat in South Africa. In an incisive analysis of the Fees Must Fall protests, Jonathan Jansen, a former vice chancellor of the University of the Free State, offered a scathing criticism of the state's leadership inertia and their abdication of responsibility (Jansen 2017).

The year 1994 was a watershed moment in South Africa's history. As a 'darling' of the international community following its unprecedented peaceful transition to democracy under the leadership of Nelson Mandela, powerful Western nations looked to South Africa to show leadership and innovation in relation to education provision. Instead, the newly democratic state somewhat blindly borrowed policy, adopting an outcomes-based education system, which has since been roundly criticised as inappropriate to the country's severely under-resourced schools. To their credit, through the efforts of Nelson Mandela and his successor Thabo Mbeki, South African leaders attempted to assert their vision of an African Renaissance, which sought to better position Africa, and African education, for engagement with the international community. However, these good intentions were not sufficient. Decisive action was required, and its absence has had consequences that the naive South African polity did not adequately anticipate.

In a paper on the relationship between South Africa and its neighbours, Zimbabwe and Swaziland, Lalbahadur (2015) argued that South Africa's attempt to advocate for transformation in governance has been largely benign and wholly ineffective. Similarly, attempts to develop a regional educational qualification framework failed to gain traction in the region. The enormous potential for substantive regional collaboration on education and higher education remains untapped.

Mentorship and collaboration in a flammable and schizophrenic environment

Shore (2010) traced the emergence of the 'schizophrenic university' – marked by confounding imperatives and the overloading of responsibilities – that is, the university that tries to do and be too many things at the same time. Globally, the dominance of neo-liberal discourse has altered the traditional Humboldtian vision of higher education, making it increasingly market-driven. The international rankings that epitomise the globalisation of the higher education enterprise are stoking the conflagration (Haywood et al. 2011). The effect is a constant reshaping of the knowledge economy into one in which 'profitable' knowledge takes precedence over 'soft' knowledge that is not readily convertible into forms that serve economic ends. As a result, a narrowly defined economic utilitarian mentality shapes the higher education market and its offerings in particular ways, leading to increasing competition for financial and human resources.

While healthy collaboration does still occur within and between some higher education institutions, neo-liberal forces often detract from the vision of community and the social pact that has guided the academic community for centuries. Meanwhile, prescriptive funding criteria, such as a cross-regional collaboration requirement, can create contrived relationships that are seldom based on pre-existing and sound foundations. Contextual issues, such as differing research cultures, data-collection constraints and financial-accountability mechanisms pose real challenges to cross-regional collaboration. This raises the issue of how universities can constructively align with international partners, with a view to developing and strengthening collaboration in relation to mentoring novice academics to respond to global challenges and opportunities. Included in this are how such academics navigate this competitive environment, the gains that can accrue from healthy competition as well as the costs of this competition for the higher education sector. For academics to thrive and function effectively, a particular kind of mentorship is necessary.

In acceding to the demands of a neo-liberal environment, higher education institutions begin to subject their human resources to stringent demands and particular types of performance (Maistry 2012). Accordingly, the human resource departments then impose performance and accountability models from the corporate world onto academics in an attempt to measure productivity levels. This often occurs at the expense of social justice, and is likely to subvert the achievement of the SDGs.

What kind of mentorship is required to avoid the systematic suffocation of the academic as institutions react to the neo-liberal squeeze? Of significance in answering this question is to achieve clarity about the expectations and roles of academics as they help to shape research agendas and course curricula, as well as guiding students. In the discussion that follows, we attempt to open a debate about how this question might be addressed by signalling key issues worth consideration.

The assumption at many higher education institutions is that existing academic staff (faculty members) will autonomously work out the competencies necessary to educate future global citizens (albeit within a neo-liberal performative frame). This is a somewhat risky assumption. Tacit knowledge and anecdotal experience indicates that the experiences of novice academics, as they attempt to come to terms with the teaching, research and community service dimensions of their job descriptions, are not well-understood or acknowledged.

From quantity to quality and back again: the lack of 'pluriversal' knowledge in the SDGs

Political and technocratic support for the SDGs is widespread. Like the Millennium Development Goals (MDGs), the SDGs are likely to have far-reaching consequences for development practice globally, and for education in particular. In 2016, the Inter-Agency Expert Group on the SDG Indicators presented a global indicator framework to measure progress towards the SDGs (UN 2016). In many contexts, indicators are vital quantifying measures and constitute a key tool. However, not all knowledge is easily quantifiable.

In a development context, for example, Jerven (2015) has questioned the usefulness of quantifiable measures and shown how these supported consensus around dubious policy making processes. In terms of education in a post-political development context, local and indigenous practices – also known as 'pluriversal knowledge' – can be useful in challenging hegemonic knowledge, knowledge practices, as well the indicator apparatuses linked to the SDGs.

Considering how education shapes societies, such concerns are crucial. While MDG 2 was about universal access to *primary* education, SDG 4 concerns access throughout the educational span, and addresses education *quality* in particular. The key indicator for MDG 2 was the primary school net enrolment rate, which increased from 83 per cent in 2000 to 91 per cent in 2015, globally (UN 2015). This represents progress. However, education's relevance for improving the economic, social and political aspects of a society is not taken into account when only inputs are measured and not outcomes or impact. While the strength of the MDGs was that they constituted straightforward and manageable goals, they were criticised for lacking focus on the societal implications of their outcomes and impacts (Loewe 2012). Further, more data gaps than actual observations were recorded (Jerven 2017).

Consequently, the SDGs place a stronger emphasis on their own social implications. To paraphrase Le Blanc (2015), the SDGs aim to cover the entire sustainable development universe.

Measure what we treasure

Since the 1980s, quantitative methods have replaced qualitative and historical methods of learning assessment. This is a rising trend in low- and middle-income countries, supported, to a large degree, by donor agencies (Lockheed 2013). In line with this, the OECD's Programme for International Student Assessment (PISA) has affected education policies and curricula globally, and best practices as defined by the OECD have been adopted in several countries as blueprints for educational reform (Kamens 2013). One consequence of this is that a particular kind of education assessment has been embedded into the SDG agenda. This includes a general shift towards large-scale quantitative assessments.

Concerns about and critiques of this 'measurement dogma' can be addressed in different ways. One comes from the field of post-politics (see, for example, Swyngedouw 2007), which scrutinises where decisions are made, and focuses on the rising power of technocrats and the diminishing power of the education and research community. This is a productive framework for identifying stakeholders and decision-making processes as well as relative levels of power and legitimacy in relation to decision-making.

In the Nordic context, a vital debate challenging the PISA approach to education has taken place. Social media groups,[2] op-eds and newspaper articles[3] have criticised and debated the role of testing, measurement and indicators within target-driven, neo-liberal education policies. This has taken the form of bottom-up resistance in which teachers, parents, researchers and some politicians have challenged the existing system. Meanwhile, the system has been defended by technocrats, neo-liberal politicians and conservative think tanks – the same actors who decided to adopt the PISA system and facilitated its implementation. Teachers and researchers in the education sector were to a large degree excluded from both the decision to adopt PISA and its implementation.

Another approach is evident in the concepts and tools of post-development scholars, such as Escobar (2012), who argued against the 'universal and homolingual thrust of modernity' evident in many development practices and agendas, including in our view, the SDGs. Escobar (2012) and Höne (2015) are highly critical of development based in universalist modus operandi that overemphasise scientific methods. They argue that this 'path to modernity' involves the invention of the so-called Third World through education programmes, health programmes and industrialisation, and that development is little more than a strategy for cultural and social domination.

The concept of the pluriverse, on the other hand, offers a critique of neo-liberal policies and universalistic apparatuses such as the SDGs. It aims to reveal a plurality of alternatives, options and solutions instead of a single linear and universally applicable path to a singular, linear and universal model of modernity, development or sustainability.

It is important to note that a wide range of voices were included in the negotiations that led up to the formulation of the SDGs. However, the indicator framework for assessing the quality of global education has created a universalistic apparatus that excludes the pluriverse once again. This is a significant challenge, and one that the education sector must address, regardless of the SDG indicator apparatus. Multiple voices that problematise diverse aspects of education quality must be heard and respected.

Another challenge concerns the collection of data for the indicators. Jerven (2017: 46) estimates that of the 230 indicators, half are lacking in 'acceptable country coverage, agreed-upon methodologies, or both'. Many countries lack the data (or the infrastructure required to collect the data) to measure progress on achieving the SDGs. This means that monitoring and implementing the SDGs will require enormous investment from the very countries that already have the fewest resources (Dunning 2016). Jerven (2017) argues that the total cost of measuring the indicators connected to each target, based on a modest estimation of the costs involved in measuring the 60 MDG indicators ($24 billion), is unrealistic. With more than 200 indicators, the SDGs require complex methodologies to be followed in countries where data collection can be extremely difficult and highly contested. If the indicator framework is designed such that the costs of data collection alone are unrealistic, we should surely be very worried about the implementation of the SDGs themselves.

Of course, the education and development sectors are in need of statistical data to provide reliable information for policy implementation. However, it is crucial for us to engage in the SDG debate, especially around SDG 4. The ten targets under SDG 4 entail an all-inclusive approach to education, from primary to tertiary education and vocational training. The 11 corresponding indicators are designed to improve data collection by measuring: the proportion of learners at different levels in the education system; participation rates and parity indexes; and the extent to which global citizen education and education for sustainable development are mainstreamed in national education policies, curricula, teacher education and student assessment (UN 2017). Bexell and

Jönsson (2017) express a concern that the development of the quantitative indicators is a political process as much as a technical one. The indicators will have strong steering effects before and beyond the evaluation phase, and measurements will be a trade-off between poor statistical data availability on one hand, and addressing urgent needs on the other. Without clarity on what kinds of measurements will be taken, for whom, what purposes the data will be used for, and what kinds of policies are at stake, a range of unintended negative consequences may materialise (Jerven 2017), giving rise to exactly what Escobar (2012) warned against – a failure to take the pluriverse into account.

Opening up new conversations

In this chapter, we have attempted to offer some insights into the fragility and volatility of the higher education sector. We pointed out some of the complex challenges involved in developing and mentoring academics in a milieu of perennial conflict and contradiction, especially as the education project is increasingly held hostage to a neo-conservative and neo-liberal agenda. In addition, we touched on a possible approach to encouraging a range of approaches to understanding the world, and the world of education in particular.

As we wrote, a range of key questions emerged around the strategic competencies that need to infuse mentorship programmes for new academics as they construct their careers and envisage doing research in the context of the SDGs. In our view, challenging the universalistic nature of the indicators and integrating the notion of the pluriverse into education policy, invites further critical study. We offer the following questions in the hope that they might be useful in framing such studies:

- What competencies do academics need to avoid becoming merely a subject/instrument of the neo-liberal agenda?
- How can we develop higher education communities of practice or knowledge communities that serve the UN development agenda without being subservient to it?
- How might we deepen understandings and create higher levels of awareness of the threats posed by neo-liberalism, with a view to resisting and challenging it?
- How do we develop an epistemology of scepticism through the programmes and curricula we construct and deliver?
- How can we promote higher education as necessarily a political experience and disrupt the notion of training 'human capital'?
- What should a new North–South social compact consist of?

- What might it take to re-centre the human subject at the heart of the educational enterprise?
- How can we shape and reshape the discourses around what it is to be an academic operating in a global space?

Notes

1 The notion of the pluriverse was coined to encapsulate 'the coexistence of a rich multiplicity of moral languages, concepts and discourses' (Esteva and Prakash 2014). Held within the concept is a strong critique of capitalism, patriarchy and imperialism, which identifies and targets conditions of coloniality (Höne 2015).
2 https://www.facebook.com/groups/706685366093232/?fref=ts, https://www.facebook.com/Foreldreoppr%C3%B8r-i-Osloskolen-420548688118979/?fref=ts
3 Some examples discussing education and PISA in a Norwegian context: http://www.dagsavisen.no/nyemeninger/nyemeninger-search-7.802117?sortby=date&q=skole+pisa

References

ASSAf (Academy of Science of South Africa) (2010) *The PhD Study: An Evidence-based Study on How to Meet the Demands for High-level Skills in an Emerging Economy.* Pretoria. Available online.

Bexell M and Jönsson K (2017) 'Responsibility and the United Nations' Sustainable Development Goals' *Forum for Development Studies* 44 (1): 13–29. doi: 10.1080/08039410.2016.1252424

Dunning C (2016) *230 Indicators Approved for SDG Agenda.* Washington, DC: Center for Global Development. Available online.

Escobar A (1995/2012) *Encountering Development: The Making and Unmaking of the Third World.* Princeton, NJ: Princeton University Press.

Esteva G and MS Prakash (1998/2014) *Grassroots Post-Modernism: Remaking the Soil of Cultures.* London and New York: Zed.

Gelb A (2001) *South Africa's Role and Importance in the Development of Africa and the African Agenda.* Johannesburg: Edge Institute.

Habib A (2013) *South Africa's Suspended Revolution: Hopes and Prospects.* Johannesburg: Wits University Press.

Harvey D (2007) *A Brief History of Neoliberalism.* Oxford: Oxford University Press.

Haywood H, R Jenkins and M Molesworth (2011) 'A degree will make your dreams come true: Higher education as the management of consumer desires' in M Molesworth, R Scullion and E Nixon (eds), *The Marketisation of Higher Education and the Student as Consumer.* London: Routledge.

Höne K (2015) 'What quality and whose assessment: The role of education diplomacy in the SDG process – A new diplomacy for a new development agenda?' paper presented at the 3rd Nordic Conference on Development Research, Gothenburg, Sweden, 5–6 November 2015.

Jansen J (2009) *Knowledge in the Blood: Confronting Race and the Apartheid Past.* Cape Town: UCT Press.

Jansen J (2017) *As by Fire: The End of the South African University.* Cape Town: Tafelberg.

Jerven M (2015) *Africa: Why Economists Get it Wrong.* London: Zed.

Jerven M (2017) 'How much will a data revolution in development cost?' *Forum for Development Studies* 44 (1): 31–50. doi: 10.1080/08039410.2016.1260050

Kamens D (2013) 'Globalization and the emergence of an audit culture: PISA and the search for "best practices" and magic bullets' in H-D Meyer and A Benavot (eds), *PISA, Power and Policy: The Emergence of Global Educational Governance.* Oxford: Symposium.

Lalbahadur A (2015) *South Africa's Foreign Policy: Tempering Dominance Through Integration.* Johannesburg: South African Institute of International Affairs. Available online.

Le Blanc D (2015) 'Towards integration at last? The Sustainable Development Goals as a network of targets' *Sustainable Development* 23 (3): 176–187. doi: 10.1002/sd.1582

Lockheed M (2013) 'Causes and consequences of international assessments in developing countries' in H-D Meyer and A Benavot (eds), *PISA, Power and Policy: The Emergence of Global Educational Governance.* Oxford: Symposium.

Loewe M (2012) *Post 2015: How to Reconcile the Millennium Development Goals (MDGs) and the Sustainable Development Goals (SDGs)?* Briefing Paper 18, German Development Institute, Bonn. Available online.

Maistry SM (2012) 'Confronting the neoliberal brute: Reflections of a higher education middle-level manager' *South African Journal of Higher Education* 26 (3): 515–528.

National Planning Commission (2012) *National Development Plan 2030: Our Future Make it Work.* Pretoria: Office of the Presidency – Republic of South Africa. Available online.

Nussbaum MC (2010) *Not for Profit: Why Democracy Needs the Social Sciences.* Princeton: Princeton University Press.

Sen A (2009) *The Idea of Justice.* London: Allen Lane.

Shore C (2010) 'Beyond the multiversity: Neoliberalism and the rise of the schizophrenic university' *Social Anthropology* 18 (1): 15–29.

Singh S (2012) 'Re-inserting the "public good" into higher education transformation' in B Leibowitz (ed.), *Higher Education for the Public Good: Views from the South.* Stoke on Trent: Trentham.

Statistics South Africa (2017) *Quarterly Labour Force Survey.* Pretoria: Stats SA. Available online.

Stronach I (2010) *Globalizing Education: Educating the Local.* London: Routledge.

Swyngedouw E (2007) 'Impossible/undesirable sustainability and the post-political condition' in JR Krueger and D Gibbs (eds), *The Sustainable Development Paradox: Urban Political Economy in the United States and Europe.* New York: Guildford.

Teferra D (2015) 'Manufacturing and exporting excellence and "mediocrity": Doctoral education in South Africa', *South African Journal of Higher Education* 29 (5): 8–19.

UN (United Nations) (2015) *The Millennium Development Goals Report 2015*. Available online.

UN (2016) 'UN Statistical Commission agrees on global indicator framework', United Nations website, 11 March 2016. Available online.

UN (2017) *Sustainable Development Goal 4*. Available online.

Žižek S (2011) *Living in the End Times*. London: Verso.

PART II: **NORTH–SOUTH COLLABORATION**

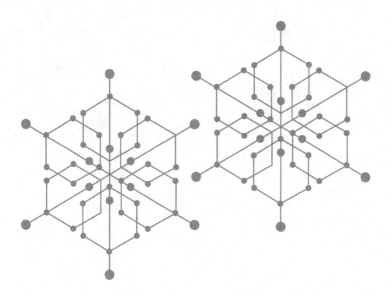

Chapter 7

Contributing to the agenda for sustainable development through North–South educational partnerships: An analysis of two Linnaeus-Palme staff–student exchanges between Sweden and South Africa

Kate Rowntree and Roddy Fox

THE GEOGRAPHY DEPARTMENT AT RHODES UNIVERSITY in Grahamstown, South Africa, has participated in three Linnaeus-Palme exchange programmes with Swedish universities, two with Högskolan Väst, from 2003 to 2010, and one with Linköping University, from 2013 to 2015. All three programmes involved student and staff exchanges between the participating universities. As participating staff from Rhodes University are now retired and will not take part in any future exchanges, this is an appropriate moment to draw together our experiences. We do this in a number of ways. First, we evaluate our exchanges within the context of the Millennium Development Goals (MDGs), the Sustainable Development Goals (SDGs), and international and institutional policies relating to internationalisation, sustainable development and the environment. We then present reflections from students who participated in the exchanges to show the extent to which the programmes have heightened their awareness of their own and partner cultures, and might have contributed to the achievement of the MDGs and SDGs. We also discuss the curriculum of the last exchange, in which we used a range of active learning methods to promote deep learning about sustainable water resource management in Africa. We conclude by relating our experience of designing, developing and participating in these exchange programmes to the broader context of North-South collaboration and consider how aspects of what we have learned might be applied to future programmes of this nature.

The Millennium Declaration of 2000, the Millennium Development Goals and the Sustainable Development Goals

The frameworks and protocols established by the United Nations Millennium Declaration of 2000 were developed and promoted as we began planning for our first exchange with Högskolan Väst. Thus, they are a useful starting point for this paper. The Millennium Declaration was subsequently encapsulated as the eight MDGs that nations were to meet by 2015. In September 2015, our last Linnaeus-Palme exchange programme ended just as the MDGs were superseded by the SDGs. The 17 SDGs, to be met by 2030, have set an ambitious agenda for people, the planet, prosperity, peace and partnership. Two of these in particular, the planet and partnership, are arguably common threads running through global obligations since 2000.

The Millennium Declaration starts by spelling out its core values and principles. Article I.6 details the six values that are fundamental to international relations: freedom, equality, solidarity, tolerance, respect for nature and shared responsibility. It is fair to say that two of these, in particular, have been especially important to our curriculum and exchange activities. They are quoted below (UN 2000: 2):

> *Solidarity.* Global challenges must be managed in a way that distributes the costs and burdens fairly in accordance with basic principles of equity and social justice. Those who suffer or benefit least deserve help from those who benefit most...

> *Respect for nature.* Prudence must be shown in the management of all living species and natural resources, in accordance with the precepts of sustainable development. Only in this way can the immeasurable riches provided to us by nature be preserved and passed on to our descendants. The current unsustainable patterns of production and consumption must be changed in the interests of our future welfare and that of our descendants.

These values were subsequently translated into MDG 7 (Ensure environmental sustainability) and MDG 8 (Develop a global partnership for development). None of the MDGs were directed specifically towards higher education or sustainability in education; MDGs 2 and 3 promote universal primary education and the elimination of gender disparity from primary and secondary education.

Arguably, higher education can be said to feature in the solidarity principle that underpinned MDGs 7 and 8. In our case, the Swedish International Development Cooperation Agency's Linnaeus-Palme programme fully funded reciprocal exchanges of staff and students between higher education institutions in Sweden and countries in the South. SANORD member institutions, such as Rhodes University, Högskolan Väst and Linköping University, therefore benefitted from this funding vehicle.

The seven aims of the Linnaeus-Palme exchange programme remain strongly related to the Millennium Declaration and MDGs described above (Boman et al. 2012), and to MDG 8 in particular:

- The programme aims to raise the quality of higher education by integrating global perspectives into the learning process.
- Teachers and students participating in the exchange should gain increased competence in global issues and an enlarged contact network.
- On a departmental level, the aim is to integrate global perspectives into teaching, which will also benefit those who have not taken part in an exchange.
- Students who participate in exchanges should be better prepared for work in a global context. Teachers who participate in exchanges are expected to use and spread both their own global knowledge as well as that of their students, inside and outside of the classroom.
- Partners should be able to participate in equal collaboration that leads to mutual benefits, even if the resources may be very different.
- The programme, financed by the Swedish International Development Cooperation Agency, aims to contribute to the fulfilment of the goals set out in its strategy for capacity development and collaboration, through providing good competence and capacity both with Swedish participants and participants from developing countries.
- A longer-term aim is to contribute to the sustainable reduction of poverty. An important part of this project is to stimulate Swedish higher education institutes into increasing their internationalisation, by contributing to the strengthening of relations with countries outside Europe and North America.

Building on from the MDGs, the SDGs (UNDP 2016) focus on similar themes. Two areas of critical importance noted by signatories to the post-2015 Agenda who helped formulate the SDGs were that (UN 2015: 2–3):

We are determined to protect the planet from degradation, including through sustainable consumption and production, sustainably managing its natural resources and taking urgent action on climate change, so that it can support the needs of the present and future generations…

We are determined to mobilise the means required to implement this Agenda through a revitalised Global Partnership for Sustainable Development, based on a spirit of strengthened global solidarity, focused in particular on the needs of the poorest and most vulnerable and with the participation of all countries, all stakeholders and all people.

Sustainability is a key component of Rhodes University's own environmental policy. Thus, by focusing on sustainable water resource management in an African context in our latest exchange with Linköping University, our programmes and exchanges were directly aligned to the global initiatives outlined above and in the policy of our own university. An important aim of the Linnaeus-Palme programme is that the partners involved share collaboration and benefits despite their different resource levels. In our view, Sweden benefitted from the pedagogical developments in South Africa's higher education sector and the innovations that our African context has prompted us to develop (Fox and Assmo 2004; Fox et al. 2008). It is therefore appropriate to consider the institutional context in which Rhodes University staff contributed to the exchange. Before examining our curriculum and the exchanges themselves, however, it is useful to outline Rhodes University's institutional response to the Millennium Declaration, MDGs and SDGs. We argue that two policies, in particular, informed the success of the exchanges and the degree to which they supported the SDGs in terms of environmental policy and internationalisation. These are explained through our institutional memories, as we were role players in the development of the environmental policy.

Institutional policies at Rhodes University

It is fair to say that by mid-2017, there had been no debate at an institutional level concerning a response to the MDGs or SDGs. The university's environmental sustainability policy (Rhodes University 2015), however, predates the MDGs, and is one of a number of initiatives championed by concerned and motivated academic staff. It was adopted in 1998 at the same time as the university's cross-disciplinary environmental science programme began. It was revised again in 2015. The policy's first principle is:

> To promote, support and expand initiatives and programmes that lead to improved understanding, development and implementation of sustainability education and research across all faculties and all disciplines.

We were directly involved in both the establishment of the environmental science programme and the first environmental science committee that drew up this policy. Unsurprisingly, therefore, the geography curriculum and associated international activities support the policy, and subsequently MDGs 7 and 8.

Rhodes University formally adopted a policy that supports internationalisation in 2005. Following on from Knight's (2004) work, Rhodes University (2005a: 3) defines 'internationalisation' as:

The process of developing, implementing and integrating an international, intercultural and global dimension into the purpose, functions and delivery of higher education.

Knight focused on unravelling what internationalisation means at the institutional or sectoral level; in this chapter, we are concerned with the disciplinary and academic levels. It is clear, however, that the exchange programmes discussed below are good examples of internationalisation and, although pre-dating the university's policy, were well aligned to it. Thus, our curriculum supports both the environmental and internationalisation policies, and these, in turn, relate directly to the principles of solidarity and respect for nature expressed in the Millennium Declaration and its subsequent formulations as the MDGs and SDGs.

Internationalisation and the geography curriculum at Rhodes

Since the early 2000s, internationalisation through participation in exchange programmes has played a significant role in the curriculum development of the geography department at Rhodes University. From 2003 onwards, one of the spin-offs from the university's innovative post-graduate diploma in higher education and training, completed by Fox, was a new awareness of international academic credit systems, and opportunities available for us to design post-graduate courses in collaboration with external, non-South African partners. This meant, for example, that students at Rhodes and Högskolan Väst could complete modules of their honours (fourth-year) level courses, and undertake research projects in each others' countries, while gaining transferrable credits along the way (Fox and Assmo 2004).

Pedagogical innovations followed; some teaching was delivered online, and video conferencing took place from as early as 2003 (Fox and Assmo 2004). Furthermore, role-playing simulations such as the African Catchment Game, African Development Game and Swampfire were integrated into these exchanges (Fox et al. 2008; Rowntree and Fox 2008), facilitating deeper understandings of the African context for participants.

The undergraduate geography curriculum at Rhodes University was refocused in the early 2000s with an explicitly international and African element throughout (Rhodes University 2005b). It might seem tautological that geography as a discipline would be place specific and context dependent, but this is not necessarily the case (Fox 2005). The African continent had always featured in the Rhodes geography courses, but from the early 2000s, this was made an explicit part of the curriculum. First-year courses focused on global dimensions, the second year focused on southern Africa, and in the third year, the first semester core course examined developmental and environmental issues in Africa. Indeed, the strong African content in the curriculum, and the lack of understanding of Africa in the Nordic countries, has been one of the benefits that Rhodes geography department brought to its internationalisation activities. The section on the Linköping curriculum below shows how this played out in our last exchange programme.

By 2001, the department had packaged its honours options into four marketable streams: geography honours, spatial development honours, environmental water management honours, and landscape process and management honours (Rhodes University 2005b). None of the four streams explicitly targeted the MDGs, but sustainability was a key thread running through all of them. Significantly, the Linnaeus-Palme exchange with Högskolan Väst (in economic or human geography) helped support the viability of the honours programme by attracting students who were interested in human geography. The environmental water management programme provided an honours level option that was attractive to geographers with a scientific background. The second exchange with Linköping University targeted this group.

The exchange programmes
External funding was found for staff and student exchanges through Sweden's Linnaeus-Palme programme from 2002 to 2015. From 2003 to 2010, the exchange was with Högskolan Väst; a second initiative began in 2012 with Linköping University.

The exchange programme with Högskolan Väst ran in two phases. The first ran from 2003 to 2006, and involved fourth-year students from Rhodes University and what was then known as Högskolan Trollhättan-Uddevalla. All students undertook a common online course in research methodology and philosophy that was worth 7.5 credits in the European Credit Transfer System (ECTS). This was followed by a minor research project (15 ECTS credits) conducted in each other's country. When Högskolan Trollhättan-Uddevalla became Högskolan Väst in 2006/2007, the economic geography programme was discontinued and a new international undergraduate programme in politics and economics (IPPE) was designed with our input. From 2007 to 2010, Rhodes students went on exchanges built around research projects in Sweden, while Swedish students could obtain undergraduate coursework credits at Rhodes by taking courses with a strongly African focus. These credits counted towards the international component of their IPPE curriculum.

As mentioned, the exchange with Linköping University ran from 2012 to

2015. South African master's and honours students who went to Sweden all participated in master's courses. For honours students, the courses counted towards their Rhodes degree. For master's students, however, the courses were seen as supplementary to their required research activities, which started only after they had returned to South Africa. The benefit of the exchanges for master's students was to experience a different country and academic culture in addition to scholarly networking, but they did not accrue any credits towards their degree from Rhodes University. The courses taken at Linköping were: climate science and policy (15 ECTS credits), sustainable resource management (15 ECTS credits) and Nordic culture (15 ECTS credits).

The Swedish master's students who came to Rhodes University gained credits towards their Linköping degrees by attending fourth-year courses in geographic information systems, and environment and development in Africa. These were compatible with their curriculum on science for sustainable development.

In 2013 and 2015, staff from Rhodes visited Linköping's thematic studies department and taught a three-week course component on environmental change (worth 15 ECTS credits). This was a contribution to a course on sustainable resource management, which was part of their master's programme in science for sustainable development. We focused on water resource management for sustainable development in Africa. In 2014, another staff member from Rhodes contributed to an introductory course on sustainable development (7.5 ECTS credits) linked to this same degree.

Clearly, the two exchange schemes operated in different ways. The Högskolan Väst–Rhodes University exchange was research focused, while the Linköping–Rhodes University exchange was coursework focused. Participating students therefore had quite different experiences in the two programmes, and this is reflected in some of their responses as detailed below. Students who did their research through the Högskolan Väst exchange had less contact with the university departments but more with people and structures outside of the university, such as homeowners and municipal officers. The Linköping exchange integrated students more into the university environment and, in the case of South African students, gave them opportunities to interact with a wide range of international and Swedish students. They had less engagement outside the university.

The impact of the exchanges on participating students

In 2015, we asked the 61 students who participated in the exchanges about their experiences. We mailed a questionnaire to the different groups, and engaged in face-to-face and email follow-up reminders with those who responded. Some were difficult to trace, as by then it had been many years since they had completed their studies and left the university. We managed to find most of them, however, via social media. Of the 54 students who went on the Högskolan Väst exchange from 2003 to 2010, we received responses from only 16. Significantly those who responded either had gone on exchange relatively recently or had made lasting friendships while away. From the Linköping exchange, five of the total of seven students responded, four of these from South Africa. Of the 61 students who participated in the exchanges, the majority (44) were female, which was a small, and deliberate, over-representation of the gender distribution of our students.

The questionnaire consisted of three sections with three or four questions in each. The preliminary questions regarding personal details of age, sex and year of exchange were followed by: first, a section on their personal and social connections; second, their spatial and place-based connections; and lastly, their experience of the exchange and research or learning experience. The questions we asked were relevant to the seven aims of the Linnaeus-Palme programme mentioned above (Boman et al. 2012), and while it was not our intention to evaluate the programmes against each of the seven aims, the responses we had certainly show that our exchange had fulfilled many of them. In addition, as geographers involved in internationalisation, it was also important for us to understand the spatial, geographical context of the students, and the questions were designed to help us obtain some insight into this.

Fifteen of the respondents were from Rhodes University, and six were from Högskolan Väst and Linköping. All 21 respondents indicated that they had made social connections or friends during the exchange. Ten said that they had made work-related connections, and half of these reported that they had maintained these connections since their exchange.

Three of the students from Högskolan Väst had already been to Africa before their exchange. All those from Sweden visited places other than Grahamstown during their exchange, and two have returned to South Africa since. Two Rhodes students and one Swedish student had returned to visit the friends and connections they had made in their host countries. All respondents reported that they had benefitted from the exchange, and all but one indicated that the exchange had influenced their life and work. The open-ended responses showed that the exchange had a major impact on most of the students. The quotes below have been selected to exemplify the main recurring themes.

Increased global awareness and preparation for work in a global context are pre-requisites for the global partnerships envisaged in the MDGs and the SDGs. They also relate to aims two and four of the Linnaeus-Palme programme. Typical responses from former students included, 'There is a large cultural difference between South Africa and Sweden,' and 'International studies benefitted my employability'.

Many of the responses highlighted an appreciation for differences, learning opportunities, confidence gained, skills mastered and people encountered: 'I came back a different person so it has influenced everything' said one. 'I learned a lot about differing views, social, economic and environmental with many students from all over Europe' said another.

It is clear that the students experienced new cultures and geographical settings and broke down some stereotypes. As one respondent noted, 'Sweden does have social issues, largely drug related, I was expecting the "perfect" country...people were a lot friendlier than I had imagined.'

Geographically, the survey responses reveal an enhanced appreciation of space and place. They also show that the Linnaeus-Palme exchanges supported the aims of both the Linnaeus-Palme programme and Rhodes University's internationalisation policy. It can also be argued that the exchanges offered an effective way of upholding the principle of mutuality in North–South partnerships and supporting the Millennium Declaration's call for international solidarity.

Raising awareness about sustainable development in Africa
In 2013 and 2015, we taught a three-week component at Linköping University that focused on water resource management for sustainable development in Africa, as a contribution to a course in sustainable resource management. Our aim was to raise awareness among Linköping students of the role of water in sustainable development, using Africa as a case study. Some outcomes of the 2015 course are highlighted below.

Twenty-one students attended the 2015 course. They comprised an international group, with six students from Sweden, nine from other European countries, three from Africa (including the two students from Rhodes), and one each from China, Mexico and Bangladesh. The course was taught in English, a second language for the majority of students. Their academic background was also highly variable.

Our course examined the distribution and development of water resources in Africa in relation to more general development issues on the continent. The principles of integrated water resource management provided the theoretical context. Our aim was to help students gain a better understanding of the complex issues around water and the key role it plays in the environment, social welfare and economic growth. We used a range of different learning activities that we have developed in a number of different curriculum contexts (see Assmo and Fox 2015; Fox et al. 2008; Fox et al. 2013a; Fox et al. 2013b; Rowntree and Fox 2008; Rowntree et al. 2009). These included:

- Formal lectures and seminars on readings.
- A geographic information systems exercise using Fusion Tables (an open-access platform) in Google Drive to map water use in Africa.
- Two self-guided exercises on climate change and water use in Africa using the online learning platform MetEd.
- A water futures workshop, drawing on experience gained from working with colleagues from Turku University as part of a Finnish North–South–South exchange programme.
- A seminar on water for development based on the themes of World Water Week organised by the Swedish International Water Institute.

Key learning outcomes were that Africa is a diverse continent and that there is no one-size-fits-all solution. More specific knowledge outcomes included:

- Drier countries are often the best developed.
- Vulnerability to climatic hazards such as floods and drought is increased in poor countries through the lack of investment in infrastructure.
- The widely promoted integrated water resource management (IWRM) is a useful theoretical concept but hard to apply in practice, especially in a developing country.

Awareness of the SDGs was developed through a mini-conference at the end of the course in which students presented on four perspectives: global to local; growth and development; human and social; and ecosystem and pollution. The presentations, which covered a range of issues relating to water management in eight African countries, clearly showed how the four perspectives intersect, highlighting again the diversity of water management issues in Africa.

Two questionnaires were sent to students involved in the two exchanges between Linköping and Rhodes. That is, students who took part in exchanges were asked whether their participation in the courses had added to their learning experience and how they viewed their fellow students' knowledge of their own continent. All four South African students and one Swedish student responded. Then, all students who participated in the course we taught were sent a different questionnaire. Seven of the 21 students who attended the course responded.

Our first question to the exchange students asked whether living in Sweden helped South African students to understand their own country better. All agreed that it did. It helped them to reflect on their own circumstances and to compare countries. The significance of a colonial history was brought home to one South African student; another said she had met people from several African countries in her Swedish university residence in Linköping and on public transport and had learned about other African countries in this way.

When asked whether people from the developed world understand what it is like to live in Africa, all the exchange students, irrespective of whether they were from South Africa or Sweden, responded negatively. One South African student said that she found that, while many people were able to sympathise with issues such as poverty or food availability, subtler issues such as racial sensitivity and the importance of cultural heritage were things they had never been exposed to. Other non-Africans found it hard to grasp the widespread nature of poor service delivery that resulted in electricity outages and water shortages in South Africa. Some had started out with a simplistic view of life in different African countries. The Swedish student who had come to South Africa commented on the vast diversity within the continent, noting that even within South Africa, big differences exist.

In a follow-up question we asked whether the presence of South African exchange students in the class had helped other students to understand Africa better. There was general agreement that they were able to help other students understand the nuances of Africa. South Africans noted that, during the course, European students tended to apply a 'first-world mindset' and had little understanding of the political or cultural context of development issues in Africa. Two examples mentioned were the impact of apartheid and the cultural value of natural resources. Non-African students also tended to assume that all African countries were the same. The teaching activities described above helped to dispel these notions.

By participating in the exchange, the South African students' awareness of African issues was typically heightened, and they were also able to share some of their insights with other students in the class. The exchange was thus seen to benefit all students to some extent and had increased their competence to address global issues.

Discussion

The two Linnaeus-Palme exchange programmes spanned the period in which the MDGs were implemented; they ended as the SDGs were published. In this section, we consider the extent to which the exchange programmes promoted these goals.

The teaching exchanges benefitted from the in-depth knowledge of Africa gained over many years by the Rhodes geography department. We were able to offer insights into development problems that someone not resident in Africa would be less able to do. The curricula we developed at Rhodes have all been closely aligned to the principles and values underpinning the Millennium Declaration, MDGs and SDGs, taking cognisance of global and local priorities, challenges and mechanisms. For example, the first-year course on global development considered sustainable development both as a concept and in practice. In the second year, an analysis of natural resources in southern Africa necessitated examining the reasons for the degradation of soils and water through unsustainable practices. At Linköping our offering encouraged students to appraise the opportunities for and constraints on the sustainable management of African water resources. Thus, it can be argued that the exchanges enhanced and expanded participants' capacities to address the key challenges of MDG 7 (ensure environmental sustainability) and SDG 6 (clean water and sanitation).

Obviously, appropriate curriculum design and content can promote awareness about the need for sustainability, but can an exchange scheme contribute directly to the SDGs? We believe the Linnaeus-Palme programme has done so through promoting a global partnership for sustainable development and contributing to strengthened global solidarity. Both South African and Swedish exchange students came away with more nuanced understandings of the issues underlying poverty and vulnerability that are likely to enhance their capacity to contribute to the achievement of the SDGs in future. The Linnaeus-Palme exchanges also clearly addressed MDG 8 (develop a global partnership for development) and SDG 17 (partnerships for the goals).

The SANORD network is a good example of an organisation based on the principle of global solidarity. Our exchange programmes certainly promoted awareness of SANORD and, as Rhodes was an early member of the network, this led to our Linnaeus-Palme partners (Högskolan Väst and Linköping University) also joining. The exchanges are good examples of the mutuality that underpins the network and of the high regard that has developed between Nordic and southern African universities.

Promoting internationalisation

The teacher and student-exchange programmes have played a valuable role in curriculum development at Rhodes, helping to sustain internationalisation over a long period of time. In this section, we assess the level to which we attained internationalisation through the framework developed by Bell (2004).

Bell proposed that academics could be categorised with respect to four levels of acceptance of an international curriculum. Level one, where internationalisation is seen as having a negative impact, and level two, where it is deemed to be inappropriate, lie on one side of what she refers to as Ellingboe's Great Divide. On the other side of the divide is level three, where internationalisation is viewed as possible, through to level four where internationalisation is integral to the curriculum. The two dimensions through which she allocates academics and their programmes to this spectrum are the pedagogical approaches they adopt and the way they view disciplinary content (Bell 2004).

Using Bell's classification system, internationalisation was clearly integral to our exchange curricula. Pedagogically, these were learning-focused, interactive, dialogic, inclusive and critical, all keywords that Bell uses to exemplify level-four acceptors. The curricula were also contextual, experiential and international; that is, we developed disciplinary content that was intrinsically international.

The range of pedagogic activities embraced in the Linköping course clearly positioned the curriculum in level four of Bell's (2004) typology. Although the course had a specific African focus, students completing the learning activities would have been well equipped to apply the underlying principles to other regions of the world. As teachers, we met the first aim of the Linnaeus-Palme programme: to integrate global perspectives into the learning process, and our students were asked to apply their learning to global issues.

Opportunities and challenges for future exchange programmes

One reason for the longevity of the first exchange programme was the concurrent development of our knowledge of curriculum design, international best practice in quality assurance, assessment and web-based learning. This was, in part, a consequence of the post-graduate diploma in higher education that Rhodes University launched in 2002. This enabled us to readily harmonise our marking schemes and credit values to suit not only the old Swedish system, but also the new ECTS and Rhodes's own grading and credit value systems. We managed to do this in ways that had little impact on our colleagues at Rhodes, so that they implicitly became typical of Bell's (2004) level three – in that they realised that internationalisation is possible. We strongly recommend that other southern African institutions intending similar exchanges make themselves familiar with the European credit systems.

In addition, our international partners were willing to adapt their course scheduling to suit both the sending and receiving institutions. This was imperative, as South Africa and Sweden have markedly different semester dates and durations. Being able to give the correct credit weights to Rhodes undergraduate courses, which are typically of six- and seven-week term length, was also important, and we frequently had to develop separate and extra assessment tasks to facilitate this. We also had to be willing to take on the end-of-semester undergraduate-examination marking for teaching undertaken by exchange colleagues who had returned to Sweden, an additional burden on our own time.

One advantage of the early Linnaeus-Palme exchanges with Högskolan Väst was that the same lecturers were able to participate and collaborate over several years. This provided opportunities for those involved to develop a good understanding of the different learning environments and to develop our teaching styles appropriately. Conversely, a pedagogic challenge related to the Linköping exchange was the short contact period (of only three weeks) together with the limited two-year period over which the exchange took place. The short contact period in particular did not allow time to develop a common knowledge base with the students on which to build more critical concepts. Moreover, for personal reasons, we ourselves were only able to participate in two years of the three-year Linköping programme. A more sustained programme over several years, as was the case for the Högskolan Väst exchange, allowed both institutions to achieve maximum benefit and also allowed for a closer harmonisation of our activities with the goals of the donor organisation.

A number of factors tend to mitigate against exchange programmes lasting for long periods. Staffing is one issue: for example, the continuation of our second exchange was jeopardised when the Swedish programme leader's contract was not renewed. A commitment from all staff involved in an exchange, and a personal interest in travelling to and maintaining links with the reciprocating country, is required to ensure its longevity.

Many higher education institutions and academic networks aim to promote opportunities for student mobility and staff exchanges in relation to research and educational collaboration. Our experience shows that this can be sustained *only* if participating universities embrace internationalisation in a meaningful way, ensuring that participants receive accreditation appropriate to their institution.

In addition, the funding we received was for mobility and subsistence only; staff and students were exchanged on a quid pro quo basis. No additional income accrued to either of the universities through student registration fees or payment for staff time. The additional administrative costs were borne by the hosts in each case. This kind of arrangement means that strong institutional support will only be forthcoming if institutions recognise the intangible benefits of internationalisation and the sharing of best practices for teaching and learning.

Academic networks like SANORD could play a vital role by encouraging the development of institutional structures that support such exchanges. Without these, institutions can so easily obstruct such programmes. For example, at Linköping University, a research levy meant that funding for exchange programmes was 'top-slicing' by as much as 40 per cent or 50 per cent. This meant that money intended for staff and student movement – the very rationale for the exchange – instead went towards the host university's administrative costs. Ultimately, this made the exchange unsustainable. Higher education institutions also tend to frequently restructure and rationalise in ways that impact on exchange activities. Högskolan Väst, for example, centralised onto one campus and revised its curriculum so that our first exchange had to be rapidly re-organised in order to continue.

University-based academics are under much pressure to conduct research, supervise post-graduate students and publish – activities that often take precedence over undergraduate teaching. Being strictly a teaching exchange, the Linnaeus-Palme programme did not allocate time for research and publications, nor did it free up time spent in the lecture room. In terms of research output, none of the 40 minor field studies completed under the exchange with Högskolan Väst resulted in publications due to time constraints and other pressures on participating staff. Eight of the Rhodes students, however, went on to pursue master's degrees (by research) at their home university, which also elicited significant income for the university by way of government funding. However, such programmes open up vast potential for research collaboration where alternative funding can be accessed (see, for example, Assmo and Fox 2015).

Despite the problems referred to above, our experiences with internationalisation and teaching sustainability have left a rich legacy. Over 90 student and staff exchanges have taken place and, as we have argued, they have likely succeeded in building capacity to address key challenges raised in the SDGs. On a theoretical pedagogical level, our analysis and reflections indicate that meaningful exchange of staff and students combined with curriculum innovations facilitated by the exchanges enhanced deep learning about sustainable development, enhanced North–South understanding and strengthened global solidarity.

References

Assmo P and RC Fox (2015) 'International collaboration for pedagogical innovation: Understanding multiracial interaction through a time-geographic appraisal' in T Halvorsen, H Ibsen and VRP M'kumbuzi (eds), *Knowledge for a Sustainable World: A Southern African–Nordic Contribution*. Cape Town: African Minds. Available online.

Bell M (2004) 'Internationalising the higher education curriculum: Do academics agree?' *Research Development in Higher Education* 27: 50–61.

Boman J, N McKnight, Å Nilsson and L Sjölin (2012) *The Linnaeus-Palme Exchange programme: A programme evaluation report for the period 2006–2012.* Available online.

Fox RC (2005) 'Geography of African development: An alternative curriculum', *South African Geographical Journal* 87 (1): 1–9.

Fox RC and P Assmo (2004) 'The development of a research philosophy and methodology course using web-based learning: An international collaboration' in WA Kent, E Rawling and A Robinson (eds), *Geographical Education: Expanding Horizons in a Shrinking World: Proceedings of the 30th Congress of the International Geographical Union Commission on Geographical Education.* Glasgow: International Geographical Union.

Fox RC, P Assmo and H Kjellgren (2008) 'Role playing African development: An international comparison', *The Independent Journal of Teaching and Learning* 3 (1): 31–40.

Fox RC, KM Rowntree and LM Fraenkel (2013a) 'Learning about water management through the African Catchment Game', *Investigaciones Geografica* 45: 91–102. doi: 10.5354/0718-9575.2013.27599

Fox RC, KM Rowntree and J Kaskinen (2013b) 'Futures studies for the southern African region' in J Seeberg (ed.), *Strengthening the Role of Universities as Hubs of Development.* Aarhus: Aarhus University. Available online.

Knight J (2004) 'Internationalization remodeled: Rationales, strategies and approaches', *Journal for Studies in International Education* 8 (1): 5–31. doi: 10.1177/1028315303260832

Rhodes University (2005a) *Internationalisation Policy.* Available online.

Rhodes University (2005b) *2005 Academic Review Report.* Available online.

Rhodes University (2015) *Environmental Sustainability Policy.* Available online.

Rowntree KM and RC Fox (2008) 'Active learning for understanding land degradation: African Catchment Game and Riskmap', *Geographical Research* 46 (1): 39–50.

Rowntree KM, LA Fraenkel and RC Fox (2009) 'Exploring risk related to future climates through role-playing games: The African Catchment Game' in M Koskella and M Vinnari (eds), *Future of the Consumer Society.* Turku: Finland Futures Research Centre, Turku School of Economics.

UN (United Nations) (2000) *United Nations Millennium Declaration.* Resolution adopted by the General Assembly 55/2. Available online.

UN (2015) *Draft Outcome Document of the United Nations Summit for the Adoption of the Post-2015 Development Agenda.* Available online.

UNDP (2016) *A New Sustainable Development Agenda.* Available online.

Chapter 8

Preparing to build researchers' capacity in development and community mobilisation: Towards sustainable North–South collaborations

Thembinkosi E Mabila and Rachael J Singh

IN THIS CHAPTER, we report on a pre-collaboration study that we conducted to establish potential participants' expectations of a Southern African–Nordic Centre (SANORD) project aimed at enhancing research capacity at the University of Limpopo in South Africa. The SANORD project, entitled 'The politics of development and community mobilisation', is aimed at deepening researchers' capacity in relation to these issues, as well as strengthening relations between two higher education institutions in southern Africa (the University of Limpopo in South Africa and the National University of Science and Technology in Zimbabwe) and one from a Nordic country (the University of Bergen in Norway).

The pre-collaboration study was conducted at the University of Limpopo's Turfloop Campus. One of South Africa's historically black institutions, Turfloop is located in the country's northern-most and largely rural province of Limpopo. Our inquiry sought to ensure that participants at the university were prepared for the collaborative project in a timely manner ahead of its implementation.

As co-ordinators of the project at the University of Limpopo, we adopted the motto, *nihil de nobis, sine nobis* (nothing about us without us). Our intention was to engage potential participants in the project on our campus by giving them a chance to communicate their ideas to us first. Our hope was that this would help them to be clearer and more articulate when communicating with partners on other campuses and so contribute to the design and implementation of the project.

Aware that the collaboration would involve actively working with local communities in Limpopo province, we interviewed heads of university departments or units that would be participating in the project, namely, the

Turfloop Graduate School of Leadership, the School of Social Sciences, the School of Economic and Management Sciences, and the Rural Innovation and Development Hub. The following questions were used to guide the inquiry:

- How can a collaboration between Southern and Northern higher education institutions contribute to community mobilisation in the South?
- What are the relevant political issues pertaining to community mobilisation in our area?
- What are the perceived roles of stakeholders in the development of capacity related to community mobilisation?
- Are any particular skills needed to ensure that the collaboration works effectively?

While foregrounding these four questions, we also kept the Sustainable Development Goals (SDGs) in mind, particularly SDG 4 (quality education) and SDG 17 (partnerships for the goals). We contextualised these as follows:

- To what extent could the SANORD project ensure high-quality research training that is both inclusive and equitable while promoting lifelong learning opportunities for all stakeholders in the project?
- How could our study help to strengthen the means of implementation and so help to revitalise future global partnerships for sustainable development?

International collaboration linked to research-capacity development has become an important feature of South Africa's research landscape. As Sooryamoorthy (2013) pointed out, this has become an accepted and productive norm, partly because science is no longer a centralised activity located in a single place but is dispersed far and wide. Hence, a report on the European Union's access to South Africa's research innovation programmes (SACCESS 2013) suggests that South African researchers' collaboration with their European counterparts positively facilitates the flow of knowledge and other resources to South African innovation systems. Moreover, South Africa's post-graduate sector has also endorsed international collaboration and research partnerships as a key strategy for achieving the SDGs. Examples include the strategic establishment of institutes such as the Stellenbosch Institute for Advanced Study, the African Doctoral Academy, and the Johannesburg Institute for Advanced Study, where according to Vale (2010) 'academics from all over the world are invited to fulfil their true calling – to read, to think, to write and to talk'.

Nevertheless, experts on North–South research partnerships attest that the agenda-setting process remains a formidable obstacle in many international collaborations. Bradley (2008: 674), for instance, pointed out that the 'literature on North–South research co-operation often laments the continued domination of collaborative agendas by the interests of Northern donors and scholars, and almost invariably calls for more equitable Southern engagement in agenda-setting processes'.

In this chapter, we report on the ways in which we sought to foreground the voices, expectations and needs of southern African participants in an international research partnership. The collaboration was deemed crucial for capacity building among researchers and for contributing to the achievement of SDG 4. The collaboration was also deemed important in the three institutions' efforts to 'strengthen the means of project implementation and revitalise North–South partnerships, and by implication ensure a sustainable development agenda', as advocated by SDG 17.

We hoped to achieve these ends through the promotion of North–South and South–South partnerships, built on the shared principles, values, vision and goals that seek to 'place people at the centre of development' (Dahl 2014). It was our view that eliciting the views of Southern stakeholders from the very beginning would be crucial for enhancing their buy-in, and help to sustain the North–South collaboration that spurred the study. For this reason, two key ideas formed the basis for our research; the first is that it is crucial for Southern partners to voice their concerns and be heard during the preparatory stages of North–South collaborations; the second is a concern to ensure the sustainability of North–South collaborations. The next section reviews these concepts in the light of the local and international literature.

Reviewing the literature

Many scholars have commented on the complexities of establishing mutually beneficial collaborations between North and South. Ashman (2001) and Kruckenberg (2015) point out that the most serious challenges relate to issues of power sharing and power relations. Simon et al. (2003) allude to the political and environmental complexities in and around the locations where collaborative work takes place. Similar to the arguments we advance here, Bradley (2008) refers to the complexity of the agenda-setting process, but stops short of referring to the crucial issue of involving all stakeholders in agenda setting during the preparatory stages of a collaborative process. Meanwhile, Termeer et al. (2010) indicate that professionals facilitating such partnerships can expect to be challenged in terms of their ideology and values as these relate to politically loaded relationships and fragile social trust, financial dependence or independence, and cultural and physical distance. Surprisingly, they do not suggest addressing these issues in the preparatory stages of a collaboration. In addition, Onokerhoraye et al. (2012: 128) lament two weaknesses in research collaborations. The first is that 'the impact of North–South partnerships on research capacity building has often related more to individual rather than institutional capacity building'. The second is that such partnerships tend to focus 'too much on the one-directional transfer of capacity from North to South, which is usually at the expense of effective partnership work, mutual learning and responsiveness to the peculiar needs of institutions in both the North and the South' (2012: 128).

Without question, North–South collaborations can be challenging and disconcerting. Yet, despite reviewing a considerable body of scholarly literature, we found no studies that described or discussed consultations between stakeholders during the preparatory stages of a collaboration to ascertain their views and needs prior to project implementation. The only mentions of participatory decision-making in the collaborations we reviewed seemed to take place during and not before the implementation phase. For example, Simon et al. (2003) comment on the politics of participatory decision-making in a capacity-development project; Schelling et al. (2008) argue for an integrated approach to the planning of a capacity-development project; Atkins et al. (2016) advocate e-learning because they see it as inherently more participatory than other approaches.

Combining their own observations with feedback from the co-ordinators of a medical post-graduate capacity-development project, Amare, et al. (2017) list the strengths of effective collaboration programmes as: good planning, close supervision during implementation, appropriate budget utilisation, regular communication and periodic evaluations. In our own project, we sought to achieve 'good planning' and ensure that participants from the South would share ownership of the project from the very beginning through a pre-implementation needs-determination process.

When it comes to studies of research-capacity building at higher education institutions in South Africa, we found four that usefully highlight the importance of context and sustainability.

In the first study, Singh (2015) explored the challenges and successes of research-capacity building at the University of Limpopo. The many programmes at the university that were engaged in research-capacity building both for staff and post-graduate students were examined. It was found that a multipronged approach was being used to advance the institution's research culture. Various strategies were applied, including supervisor training, support for doctoral programmes, women in research and post-graduate students, as well as incentives for staff engaged in research, participation in funded projects and in community-linked research activities. Singh's study revealed that higher education institutions in South Africa lag behind in terms of research capacity because of challenges pertaining to staff qualifications and staff retention, a lack of infrastructure and an underdeveloped research culture. In addition, Singh explained that:

> Research capacity building in a rural environment is also challenging, for example: experienced researchers are often 'poached' by other HEIs; funding for research capacity building initiatives is limited; the culture of research is adversely affected by poor supervisory skills; and the language of research (English) is a second language for the majority of students and academics. (2015: 184)

Two recommendations emerged. The first was that capacity-building initiatives must be designed to ensure sustainability (see also Frantz et al. 2014; Puukka 2008). The second was that capacity builders should give careful consideration to contextual factors (see also Segrott et al. 2006).

In the second study, Frantz et al. (2014) examined a research-capacity development project in an unnamed South African higher education institution that was initiated as part of a North–South research collaboration. The researchers adopted a framework informed by the United Nations Development Programme (UNDP) in which capacity development is conceptualised as a process through which researchers' abilities to perform functions, solve problems, and set and achieve objectives are fostered in a sustainable way. The UNDP framework has five steps, the first of which parallels the main idea of this chapter, namely: 'engaging the partners and building consensus' before embarking on a collaborative journey. The UNDP framework was also used to analyse the project's outcomes. According to the study, the international collaboration improved the potential for capacity building and networking as the institutional partnership between the collaborating universities focused on building capacity at the individual and institutional levels. The institution's operational plans and existing North–South partnerships were identified as core assets, and the strategy was to develop participating researchers and the institution through improving staff qualifications, supervision capacity and research output. Clear targets were set and the project was implemented between 2000 and 2012. Monitoring and evaluation were conducted using existing quality assurance infrastructure. Learnings that emerged included that collaboration is time consuming and challenging; multiple strategies are needed to build capacity; co-supervision with Northern partners was necessary to enable staff to achieve master's and doctoral qualifications. Frantz et al. (2014: 1216) concluded that through this collaboration, participants 'were able to develop intra- and inter-disciplinary partnerships' that maximised 'capacity-building efforts'. Although there are similarities in the approach taken in that study and ours, Frantz et al. (2014) simply assessed the capacity of the partnering groups at the start of the partnership, whereas our project deliberately built in a mechanism to give the Southern stakeholders the space to determine the direction that the initiative should take.

The third study was conducted by Balfour and Lenta (2009). They examined research-capacity development at the University of KwaZulu-Natal between 2003 and 2007 in the context of the merger of two higher education institutions with widely differing research cultures and levels of expertise. Their strategy was to increase the research output of the newly merged institution through a process of transformation that involved mentoring, holding seminars and the co-authoring of articles. They recorded successes by using this approach, and were able to attract funding for further research.

The final example linked a university and a government department. In the study, Nesamvuni (2014) described a model for collaboration related to agricultural research and development in Limpopo province. Arguing that effective research and development requires new forms of collaboration based on opportunities offered by willing stakeholders, the author set out to assess the research capacity of the Department of Agriculture in Limpopo and to make suggestions for establishing an effective programme of collaborations. A PESTEL analysis was used to measure the (political, economic, social, technological, environmental and legal) impact of the collaboration project on crop and livestock production. Nesamvuni identified some weaknesses which were ascribed to, among other things, a lack of involvement from relevant stakeholders, demotivated and uncooperative participants, and limited attention paid to suggested policies or strategies. Hence, the recommendations that emerged from this study included the need to involve stakeholders in more meaningful ways, and to combine research capacity, environments, and technologies with appropriate institutional arrangements (Nesamvuni 2014).

Our comparison of these four studies revealed that strategies and models for building research capacity probably need to differ depending on context. This reinforced our view that any new research-capacity building programmes needed to be carefully and thoroughly planned – communities differ, as do their needs. Swilling (2014) usefully emphasises the need to re-think the science–policy interface in South Africa. He suggests experimenting with knowledge production, using, for example, a reflexive approach that deconstructs the discourses of participatory policy making as well as transdisciplinary approaches that legitimise researchers as active change agents (Swilling 2014).

Research methodology

For this study, we took a qualitative approach, using an instrumental case-study design (Stake 2005). As noted, our aim was to gain an understanding of the needs and priorities of the southern African partners in the SANORD collaboration, which would then inform the planning and delivery of the capacity building project for community mobilisation. Thus, we conducted an in-depth inquiry into stakeholders' perceived requirements, views and expectations regarding the upcoming project. Data were collected via interviews with the prospective participants in the project and analysed thematically.

As noted, the participants came from different departments within the university. Of common concern was their involvement in community development and mobilisation through their undergraduate and post-graduate programmes. The sample consisted of twelve participants who were representative of those who would be involved in the forthcoming collaborative project. Included were post-graduate candidates at master's and doctoral levels, as well as staff, school directors, programme managers and heads of the identified departments, since they would be at the forefront of research development activities to follow.

Participants had varying levels of experience in collaborative efforts that included working with a number of researchers from the Netherlands, and Belgium, as well some of the Nordic countries, including Finland and Norway. The interviews were held in the participants' offices and were guided by, but not limited to, the following six key questions that served to create space for wide-ranging discussions:

- How can higher education institutions contribute to community mobilisation in the South?
- What are the relevant political issues pertaining to community mobilisation?
- What is your opinion of the envisaged SANORD collaboration in the light of the politics of community mobilisation?
- What roles can other university stakeholders play in the development of capacity in relation to community mobilisation?
- What role do you think the Northern partner should play in this collaboration?
- What skills do you think are needed for the effective development of a community mobilisation project?

Prior to conducting the inquiry, we informed the participants about the aims and objectives of the envisaged community mobilisation study, and obtained their consent to use their responses in our research. In addition, we assured the participants that their identity would be kept confidential at all times, and ascertained that their participation was voluntary. Accordingly, respondents are quoted below but are not named.

During the interviews, we made notes of the participants' responses. These notes were then consolidated at a debriefing session immediately after each interview. The data were then analysed thematically following the prescripts of thematic analysis advocated by Braun and Clarke (2006), and in accordance with the following steps: i) familiarisation with the written data; ii) generation of initial codes; iii) collation of codes into potential themes; iv) generation of a thematic map; and v) definition and naming of identified themes. After completing our analysis, we asked respondents to confirm the themes and data interpretations before we prepared a final report that was then shared between the two collaborating institutions in the South.

Findings and discussion

The key themes that emerged from the interviews were considered crucial in determining elements of the larger project that all participating departments needed to discuss. The themes identified were stakeholder co-operation, knowledge co-generation, power relations, skills development, and policy development. Certain facets of participants' contributions transcended these thematic classifications; in our view this indicated that the prospective collaborators held a common understanding of what would be essential for the successful implementation of the larger project.

Stakeholder co-operation

Stakeholder co-operation will play a key role in the achievement of the SDGs since the ability to enhance knowledge, learn together, facilitate capacity development, collaborate and jointly create solutions to development challenges is often well served by good stakeholder co-operation (OECD and Camoes Institute 2016). Hence, it is not surprising that this theme cut across all participants' responses in our study. When asked about their perceptions and expectations of the envisaged collaboration, they were explicit that the project should: 'add value for all parties'; 'enhance co-operation between different faculties within the university'; and ensure 'representative community participation'.

Our view was that the SANORD project would meet these requirements, as the project grant vividly pronounced on the need to foster an equal partnership that would mutually benefit all participants. Hence, we were pleased when a respondent in our preparatory study elaborated on this, adding that 'through the envisaged collaboration, the university will sharpen activities such as experiential learning, volunteerism and engaged research'. This view also reflected the notion of enhancing workplace readiness in students who would be involved in the project. Other comments highlighted participants' hopes that the project would benefit from resource sharing and that they themselves would gain knowledge and skills that would enable them to enhance stakeholder co-operation. As one respondent put it: 'There are multiple avenues to be explored here, and each faculty or department will have different angles that they can contribute, so collaboration within this diverse society is important.'

The fact that countries differ both culturally and politically has major implications for the ways in which higher education is organised, and how quality within the different higher education institutions is perceived (NOQA 2011). For several years, the Nordic Quality Assurance Network in Higher Education has included stakeholder co-operation as an element in measuring the quality of higher education (NOQA 2011). This is especially important in relation to international co-operation and partnerships that aim to help countries build on the achievements of the Millennium Development Goals (MDGs) and to make more rapid progress towards the realisation of the SDG targets (Osborn et al. 2015). Participants in our inquiry agreed with the NOQA (2011) that the central goal of stakeholder co-operation is to ensure that close contacts are maintained with stakeholders in the higher education and community sectors, and to ensure the delivery of quality projects.

Consideration of these issues is key to the successful implementation of such projects because, as Osborn et al. (2015) suggest, the SDGs pose a transformational challenge. High-income countries, particularly, are facing a paradigm shift – from conditions in which knowledge generation and transfer were unidirectional from North to South, to conditions in which *mutual* benefit is expected to be derived from an *interchange of knowledge*. Participants in our inquiry were clear: in the larger collaboration, the benefits must not be one-sided.

Knowledge co-generation

The role of international co-operation among universities has become more marked in recent years. This coincides neatly with the United Nations' development agenda, sharpened and spelled out through the SDGs, which strive towards a world in which learning and knowledge-generation are widely advocated. The traditional functions of educating and conducting research, as well as the importance of a wider interface between university and society, need hardly be emphasised here (Aranguren et al. 2012).

All participants in our study stressed the importance of the envisaged project as an opportunity for stakeholders to contribute to knowledge co-generation. They all emphasised that the most important issue would be to define what community mobilisation is. The reasons given for this were: i) there is a gap between theory and practice when it comes to community mobilisation, and this collaboration has the potential to help bridge this gap, thereby adding real meaning to the concept; ii) the project needs to clarify what sorts of partnerships can drive and sustain community mobilisation; iii) defining the concept will enhance knowledge co-generation and help to create a space in which to rethink, transform and produce knowledge collectively; iv) the definition will help researchers and community members to better understand the relevance of community mobilisation in initiating peaceful change.

According to Odebode (2012), the role of knowledge co-generation cannot be overemphasised given the effect it has on rural communities, and particularly on community projects geared towards rural development. In their understanding of and explicit association with the value of knowledge co-generation, participants in our study concurred with Odebode's (2012) observations that the success of such projects is largely due to the positive relationships that researchers can build with communities.

Power relations

In their review of the SDGs, Deacon and St Clair (2015) show that a plethora of studies attribute persistent poverty to global, national and local power relations that enable dispossession, inequity and disrespect for people's rights and dignity. Like Nyasimi and Peake (2015), they conclude that unless dealt with effectively, such power relations will create serious obstacles for the realisation of the SDGs. Turning to research collaborations between universities, Atkins et al. (2016) remark, 'the traditionally inequitable balance of power and resources between northern and southern institutions has often led to what has been described as scientific colonialism.' Our participants' opinions differed on political issues pertaining to community mobilisation. One thought the project would 'help clarify issues of power relations in community mobilisation.' Another asked, 'Whose reality counts, because there are different power relations?' A third noted that: 'It is difficult to implement community mobilisation effectively within highly prescriptive environments.'

Commenting on these issues, Steenkamp and Uhr (2000) point to the critical role that power relations play in community mobilisation. They cite the case of the Makuleke Land Claim, in which power relations around a community-based resource-management project and a land claim initiated by the community had the unintended consequence of weakening the community's bargaining power relative to the state. They conclude that skewed power relations negatively affected the Maluleke community's ability to develop and pursue an independent bargaining strategy with respect to the land claim.

A very different view came from one participant in our study who wondered whether there was a place for politics in the research-capacity development project, and asked: 'I'm not sure why SANORD would want to be involved with politics.' Schneider (2002: 145) raised similar concerns, asking: 'In the context where the state has had the power to implement major policy initiatives…why has conflict persisted as high politics.' What this signifies is the importance of our pre-collaboration inquiry in affording participants the opportunity to clarify their concerns and thus contribute more effectively to the planning phases of the project.

Skills development

A report compiled by researchers from the Earth Institute of Columbia University strongly suggests that information and communications technologies (ICTs) will play a special role in the future of low-income countries (Ericsson 2015) – a point strongly and cogently echoed by the United Nations Broadband Commission. The Earth Institute's researchers suggest that 'in essence, ICTs are "leapfrog" and transformational technologies, enabling all countries to close many technology gaps at record speed' (quoted in Ericsson 2015: 2). This supports the view of Seegolam et al. (2015), who contend that ICTs are an important development factor around the world. In this, they support the United Nations' view that ICTs have the potential to help enable the achievement of SDGs, and place strong emphasis on the provision of ICT infrastructure and skills. Referring to the role of collaboration in skills development, Herbert-Cheshire (2000) revealed that many contemporary strategies for rural development are based upon notions of self-help and bottom-up, community-based initiatives which are said to 'up-skill' individuals. Nelson and Stroink (2012) added that, since the role of the university in society is to be a place of exploration, reflection, experimentation and innovation, such collaboration projects create breeding grounds for skills development.

In our inquiry, consensus emerged that skills development was a major potential benefit of the envisaged collaboration. Respondents noted that 'multiple soft and hard skills' (including ICT-related skills) would likely be acquired by prospective participants. The dominance of these views about ICT were interesting because they support our own experience of research development at the university, where the majority of past and present capacity-development projects supported by Northern partners have focused on ICT-related skills. These have included the use of computer-based research and data-analysis programmes such as Nvivo, AtlasTI and STATA.

Policy development

In September 2015, when nations across the world adopted the 2030 Agenda for Sustainable Development and its associated SDGs, it was hoped that this would prove highly catalytic in influencing policy related to development. In theory, the SDGs should create an environment fertile for communities (including children, young women and men) to participate in policy development as 'critical *agents of change*' (Olaiya 2016: 34). Our inquiry yielded mixed views on this. Our interview notes reveal participants' concerns about the role of the future collaborative project in empowering prospective participants as agents of policy development. Some comments reflected participants hopes related to 'gaining new insights'. One participant said: 'For all, it will unpack new and emerging policy issues that seek to enable the exploration of intellectual highways which may or may not cut across each other in trying to understand the flows and fluxes in development and community mobilisation.' This echoes the views of Barrett et al. (2011: 40) who suggested that such 'partnerships have an increased potential to build interdisciplinary research capacity in order to positively affect policy and good practice within diverse contexts or settings'. An opposing view on this theme was expressed by some participants who were concerned about the 'envisaged project's focus' on politics rather than on 'more important policy issues'. One participant asked, 'Why not pick up on some policy issue like the DST's grand challenges[1] [or something like that]?'

Referring to collaboration and policy development, Nelson and Stroink (2012: 3) explain that proper consultation in collaboration projects contributes to 'the democratisation of knowledge creation, as it is then no longer seen as the exclusive domain of academia'. For this reason, we hope that, by taking a more flexible and fluid approach to community involvement and mobilisation, the university might serve as a knowledge-creation hub in ways that are accessible to anyone seeking new knowledge and advanced thought.

Conclusion

Our findings indicate that, based on previous experiences, most participants in the forthcoming project saw North–South relationships as involving unidirectional transfers of knowledge that tend to mostly benefit the Northern partners from whom project funds and certain kinds of expertise are sourced. Nevertheless, most respondents also indicated their belief that collaboration remains paramount for higher education institutions in the South, and specifically for success in projects like the planned one on development and community mobilisation. These findings led us to conclude that, for our project to succeed, stakeholders from South and North needed to co-operatively determine the project's purpose and objectives.

In a nutshell, the lessons we learned were that consultation ahead of project implementation can help to create an inclusive environment that is conducive to wider buy-in from participants, as well as strengthen the means of project implementation and, by implication, extend opportunities for lifelong learning. If well conceptualised, projects that engage all partners from the start have the potential to help revitalise global partnerships in ways that enhance their sustainability and effectiveness, as well as involving lower-income-country partners as the architects of their own destiny. Hence, we argue that preparing and organising such collaborative processes should be a team effort that fully includes all participants, from teaching staff to those who plan and implement the policies that encourage such initiatives.

Our findings highlighted important areas to plan for within the envisaged SANORD collaboration. In particular, it became clear that to enhance knowledge co-generation the collaboration would need to foster stronger stakeholder co-operation. Participants in our study were positive about the project because, in their view, it had the potential to deepen the understandings of all stakeholders of the power relations inherent in community mobilisation. Furthermore, their hopes that the collaboration would help ensure skills development, as well as empower participants to contribute to policy development, were articulated and acknowledged.

The sentiments expressed in the interviews made it clear that the participants were confident that benefits would flow from the project. By way of warning, however, it is useful to note the caution expressed by Hogue (1993), that when communities do not develop a pattern of collaboration, the potential for community development diminishes. A lack of collaboration, he argues, results in a lack of direction, win/lose behaviours, a lack of commitment, and poor planning.

In the light of this, participants concluded that the planned collaboration needed to be tailor-made to ensure that fertile ground was created to address the six key questions highlighted in the pre-project inquiry. This approach should also align the implementation of the project with SDGs 4 and 17, as well as with targets related to capacity building that are embedded in several of the other SDGs. Finally, careful tailoring should help to direct the project towards the kind of international co-operation between North and South that brings change and new knowledge to all partners involved, and not only to those in the lower-income countries.

Note

1 South Africa's Department of Science and Technology (DST) has identified five 'grand challenges': namely, a) strengthening the bio-economy, b) contributing to space science and technology, c) meeting energy security needs, d) responding to global change (with an emphasis on climate change), and e) contributing to a global understanding of shifting human and social dynamics' (see https://nationalgovernment.co.za/suppliers/view/152/department-of-science-and-technology; accessed September 2017).

References

Amare BL, J Lutale, M Derbew, D Mathai and N Langeland (2017) 'The impact of a model partnership in a medical post-graduate program in North–South and South–South collaboration on trainee retention, program sustainability and regional collaboration' *International Education Studies* 10 (3): 89.

Aranguren MJ, M Larrea and JR Wilson (2012) 'Academia and public policy: Towards the co-generation of knowledge and learning processes' in BT Asheim and MD Pariilli (eds). *Interactive Learning for Innovation*. London: Palgrave.

Ashman D (2001) 'Strengthening North–South partnerships for sustainable development' *Nonprofit and Voluntary Sector Quarterly* 30 (1): 74–98.

Atkins S, S Marsden, V Diwan and M Zwarenstein (2016) 'North–South collaboration and capacity development in global health research in low-and middle-income countries: The ARCADE projects' *Global Health Action* 9.

Balfour RJ and M Lenta (2009) 'Research capacity development: A case study at the University of KwaZulu-Natal, 2003–2007' *South African Journal of Higher Education* 23 (1): 8–20.

Barrett AM, M Crossley and HA Dachi (2011) 'International collaboration and research capacity building: Learning from the EdQual experience' *Comparative Education*, 47 (1): 25–43.

Bradley M (2008) 'On the agenda: North–South research partnerships and agenda-setting processes' *Development in Practice* 18 (6): 673-685.

Braun V and V Clarke (2006) 'Using thematic analysis in psychology' *Qualitative Research in Psychology* 3 (2): 77–101.

Dahl AL (2014) 'Putting the individual at the center of development: Indicators of well-being for a new social contract' in F Mancebo and I Sachs (eds), *Transitions to Sustainability*. Dordrecht: Springer.

Deacon B and AL St Clair (2015) 'End poverty everywhere in all its forms' in ICSU and ISSC, *Review of Targets for the Sustainable Development Goals: The Science Perspective*. Paris: ICSU. Available online.

Ericsson (2015) *ICT & SDGs: How Information and Communications Technology can Achieve the Sustainable Development Goals*. Available online.

Frantz JM, L Leach, H Pharaoh, SH Bassett, NV Roman, MR Smith and A Travill (2014) 'Research capacity development in a South African higher education institution through a North–South collaboration' *South African Journal of Higher Education* 28 (4): 1216–1229.

Herbert-Cheshire L (2000) 'Contemporary strategies for rural community development in Australia: A governmentality perspective' *Journal of Rural Studies* 16 (2): 203–215.

Hogue T (1993) *Community-based Collaboration: Community Wellness Multiplied.* Portland: Oregon Center for Community Leadership, Oregon State University.

Kruckenberg LJ (2015) 'North–South partnerships for sustainable energy: Knowledge–power relations in development assistance for renewable energy' *Energy for Sustainable Development* 29, 91–99.

Nelson C and M Stroink (2012) 'Hubs of knowledge creation: Exploring the potential for knowledge co-generation with the post-secondary academy' *Interact* 3: 3–4, Newsletter of the Association of Commonwealth Universities Extension and Community Engagement Network.

Nesamvuni E (2014) 'Effective collaboration model for agricultural research and development in Limpopo province of South Africa' *Journal of Public Administration* 49 (4): 1196–1212.

NOQA (Nordic Quality Assurance Network in Higher Education) (2011) *Stakeholder Cooperation Within the Nordic Agencies for Quality Assurance in Higher Education: Similarities, Differences and Examples of Good Practice.* Available online.

Nyasimi M and L Peake (2015) 'Achieve gender equality and empower all women and girls' in ICSU and ISSC, *Review of Targets for the Sustainable Development Goals: The Science Perspective.* Paris: ICSU. Available online.

Odebode S (2012) 'Knowledge co-generation: A case study from the University of Ibadan' *Interact* 3: 1–3, Newsletter of the Association of Commonwealth Universities Extension and Community Engagement Network.

OECD and Camoes Institute (2016) Triangular co-operation: Promoting partnerships to implement the Sustainable Development Goals. Summary of discussions at an OECD Meeting on Triangular Co-operation, Lisbon, 19 May 2016. Available online.

Olaiya HBA (2016) 'Transforming our world: The 2030 Agenda for Sustainable Development and the International Decade for People of African descent' presentation to the European Network Against Racism's Steering Group on Afrophobia, Brussels, 21 March. Available online.

Onokerhoraye AG, E Maticka-Tyndale and the HP4RY Team (2012) 'Meeting the challenges of North–South collaboration: The case of HIV prevention for rural youth, Edo State, Nigeria' *African Journal of Reproductive Health* 16 (2): 127–146.

Osborn D, A Cutter and F Ullah (2015) *Universal Sustainable Development Goals. Understanding the Transformational Challenge for Developed Countries.* London: Stakeholder Forum. Available online.

Puukka J (2008) 'Mobilising higher education for sustainable development: Lessons learnt from the OECD study' in *Proceedings of the Fourth International Barcelona Conference on Higher Education.* Barcelona: GUNI Network. Available online.

SACCESS (2013) *Supporting EU Access to South Africa's Research and Innovation Programmes*. Pretoria: Department of Science and Technology.

Schelling E, K Wyss, C Diguimbaye, M Béchir, MO Taleb, B Bonfoh, B Tanner and J Zinsstag (2008) 'Towards integrated and adapted health services for nomadic pastoralists and their animals: A North–South partnership' in G Hirsch Hadorn, H Hoffmann-Riem, S Biber-Klemm, W Grossenbacher-Mansuy, D Joye, C Pohl, U Wiesmann and E Zemp (eds), *Handbook of Transdisciplinary Research*. Berlin: Springer.

Schneider H (2002) 'On the fault-line: The politics of AIDS policy in contemporary South Africa' *African Studies* 61 (1): 145–167.

Seegolam A, A Sukhoo and V Bhoyroo (2015) 'ICT as an enabler to achieve sustainable development goals for developing countries: A proposed assessment approach', paper presented at the Institute of Electrical and Electronics Engineers' eChallenges e-2015 Conference, Vilnius, Lithuania.

Segrott J, M McIvor and B Green (2006) 'Challenges and strategies in developing nursing research capacity: A review of the literature' *International Journal of Nursing Studies* 43 (5): 637–651.

Simon D, D McGregor, K Nsiah-Gyabaah and D Thompson (2003) 'Poverty elimination, North-South research collaboration, and the politics of participatory development' *Development in Practice* 13 (1): 40–56.

Singh RJ (2015) 'Challenges and successes of research capacity building at a rural South African university' *South African Journal of Higher Education* 29 (3): 183–200.

Sooryamoorthy R (2013) 'Scientific collaboration in South Africa' *South African Journal of Science* 109 (5–6), 1–5.

Stake R (2005) 'Qualitative case studies' in NK Denzin and YS Lincoln (eds), *Sage Handbook of Qualitative Research* (third edition). Thousand Oaks: Sage.

Steenkamp C and J Uhr (2000) *The Makuleke Land Claim: Power Relations and Community-Based Natural Resource Management*. IIED Evaluating Eden Discussion Paper Series No.18. Available online.

Swilling M (2014) 'Rethinking the science–policy interface in South Africa: Experiments in knowledge co-production' *South African Journal of Science* 110 (5/6): 1–7.

Termeer CJAM, T Hilhorst and J Oorthuizen (2010) 'Facilitating North–South partnerships for sustainable agriculture' *Journal of Agricultural Education and Extension*, 16 (3): 213–227.

UNAIDS (Joint United Nations Programme on HIV/AIDS) (2016) *UNAIDS Strategy 2016–2021*. Available online.

UNDP (United Nations Development Programme) (2007) *Capacity Assessment Methodology: Users Guide*. Available online.

Vale P (2010) 'Quiet please, academics advancing' *Mail and Guardian*, 24 Sep 2010. Available online.

Chapter 9

North–South research collaboration and the Sustainable Development Goals: Challenges and opportunities for academics

Stephen Mago

NORTH–SOUTH RESEARCH COLLABORATION has a long history and is celebrated for enhancing knowledge transfer between academics and higher education institutions in the two geographic regions. Knowledge transfer between the North and South presents an opportunity for academics and institutions to contribute towards the achievement of the Sustainable Development Goals (SDGs) as set out in the United Nations Agenda for Sustainable Development 2030 (UN 2016). But does North–South collaboration enhance effective knowledge transfer? What geopolitical factors affect these collaborative efforts? And what challenges do the SDGs present for academics?

In this chapter, I offer a short summary of international research and debate about North–South research collaboration. I explore some of the potentials and pitfalls of such collaborations, examining how it can be a catalyst for knowledge transfer in the context of the SDG era. My aim is to contribute to the discourse about ways in which academics and/or institutions in the North can collaborate with those in the South to build research capacity.

The SDGs comprise a list of 17 goals and 169 targets to be achieved by 2030 (UN 2016). Building on the success of the Millennium Development Goals (MDGs), the SDGs are intended to be more inclusive and call for the whole world to be involved in their achievement. Noting this, Mohamedbhai (2015: 1) stated that unlike the MDGs, the 'SDGs were crafted by a group of no less than 70 countries, including developing ones'. The SDGs also give higher education institutions a prominent role to play in their implementation. As such, the goals present 'a unique opportunity for universities' (Mohamedbhai 2015: 1). In particular, SDG 17 (on partnerships for achieving the goals) has significance for academic researchers who are active in cross-regional research networks (UN 2016).

Higher education institutions have a prominent role to play in accomplishing the SDGs by 2030 (Van der Valk 2015). As they are already part of international networks and research collaborations, these institutions should therefore be able to play a leading role in extending and consolidating global partnerships (Halvorsen 2016), which is one of the five transformative shifts identified in the SDGs. Discussion in this regard has already begun. For example, the theme of the International Association of Universities' 15th General Conference held in Thailand in November 2016 was 'The role of higher education as a catalyst for innovative and sustainable societies'. As a follow-up, the University of Bergen (2017) organised a workshop to discuss the role of universities in the implementation of the SDGs.

In university efforts to contribute to the achievement of the SDGs, co-operation among academics will be crucial. Since academics contribute to the production of new knowledge (Bradley 2008; Halvorsen 2016), collaboration has the potential to enhance knowledge sharing to the benefit of all parties. Although research institutions in the South have capable human resources, that is, academics and professionals, they are based in countries with limited public funding for research (Breidlid 2013; Ishengoma 2016b). North–South collaboration may assist in the transfer of essential financial resources from North to South. For example, as Ishengoma (2016a) pointed out, the University of Dar es Salaam in Tanzania has benefitted significantly from collaborative arrangements with several Northern donor countries and institutions.

On the other hand, a number of challenges limit the capacity of Southern academics to participate in collaborative research. For example, South Africa is the only southern African country with advanced research facilities. The country's National Research Foundation (NRF) has helped academics and institutions to make reasonable strides in research. Academics in universities and other research institutions receive financial support through a number of NRF-sponsored research programmes. However, the majority of African countries lack similar funding bodies, hence the need for research capacity building.

In this chapter, I have three aims:

- To review some of the debates around North–South research collaboration and knowledge sharing among scholars and/or institutions.
- To reflect on the geopolitics of research collaboration between the two regions.
- To identify particular challenges facing academics from the South.

To achieve these objectives, I used 'literature research methodology', defined as 'to read through, analyse and sort literatures in order to identify the essential attribute of materials' (Lin 2009: 179). I conducted an extensive internet search using the following keywords and phrases: 'North–South collaboration', 'South–South collaboration', 'partnerships', 'knowledge sharing', 'geopolitics of research', 'academic institutions', 'sustainable development goals' and 'SDGs'. I selected literature using Wang's literature selection principles (cited in Lin 2009), namely: purpose (whether the literature is valuable), authority (whether it was written by respected authors in the field of North–South research collaboration), effectiveness (in explaining the problem under discussion) and reliability (for example, articles published in respected journals). I used a qualitative approach to summarise the debates.

Debates about North–South research collaboration

Partnership as a concept refers to a relationship between institutions or individuals based on two principles: equity (fairness) and mutual benefit (Ashman 2001). Collaboration theorists have noted six critical factors that lead to an effective partnership or collaboration: trust, co-operative relationships, mutual influence, commitment, active communication and joint learning (Ashman 2001). Based on partnerships between the Netherlands and various Southern countries, Baud (2002) has argued that North–South partnerships can create effective systems for knowledge production. Hassan (2006) has stated that collaboration is a critical driver for knowledge sharing that is global and fruitful: 'It's a trend that benefits not just the developing world, but the entire world' (Hassan 2006: 79). Further, North–South collaboration may contribute to reducing the North–South research divide, illustrated by gaps in authorship, numbers of full-time researchers and research expenditure as a percentage of GDP (Blicharska et al. 2017).[1]

While Engelhard and Box (1999) have argued that development dynamics have the potential to widen the research divide between the North and South, strengthening North–South research capacities may help to close this gap through the pooling of resources and knowledge sharing. According to Hassan (2006), North–South research collaboration could eliminate the 'research monopoly' that Northern nations enjoyed in the past. The monopoly has the effect of skewing research agendas to benefit the North more than the South. Indeed, given the North's hegemonic position in educational discourse, Breidlid (2013: 358–359) pointed out that North–South collaboration 'may be perceived as an attempt to entrench the huge disparities between the North and the South'.

To some extent, these geopolitical dynamics in education and research are shifting. Organisations, such as the Southern African–Nordic Centre (SANORD) and Nuffic (a Dutch organisation focused on educational and research support) are strengthening cross-regional research collaboration by bringing scholars together at conferences and promoting collaborative research partnerships between member universities in the North and South. Similarly, many international donor organisations now give preference to funding collaborative research projects and programmes between scholars or institutions, thus encouraging North–South research collaboration. SANORD, for example, gives preferential financial support to North–South collaborative presentations. In addition, donors such as Nuffic run training programmes for doctoral candidates and their supervisors to strengthen doctoral programmes in southern Africa. The five-year Development Research Uptake in Sub-Saharan Africa (DRUSSA) project is another example. Funded by the Department for International Development (DFID) from 2011 to 2016, the project aimed to strengthen research through increasing research uptake in twenty-two African universities.

Meanwhile, several scholars have questioned the integrity of North–South partnerships for a range of reasons. Institutions located in the North often have more power due to their generally wealthier economies. In this context, North-based institutions 'bring in funds, expertise and resources to conduct research in low-income countries' (Van der Veken et al. 2017: 1), leading to a situation where Southern partners are viewed as 'receivers', while Northern partners are viewed as 'givers' in research collaboration arrangements (Binka 2005). Such a scenario empowers institutions based in the North at the expense of those in the South. Here, Andre Gunder Frank's (1970) thesis of 'dependency theory' seems relevant, and the risk of creating a 'dependency syndrome' among Southern researchers is certainly a real one. In this regard, Carbonnier and Kontinen (2014, cited in Ishengoma 2016b: 153) compare the capacity-building objectives of North–South research collaborations to '...the colonial enterprise of "civilising" the South'. Similarly, Breidlid (2013) has criticised the North, citing Norwegian scholars and institutions in particular for having a 'what's in it for me?' mentality. Ishengoma (2016b: 149) also observed that:

> The neocolonial structure within which North–South research collaborations operate, limits their potential to impact on capacity building. In practice, Southern researchers are often the weaker partners as a result of their nations' weaker economic bases.

To enhance North–South collaboration, South–South research collaboration constitutes a potential mitigating factor in terms of power relations. Governments in the South have realised the importance of investing in research (Blicharska et al. 2017), in growing the research capacities of

Southern researchers and, empowering Southern institutions to pursue 'true partnerships' (Binka 2005) with other researchers.

The foregoing illuminates the geopolitical context in which North–South research collaborations take place. Donors, governments and other stakeholders should play a central role in promoting North–South research networks and achieving balanced relationships. The concept of 'netweaving' may be useful here. An alternative to networking (Stevenson 1998), netweaving proposes to create a stronger and sustainable social fabric for effective relationships. The idea is to avoid the creation of new boundaries; rather, netweaving aims to extend and strengthen existing networks (Krebs and Holley 2006). According to Monesson (2007), this form of networking 'transfers the focus from "What's in it for me?" to "What's in it for them?"' (Monesson 2007: 12). Thus, as partners help others to achieve their goals, with the anticipation of receiving benefits in the long run, they create stronger collaborations and partnerships.

Research, academics and the Sustainable Development Goals

The SDG framework is built on five key themes, namely: people, planet, prosperity, peace and partnerships (SDSN 2015). This model, as noted by Holden et al. (2016), 'is in conflict with the popular three-pillar model of sustainable development, which seeks to balance social, environmental, and economic targets.' The 17 goals include, among other things, the elimination of poverty, promotion of decent work and economic growth, and reduction of inequalities. Specific areas cover: agriculture, gender, health, education, equality, climate, water and sanitation, industry and innovation, energy efficiencies, sustainable cities, poverty, peace and justice, and partnerships. Further, the SDGs are expected to perform better than the MDGs, given the new goals' 'SMART target approach'. Targets from the 2030 Agenda are specific, measurable, attainable, relevant and time bound (SDSN 2014: 4).

Higher education institutions are positioned to contribute to almost all areas of the SDGs through teaching, research and community engagement (Mohamedbhai 2015). In addition, the wide acceptance of the SDGs by higher education institutions makes academics and researchers key actors in their achievement (Mohamedbhai 2015). First, higher education institutions have an active role to play in ensuring that the concept of sustainable development is well understood, through research and dissemination of information.[2]

Second, higher education institutions are positioned to receive national and international support to work towards the achievement of the SDGs. For example, in South Africa, Green Campus Initiatives (GCIs) were established at the University of Cape Town (in 2007), Nelson Mandela Metropolitan

University (in 2011) and Durban University of Technology (in 2011) in response to climate change; the GCIs were extended in support of the SDGs. GCIs involve university students and academics in the achievement of environmentally friendly institutions in response to Goal 13 (climate action) and Goal 15 (life on land). South Africa's Department of Higher Education and Training pledged to support green initiatives in the country during the launch of the extended GCI at the University of Cape Town in 2012 (BuaNews 2012). The government's pledge created a good foundation for SDG achievement.

Third, university partnerships have the potential to leverage SDG 17 (partnerships for the goals). The response of higher education institutions to the SDGs and their implementation is an important component in the development of knowledge and the achievement of knowledge sharing through partnerships. Clarke et al. (2016) argued that co-production relationships (collaborations) promote the achievement of SDGs through knowledge sharing. At the same time, universities that produce evidence-based research can contribute to the achievement of the goals. This raises the question of what specific strategies higher education institutions can put in place to contribute to the SDGs in effective and meaningful ways?

Strategies for higher education institutions

Higher education institutions can implement several strategies to enhance SDG achievement, including research and innovation, a co-ordinated institutional approach, staff and student training, and the establishment of associations.

Research and innovation

The Sustainable Development Solutions Network (SDSN 2015: 16) pointed out that:

> Through research and development (R&D) they can create and incubate new technologies, they can identify strategic priorities and best practices in strategy and innovation, and they can help to monitor the agenda through the collection, analysis, and interpretation of primary data.

At a conference on research and innovation held by Universities South Africa (USAf) in April 2016, delegates established that 'research and innovation is a key determinant in performance on the UN's Sustainable Development Goals 2030' (USAf 2016: 1). The conference's keynote session noted the importance of an integrated and transdisciplinary research approach towards meeting the SDGs, so as to widen the scope of knowledge and its accessibility. According to Halvorsen (2016: 293), 'Knowledge is everywhere and potentially accessible to anyone who seeks it out.' Multidisciplinary research is likely to increase accessibility, thus promoting the success of the SDGs.

The establishment of multidisciplinary research involves co-ordinated research activities that attempt to promote wide and deep investigations, which can potentially cover all aspects of the SDGs. Such research collaborations broaden opportunities for knowledge sharing among academics and institutions. North–South collaboration in multidisciplinary research facilitates the achievement of solid research outputs (Engel and Keijzer 2006). By addressing multiple areas of the SDGs, collaborative research relationships have the potential to promote their achievement.

Co-ordinated institutional approach

The SDGs must be incorporated into universities' strategic plans (Mohamedbhai 2015). Budgets should also be set aside to financially boost efforts towards achieving the SDGs through collaborative research. An institutionalised approach to the SDGs is the only way to ensure academics and students in higher education institutions embrace their implementation. Mohamedbhai (2015) proposed that higher education institutions could establish research units or institutes that focus on the SDGs so as to realise lasting results. Governments of the respective countries could fund such arrangements, or resources could be mobilised through collaborative programmes. For example, through its NRF, the South African government encourages universities to establish research chairs, which could be established with the aim of addressing issues around the SDGs.

Staff and student training

Academics need to be trained on the integration of SDG-related issues in curricula. The United Nations has developed PhD and master's programmes on the Sustainable Development Goals in an effort to produce graduates with a comprehensive understanding of the SDGs. These graduates may provide critical analysis of the SDGs (SDSN 2015; UN 2016). Universities also have a role to play in this regard, as 'the key nodes of higher education, training a new generation of sustainable development leaders, and playing a key role in public awareness and education as well' (SDSN 2015: 16).

Establishing associations

Associations to support collaborative research and the achievement of the SDGs should be supported at local, national, regional and international levels. At a regional level, the Association of African Universities and the

Association of Universities of Latin America and the Caribbean are two examples (Mohamedbhai 2015). Internationally, the Global Universities Partnership on Environment for Sustainability has a membership of more than six hundred universities. Such initiatives are likely to have an impact on research and the achievement of the SDGs.

Challenges for Southern academics in the SDG era

Academics based at institutions in the South face a myriad of challenges that need to be addressed to enhance success in collaborative research for the advancement of the SDGs. For South-based academics to improve prospects for North–South research collaboration, they need to embrace e-learning technologies to facilitate effective communication. The advancement of information and communications technology (ICT) has had a positive impact on collaboration and knowledge sharing. It is now easier for researchers in the North to work effectively with those in the South and vice versa.

As mentioned earlier, South–South co-operation plays a prominent role in promoting North–South co-operation. However, South–South collaboration is challenged by a lack of research funds, as South-based institutions are often limited by weak economies. Competition for resources is not helping global collaborative efforts. Halvorsen (2016: 280) lamented that the 'focus on competition between higher education institutions and their managements has been a dangerously destructive phase in the evolution of universities'. Instead, universities should collaborate in both resource mobilisation and research programming. Jostling for 'rich' research partners only creates cleavages, new boundaries and exclusions, leading to destructive forces against academic co-operation.

The absence of democracy and good governance in developing countries also impedes collaboration activities. Freedom of speech translates into freedom of research. Academics should have the freedom to research in their areas of interest and disseminate information without fear. According to Halvorsen and Skauge (2004: 141), 'students can contribute to the social capital necessary for the construction of healthy civil societies and socially cohesive cultures, achieving good governance, and building democratic political systems'. The same applies to academic researchers.

Fragmentation, which inhibits regional co-operation, is another challenge that limits research collaboration. Regional integration in Africa has created a competition for the best grouping, leading to what has been termed the 'spaghetti bowl' effect,[3] whereby countries belong to a complex and overlapping web of regional blocs (Fergin 2011; Sorgho 2016). One country can become a member of several regional blocs. For example, Kenya, Uganda, Niger and Burkina Faso are each members of four regional groupings. It can be argued that competition for membership of regional blocs weakens regional integration in Africa and weakens collaboration. Multiple memberships create multiple and complex sets of agreements that can lead to conflicts (Fergin 2011; Sorgho 2016).

Conclusion

In this chapter, I discussed the debates around effective North–South research collaboration and knowledge sharing among academics and institutions. I made an effort to illuminate the geopolitics of North–South research collaboration and the problem of imbalances created by different positions of power. I concluded that, despite such concerns, North–South collaboration can be mutually beneficial for all parties if managed well. I then discussed the potential of research collaboration to advance the achievement of the SDGs through evidence-based academic research. I examined some strategies that higher education institutions could use to support the implementation of SDGs, namely: research and innovation, a co-ordinated institutional approach, staff and student training, and establishing associations. Lastly, I briefly explored some of the challenges faced by academics in conducting collaborative research in the SDG era. I identified the following key areas of focus: the need to embrace e-learning; the need to advance South–South collaboration; the need for democracy and good governance; and the advancement of regional co-operation, which is a precursor for research collaboration. From the foregone analysis, it is clear that North–South collaboration and partnerships will not be a 'magic bullet' for the achievement of the SDGs.

Notes

1 'The World Bank's data shows that the national average number of scientific and technical journal articles produced in 2011 by researchers from Northern countries was 10 442, compared to 1 323 from Southern countries; full-time equivalent researchers per million people was 3 220 in the North and 393 in the South for the period 2005–2014; expenditure on research and development was 1.44 per cent and 0.38 per cent of gross domestic product (GDP) in Northern and Southern countries respectively for the period 2005–2014' (Blicharska et al. 2017: 22).

2 The 2015 SANORD conference in Namibia, where the SDGs were intensively discussed, was a good example of this.

3 The spaghetti bowl concept has also been used to refer to the continent's web of overlapping trade agreements, which presents an obstacle to successful regional integration and trade in Africa.

References

Ashman D (2001) 'Strengthening North-South partnerships for sustainable development' *Nonprofit and Voluntary Sector Quarterly* 30 (1): 74–98.

Baud ISA (2002) 'North-South partnerships in development research: An institutional approach' *International Journal of Technology Management & Sustainable Development* 1 (3): 153–170.

Binka F (2005) 'North–South research collaborations: A move towards a true partnership?' *Tropical Medicine and International Health* 10 (3): 207–209.

Blicharska M, RJ Smithers, M Kuchler, GK Agrawal, JM Gutiérrez and associates (nine other authors) (2017) 'Steps to overcome the North-South divide in research relevant to climate change policy and practice' *Nature Climate Change: Perspective*. Available online.

Bradley M (2008) 'On the agenda: North-South research partnerships and agenda-setting processes' *Development in Practice* 18 (6): 673–685.

Breidlid A (2013) 'Collaboration in university development: North-South, South-North. A Norwegian case' *Postcolonial Directions in Education* 2 (2): 355–380.

BuaNews (2012) 'South Africa launches Green Campus Initiative' *Brand South Africa*, 23 April. Available online.

Clarke WC, L van Kerkhoff, L Lebel and GC Gallopin (2016) 'Crafting usable knowledge for sustainable development', *Proceedings of the National Academy of Sciences of the United States of America (PNAS)* 113 (17): 4570–4578. Available online.

Engel PGH and N Keijzer (2006) *Research Partnerships: Who Decides? Review of a Design Process*. The Hague: RAWOO. Available online.

Engelhard R and L Box (1999) *Making North-South Research Networks Work: A Contribution to the Work on A Common Vision for the Future of Science and Technology for Development by the United Nations Commission for Science and Technology for Development*. New York and Geneva: United Nations Conference on Trade and Development. Available online.

Fergin E (2011) Tangled Up in a Spaghetti Bowl: Trade Effects of Overlapping Preferential Trade Agreements in Africa, Bachelor's thesis, Lund University.

Frank AG (1970) *The Development of Underdevelopment*. New York: Monthly Review Press.

Halvorsen T (2016) 'International co-operation and the democratisation of knowledge' in T Halvorsen and J Nossum (eds), *North–South Knowledge Networks Towards Equitable Collaboration between Academics, Donors and Universities*. Cape Town: African Minds.

Halvorsen T and T Skauge (2004) 'Constructing knowledge societies? The World Bank and the new lending policy for tertiary education' *JHEA/RESA* 2 (3): 139–151.

Hassan MHA (2006) 'Promoting South-South and North-South cooperation in education and research: A question of responsibility' *Globalization and Education Pontifical Academy of Social Sciences* Extra Series 7: 79–89. Available online.

Holden E, K Linnerud and D Banister (2016) 'The imperatives of sustainable development' *Sustainable Development.* Available online. doi: 10.1002/sd.1647

Ishengoma JM (2016a) 'Strengthening higher education space in Africa through North-South partnerships and links: Myths and realities from Tanzania public universities' *Comparative and International Education* 45 (1): 3.

Ishengoma JM (2016b) 'North–South research collaborations and their impact on capacity building: A Southern perspective' in T Halvorsen and J Nossum (eds), *North–South Knowledge Networks Towards Equitable Collaboration between Academics, Donors and Universities.* Cape Town: African Minds.

Krebs V and J Holley (2006) *Building Smart Communities through Network Weaving.* Available online.

Lin G (2009) 'Higher education research methodology-literature method' *International Education Studies* 2 (4): 179–184.

Mohamedbhai G (2015) 'SDGs – A unique opportunity for universities' *University World News,* 27 November. Available online.

Monesson EP (2007) 'NetWeaving - A powerful tool for developing relationships' *CPA Practice Management Forum* 3.

SDSN (Sustainable Development Solutions Network) (2014) *Principles for Framing Sustainable Development Goals, Targets, and Indicators.* Paris: SDSN Secretariat. Available online.

SDSN (2015) *Getting Started with the Sustainable Development Goals: A Guide for Stakeholders.* Paris: SDSN Secretariat. Available online.

Sorgho Z (2016) 'RTAs' proliferation and trade-diversion effects: Evidence of the "spaghetti bowl" phenomenon' *The World Economy* 39 (2): 285–300.

Stevenson T (1998) 'Netweaving alternative futures Information technocracy or communicative community?' *Futures* 30 (2/3): 189–198.

The Association of Commonwealth Universities (ACU) (n.d.) *Development Research Uptake in Sub-Saharan Africa (DRUSSA).* Available online.

UN (United Nations) (2015) *PhD and Master of Sciences on the Sustainable Development Goals.* Available online.

UN (2016) *The Sustainable Development Agenda.* Available online.

University of Bergen (2017) *Universities and the SDGs* (Workshop invitation). Bergen, 1 February 2017. Available online.

USAf (Universities South Africa) (2016) *Research & Innovation is Central to Performance on Sustainable Development Goals.* Available online.

Van der Valk E (2015) 'From MDGs to SDGs: The role of international higher education', European Association for International Education. Available online.

Van der Veken K, L Belaid, T Delvaux and V De Brouwere (2017) 'Research capacity building through North–South–South networking: Towards true partnership? An exploratory study of a network for scientific support in the field of sexual and reproductive health' *Health Research Policy and Systems* 15: 39. Available online. doi: 10.1186/s12961-017-0202-z

Chapter 10

Education for employability: A response to industry demands

Robert L Martin, Regina Krause, Martha T Namutuwa,
Evgenia Mahler and Hartmut Domröse

HIGHER EDUCATION INSTITUTIONS have implemented work-integrated learning (WIL) programmes in response to the need to improve student employability (Bhaerman and Spill 1988; Hardman and Averweg 2011; Pillai et al. 2011). Such programmes seek to address the need for non-cognitive skills, referred to broadly as employability skills (Charner 1988; Harvey 2001; Jayaram and Engmann 2014). Despite attempts to improve student employability, employers continue to report dissatisfaction with the skills and competencies of graduates (Crossman and Clarke 2010; McQuaid 2006; Maclean and Ordonz 2007).

In response to lessons drawn from the collaboration between the Hochshule Wismar University of Applied Sciences and Namibia University of Science and Technology (formerly the Polytechnic of Namibia), the Voice of Business (VoB) project was created to develop employability skills of participating students in Germany, Namibia and South Africa. Students who join the project complete an entrepreneurial leadership course and a company-provided project within a multidisciplinary student-research and development team (MSRDT). The project also aims to strengthen the curricula used by the institutions involved.

The Voice of Business project

The VoB project aims to complement and strengthen efforts to embed WIL into higher education curricula to enhance student employability skills. The programme has five main characteristics:
• Project-based learning.
• Multidisciplinary student research and development teams.
• Entrepreneurial leadership.

- An approach to emotional, social and cognitive competence development that complements the student's task-based knowledge or technical competence.
- A focus on reflection and critical thinking that aims to develop the student's competency to think and become a life-long learner.

Based on experiential learning theory, through the VoB project, companies with real business challenges provide work-related projects to students (Dressler and Keeling 2004; Kolb and Kolb 2008; McCarthy 2010). The universities then grade the project in order for the student to obtain course credit. This approach benefits all parties, as follows:
- The company receives a solution to a real business challenges as well as an opportunity to scout for new talent.
- The university strengthens its relationship with industry and receives direct feedback on the relevance of its programme offerings and curriculum.
- The student is given the opportunity to apply task-related knowledge and gain work experience.

Through the project, students receive practical experience of working in multi-disciplinary teams. This approach departs from the traditional WIL approach, as students learn not only to resolve real work problems but also how to work as part of *multidisciplinary* teams in particular. MSRDTs also offer students an opportunity to develop skills in research, entrepreneurial leadership, ideas generation and project management within a team environment. Students develop problem-solving abilities through the integration of information, data, techniques, tools, perspectives, concepts and theories to resolve work-related challenges. MSRDTs therefore enable students to work on real business problems and to respond holistically to industry needs as identified.

The course on entrepreneurial leadership uses an integral approach to develop entrepreneurial, leadership and emotional intelligence. The programme combines the concepts of entrepreneurship and leadership to develop students into entrepreneurial leaders, either as employees or as self-employed business owners.

The programme's focus on competence development aims to equip students with theoretical and task-related knowledge as well as associated competencies that enable them to reflect, learn and develop their critical-thinking abilities. The reflective-learning and critical-thinking approach allows students to contextualise learning and develop a continuous learning approach that predisposes them to life-long learning. Therefore, it emphasises the development of the three competency clusters described by Boyatzis (2008), namely: cognitive, emotional and social intelligence.

The theoretical foundations of the entrepreneurial leadership course include experiential learning theory, complex adaptive systems theory, critical thinking and intentional change theory. The programme's beneficiaries (students, university, companies and community) each form their own system. These beneficiaries, while interacting within themselves and with each other, also interact and operate with other systems. Further, different individual systems have to adapt to constant changes within the wider system in which they operate.

Experiential-learning theory proposes that learning is greatly enhanced if combined with experiential activities in a work environment (Kolb and Kolb 2008; McCarthy 2010; Sattler and Peters 2011). Student participation in a company-based project aims to strengthen students' understanding of the working world and to offer them the opportunity to put theory into practice.

Complex adaptive systems theory (also known as 'complexity' theory) seeks to understand how order emerges in complex, non-linear systems, such as galaxies, ecologies, markets, social systems and neural networks (Gill 2013; Homer-Dixon 2002). This project takes into account that all role players form part of a system, are individually a system and form part of other systems. Critical thinking, also described as higher-order thinking by Scriven and Paul (1987, cited in MacKnight 2000), is the intellectually disciplined process of actively and skilfully conceptualising, applying, analysing, synthesising and/or evaluating information gathered from, or generated by, observation, experience, reflection, reasoning or communication, as a guide to belief and action. The focus on reflection and reflective learning aims to strengthen students' critical thinking competencies. Intentional change theory proposes that most sustainable behavioural change is intentional (Boyatzis 2008; Sinatra and Pintrich 2003). The theory also recognises that leadership development involves the emergence of nonlinear and often discontinuous experiences in an iterative cycle (Boyatzis 2006).

Multidisciplinary student research and development teams: lessons learned

In 2009, Wismar University in Germany launched its first MSRDT to work on a project. The project co-ordinator engaged students to participate in the MSRDT project on a voluntary basis. Teams were formed consisting of students from different disciplines working together on a project that addressed a real-life business problem. Students from different faculties attempted to develop innovative and market-oriented products and services. However, in the early years, regional business enterprises provided ideas and professional mentoring to the student teams.

This project had two objectives, first, it aimed to create networks and improve connections between academics and industry in the region and second, it sought to merge the resources of the university and the regional economy to mutually benefit higher education and industry. Furthermore, it aimed to improve the cross-curricular training of students. For example, students from three different faculties (engineering, design and economics) were given the opportunity to work on an idea as a team outside of their area of study in order to learn and apply other sciences. This resulted in a win-win situation for the students, the industry partner and the higher education institution.

In 2012, a master's thesis evaluated the results of the MSRDT project, confirming the model's success and identifying challenges. The main challenges students faced were the need for personal responsibility, the difficulties of managing time constraints and internal conflicts within teams. The process of screening the ideas was also found to be challenging and time consuming, albeit also interesting and engaging. Initially, communication between the MSRDT and the companies that provided the projects was a challenge in terms of hierarchical procedures, as companies feared an uncontrolled outflow of trade secrets and confidential information.

Wismar University learned from these challenges and put mechanisms in place to address situations that were initially underestimated. Following the university's evaluation, a number of improvements were made:

- The university intensified student participation in MSRDT.
- The university offered complementary workshops to coach students in soft skills.
- The partnership agreements were revised to clearly define the collaboration between the companies that provided the project ideas and the MSRDT.
- The university approved start-up ideas by students as work items for MSRDT.
- The departments of the university expanded multidisciplinary networking.

This learning experience allowed Wismar University to apply the MSRDT concept in a three-year collaboration project with the Polytechnic of Namibia. First, a pilot project between the two institutions was implemented, with student teams from different disciplines working on a business idea or problem. These business ideas or problems were received from businesses that had agreed to participate in the project.

The Polytechnic of Namibia adapted the MSRDT concept used at Wismar and introduced it within the WIL framework. However, students who participated in the project in Namibia received recognition and course credit upon completion of their tasks, while in Germany students did not earn credits for the project.

Each institution prepared students participating in the project, albeit differently. Both institutions trained the student teams on team dynamics; in addition, the Namibian teams were taught self-branding and work readiness skills.

The students who participated in the pilot study in Namibia were evaluated in terms of their employability (communication skills, interpersonal skills, problem solving skills, critical thinking skills, creativity skills and workplace preparation). The two student teams were required to share their experiences through reports, but these were assessed as part of student evaluations only in Namibia. All of the participants indicated that they had gained skills through participating in the MSRDT project.

The MSRDT project's success resulted in the establishment of the VoB project, a four-year collaborative project between the Polytechnic of Namibia, the Vaal University of Technology and the University of Applied Sciences in Wismar. The project began in January 2015 and will run until December 2018. The following section reports on progress made to the end of 2015.

The Voice of Business project as an example of North–South collaboration

The German Academic Exchange Service obtained grant funding for the continuation of the initial project with the inclusion of Vaal University of Technology in South Africa. A project committee was formed to oversee the project and to ensure that project objectives are met. The committee meets regularly to develop the project strategy; to clarify partners' roles and responsibilities; and to schedule, organise and monitor the planned activities, including the co-ordination and planning of staff and student exchanges and evaluation of activities. Meetings, workshops, seminars and conferences are attended jointly and designed to strengthen relationships as well as to assess progress and identify best practices.

The first meeting was held on 16 February 2015 in the presence of all participants. To minimise administrative work, the Wismar University co-ordinator drafted internal documents related to staff's time and travel costs. Representatives from participating universities observed that the internal regulations at each institution often hindered the reimbursement process.

In terms of administrative management, in general, it was agreed that each African partner university will be responsible for the project within its own country. Wismar University, as the lead partner, is responsible for the following:

- General project management and quality assurance.
- Financial management of the project.
- Reporting to the German Academic Exchange Service on project outcomes.
- Organising and hosting partner meetings.

The co-ordinator is responsible for reimbursing all expenses incurred by the partners. At the second project meeting, a guide for reimbursement was developed and discussed with the partners, with set deadlines for submitting claims. Each partner is responsible for spending its own money, but in ways that are in line with the regulations set out in the financial guidelines. In terms of communication, apart from the project meetings, all partners communicate regularly via e-mail, phone and Skype.

At the first meeting, the project team was formed and the partners' responsibilities were determined. The discussion resulted in agreements concerning project activities, milestones, a staff-exchange programme, and the need for each institution to conduct a needs analysis to inform the structure and content of a preparatory course.

The staff exchange consisted of Wismar University in Germany hosting representatives from the Polytechnic of Namibia and Vaal University of Technology for a four-month period from May to August 2015 to work jointly on course development. During the partners' stay in Wismar, they visited the chamber of commerce and industry and several companies in order to familiarise themselves with the industries that Wismar University works with.

The new project's first phase focused on the development of the preparatory course, which intends to prepare students for the working world. The course emanated from a needs analysis completed collaboratively in July 2015 by the three partner universities. Each university consulted with local industries in their own areas to establish what skills are required from graduates. In all three countries, companies highlighted concerns about what they saw as the lack of employability skills among graduates.

Next, each institution assessed the course needs by conducting a SWOT analysis. The project developed a holistic analysis of strengths, weaknesses, opportunities and threats by comparing the differences and similarities between the different institutions. From this analysis, the need for a preparatory course to enhance student employability was identified. Similarities and differences were also identified in terms of each institution's curriculum needs, industry requirements, government regulations and levels of support for education in the three countries. For example, all three universities noted:

- The challenge of obtaining industry support.

- That their curricula are not fully geared towards developing employability competencies.
- A need to afford students the opportunity to enhance their employability competencies.
- That the project creates an opportunity for the universities to engage with the community in ways that will also contribute to improving their image and impact.
- That students might not take the project seriously if it is not fully integrated into the academic programme.

After the needs and SWOT analyses, the focus shifted to the development of the preparatory course. An extensive literature review and best-practice benchmarking exercise was conducted from April to July 2015, which led to the development of a course on employability competencies. A five-module course structure was developed, consisting of learning outcomes in emotional intelligence, team dynamics, entrepreneurial leadership, international project management and business basics. The course focuses on employability rather than employment, and on the development of skills and competencies rather than knowledge transfer. The further development of the five modules of the course were then shared between the partner university representatives, and discussions were held in meetings and workshops so that partners could agree on structure, content and deliverables of each module.

At the end of the four-month exchange programme, the course structure, course outline and handbook were drafted. Representatives from the three partner institutions made presentations to colleagues and management within their respective institutions and solicited input from them to finalise the course materials. A blended-learning approach, with a focus on student-centred learning was envisaged, and the partners will continue to fine-tune support materials and resources, such as videos, role-play activities and handouts.

Expected outcomes

All parties recognise the importance of an efficient dialogue between higher education institutions and industry in terms of relevant employability skills and competencies. The first MSRDT project's successes and challenges have proven that there is a gap between the skills of university graduates and those required by industry.

The first outcome of the VoB project was the needs analysis, which identified the employability competencies required by industry. The next phase of the project aims to match the students' competencies to the skills demanded by businesses. For this purpose, a toolkit for preparing entrepreneurial leaders is being developed, with the following expected outcomes:

- A jointly developed curriculum and a handbook for a short course on entrepreneurial leadership.
- A business simulation game will be adapted for use by students as part of the course.
- MSRDTs will be established in each institution and connected with relevant businesses.
- MSRDT participants will receive course credits according to the assessment instruments used by each partner institution.

To achieve these outcomes, a course-development team was formed. During the design and implementation phase, the course-development team took part in a number of exchange visits. As a result of this intensified staff exchange and strong collegiality, collaborative structures and knowledge transfer between the partners has improved. The development process is expected to result in a newly developed course that satisfies the accreditation criteria of the higher education councils in the two African universities. A technical working group will be formed to obtain formal accreditation for the course. It is hoped that a major outcome of this will be inter-institutional recognition by the partner universities in South Africa and Namibia and, in the longer term, by Wismar University as well.

The project outcomes are expected to have a significant impact on various stakeholder groups as outlined below.

Students

At least 24 students will acquire hands-on experience through the completion of real assignments within the host-company team. In addition, students will be given the chance to participate in specialised events during the project. Students with leadership potential from the different teams will participate in a study tour in Germany. They will be expected to present a paper at an international conference about the learning experience. Other intangible outcomes of the project activities are strengthening experiential learning and cultural and knowledge exchange among participants. Moreover, students will be able to begin to establish their own international networks.

Companies

At least six companies from South Africa, Namibia and Germany will benefit from actively participating in shaping their own leaders and potential future executives. Moreover, the project facilitates innovation transfer and exchange between the research units of the universities and participating companies. At the end of the project a web portal will be established through which interested companies can share project ideas and propose co-operative research programmes with universities in their region.

Universities

The partner universities will profit from improved collaboration with industry and will gain input regarding the relevance of their curriculum. In addition, the presence of MSRDTs on university campuses may strengthen entrepreneurial spirit, creating a favourable environment for the development of science parks and technology centres within the universities.

Regional economies

The regional chambers of commerce and industry are valuable partners in the project. The German chamber in Schwerin, for example, benefitted from the visit of African delegations during the previous project. German companies had the opportunity to present themselves and initiate cooperation with African partners. The exchange of international delegations and company visits initiated by the VoB project may facilitate the exchange of good practices and provide networking and recruitment opportunities for the participating countries of Germany, South Africa and Namibia.

Conclusions

In this chapter, we described the VoB project and outlined the project's background and progress to date. The evaluation of the pilot project shows that the student teams involved have gained valuable work experience. The employability of about 15 student participants improved, and some students found employment within the businesses they were assigned to or in related companies, while other students started their own business ventures.

Lessons drawn from the earlier collaboration between two higher education institutions led to the establishment of the VoB project, which aims to strengthen the curriculum used by the institutions involved in the project. This improved curriculum focuses on strengthening students' employability through the introduction of the employability competencies course. This course aims to expose students to real business issues; this exposure is expected to improve the employability of graduates.

It is recommended that each institution strengthens its relationship with industry partners and reviews its curriculum in order to improve the employability of graduates. Collaboration between institutions across countries should also be encouraged.

A detailed evaluation of the new programme and the project results will be presented at a final project conference in 2018. Students who participate in the project will be required to complete an evaluation form, which will contribute to a bilateral master's thesis. The conference will not only serve as a platform for dissemination of the project results and outcomes, but will also provide opportunities to network and create synergies with other projects. An add-on outcome targeted by the project consortium is the internationalisation of the model and the MSRDT concept. Potential future partners include higher education institutions in Botswana, Mozambique and Zimbabwe that have already shown interest in joining the VoB partner network.

References

Bhaerman R and R Spill (1988) 'A dialogue on employability skills: How can they be taught?' *Journal of Career Development* 15 (1): 41–52.

Boyatzis RE (2006) 'Intentional change theory from a complexity perspective' *Journal of Management Development* 25: 607–623.

Boyatzis RE (2008) 'Leadership development from a complexity perspective' *Consulting Psychology Journal: Practice and Research* 60 (4): 298–313.

Charner I (1988) 'Employability credentials: A key to successful youth transition to work' *Journal of Career Development* 15 (1): 30–40.

Crossman JE and M Clarke (2010) 'International experience and graduate employability: Stakeholder perceptions on the connections' *Higher Education* 59 (5): 599–613.

Dressler S and A Keeling (2004) 'Student benefits of co-operative education' in R Coll and C Eames (eds), *International Handbook for Cooperative Education: An International Perspective of the Theory, Research and Practice of Work-Integrated-Learning.* Boston: World Association for Cooperative Education.

Gill G (2013) *Culture, Complexity, And Informing: How Shared Beliefs Can Enhance Our Search for Fitness.* Available online.

Hardman S and UR Averweg (2011) 'Practitioner research from a critical systems perspective' *Alternation* 18 (1): 374–384.

Harvey L (2001) 'Defining and measuring employability' *Quality in Higher Education* 7 (2) 97–109.

Homer-Dixon TE (2002) *The Ingenuity Gap.* Toronto: Vintage.

Jayaram S and M Engmann (2014) 'Developing skills for employability at the secondary level: Effective models for Asia' *Prospects* 44 (2): 221–233.

Kolb AY and DA Kolb (2008) 'Experiential learning theory: A dynamic, holistic approach to management learning, education and development' in SJ Armstrong and C Fukami (eds), *Handbook of Management Learning, Education and Development.* London: Sage.

MacKnight CB (2000) 'Teaching critical thinking through online discussions' *Educause Quarterly* 23 (4): 38–41. Available online.

Maclean R and V Ordonz (2007) 'Work skills development for employability and education for sustainability development' *Educational Research for Policy and Practice* 6 (2): 123–140.

McCarthy M (2010) 'Experiential learning theory: From theory to practice' *Journal of Business and Economics Research* 8 (5): 131–140.

McQuaid RW (2006) 'Job search success and employability in local labor markets' *The Annals of Regional Science* 40 (2): 407–421.

Pillai S, MH Khan, IS Ibrahim and S Raphael (2011) 'Enhancing employability through industrial training in the Malaysian context' *Higher Education* 63: 187–204. Available online.

Sattler P and J Peters (2011) *Work-Integrated Learning in Ontario's Postsecondary Sector.* Toronto: Higher Education Quality Council of Ontario. Available online.

Sinatra GM and PR Pintrich (2003) 'The role of intentions in conceptual change learning' in GM Sinatra and PR Pintrich (eds), *Intentional Conceptual Change.* Mahwah, NJ: Erlbaum.

PART III: CASE STUDIES

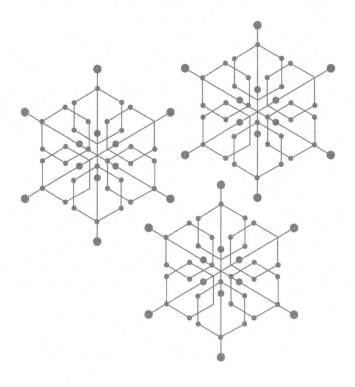

Contextual factors affecting the attainment of life satisfaction among elderly people in Zambia's North-Western province

Mubiana K Sitali-Ngoma and Emmy H Mbozi

TRANSFORMATION TOWARDS SUSTAINABILITY is a mammoth task that calls for concerted efforts from every human on planet earth. With this understanding in mind the United Nations General Assembly devised the 2030 Agenda for Sustainable Development as a platform from which children, women and men can channel their immeasurable capacities for activism into the transformation of the world, and endeavour to create a place that provides equal opportunities for all beings to fulfil their potential, enjoy prosperity, and lead lives that are free from fear and violence (UN 2015). What should be born in mind is that this transformation should go hand in hand with sustainability. In this regard, the General Assembly adopted 17 sustainable development goals (SDGs) to facilitate sustainable transformation in the world. The SDGs are designed to stimulate action up to 2030 in areas of critical importance (UN 2015).

In line with this, scholars and institutions of higher learning have a similarly mammoth task to fulfil as we have a prominent role to play in implementing the SDGs. Without North-South collaboration and the associated knowledge sharing between researchers and institutions, this task will be even more difficult. Limited funding already obstructs research initiatives, as well as their timing, quality and output. As we show in this chapter, issues related to local experiences and perspectives are also crucial if effective interventions are to be designed.

In this chapter, we report on the first two of three objectives that formed part of a larger study that took place in 2016, and looked at contextual factors influencing the attainment of life satisfaction among people aged 65 and over in the North-Western province of Zambia. The entire study was directly related to SDG 3 (good health and well-being).

The three objectives of the larger study were to:
- Establish levels of life satisfaction among elderly respondents in North-Western Zambia.
- Ascertain the factors that constrain and promote the attainment of life satisfaction among elderly respondents.
- Assess the adequacy of Zambia's national ageing policy in facilitating the attainment of a satisfying life among elderly people, and formulate guidelines as to how this might be improved.

We begin with an account of the existing literature on life satisfaction among the elderly; we then outline our objectives and explain our research design and data collection process. We present our findings and argue that research studies like this one are important in extending and challenging the general applicability of theories developed in high-income-countries where many elderly people are economically far wealthier than those in Zambia.

The literature on life satisfaction among the elderly

All human beings, if given a choice, would opt to attain life satisfaction. Those in late adulthood are no exception. Life satisfaction entails a sense of contentment and joyfulness over the span of one's lifetime. As an indicator of the quality of life (Motjuwadi 2013; Subramanien 2013), life satisfaction is considered a crucial ingredient for enhancing well-being during ageing, including mental, physical and spiritual wellness (Motjuwadi 2013; Nuehs 1990; Osborne 2009). Given its significance, gerontologists have developed various theories about its attainment. Some early ones include the activity theory of ageing, continuity theory, and disengagement theory. As summarized by Motjuwadi (2013), activity theory suggests that maintaining high levels of physical and social activity from middle age into old age brings about life satisfaction (see also Neugarten et al. 1961). Continuity theory posits that being able to continue enjoying our favourite activities into retirement will result in life satisfaction. Disengagement theory holds an opposing view, suggesting that what brings about life satisfaction in late adulthood is the ability to voluntarily reduce activity levels and social roles. The common denominator among the theories is that they all strove to identify the best possible ways of facilitating the attainment of life satisfaction among elderly people.

Since the early 2000s, research into life satisfaction in late adulthood has gained momentum. In New Zealand, Gretchen et al. (2011) undertook a study that sought to investigate ranges of life satisfaction and functioning among elderly people. Among other findings, the researchers revealed that factors that contribute to quality of life and indeed attainment of life satisfaction relate to good health, family, spouse, friends, positive attitudes towards life and independence while detractors were found to be poor health, physical impairment, poor finances, family difficulties, and age. In Germany, Humpert (2013) found that factors that had a positive impact on life satisfaction for female respondents were sport, welfare or parental activities, while hobbies increased life satisfaction for male respondents. Political activities and union membership generally had a negative effect on life satisfaction among all respondents.

In a study of determinants of life satisfaction with daily activities among retirees aged 65 years or older in 11 European countries, Bonsang and Van Soest (2012) found that respondents were generally satisfied with their daily activities, but response scales varied significantly across countries, revealing that respondents in the northern European countries tended to be more satisfied than those in central Europe or the Mediterranean countries. The Netherlands ranked first in terms of satisfaction; Sweden and Denmark came second and third. The interpretation that Bonsang and Van Soest offered was that elderly people in the Netherlands often participate in satisfaction-enhancing activities such as voluntary or charity work, belonging to sports or social clubs, and looking after grandchildren. Interestingly, elderly people in the Netherlands seem to experience fewer health problems than respondents from any other country in the study. Poland and the Czech Republic were at the bottom end of the satisfaction scale, and these were also the countries where health problems were the most common.

In a review of various research studies conducted in different countries spanning twenty years, Wang and Hesketh (2012) identified a myriad of factors that influenced the attainment of well-being. They grouped these factors into five categories (that is: individual attributes, pre-retirement job-related factors, retirement-transition factors, post-retirement activities, and family-related factors). They then suggested that these factors all influence three aspects of well-being: fiscal, physical and psychological well-being. Thus, for example, factors such as a decline in physical health, a high number of dependents and costs related to dependent care, losing a partner, and work-related physical demands, had a negative impact on the fiscal, physical and psychological well-being of retired persons. Factors such as sound financial status and physical health, marital quality, financial literacy and healthy lifestyle choices all had a positive impact on the fiscal, physical and psychological well-being of retired persons. Meanwhile in Spain, Prieto-Flores et al. (2012) found that family, neighbourhood, finances and health had more impact on life satisfaction than participation in leisure activities.

In terms of research conducted in Africa, Fisher (1992) identified factors that influence the experience of life satisfaction in retirement as good health, financial stability, contact with family and a general fulfilment of life expectations. In Mauritius, Subramanien (2013) established that good health, family attention and care, a reasonable income, a decent place to live and good social relations act as drivers of well-being in old age, and conversely that a lack of these detracted from the well-being of elderly persons. In South Africa, Motjuwadi (2013) found that retirees with sturdy and stable financial resources had higher levels of life satisfaction and adjusted better to retirement than their counterparts who had more limited financial resources. He also found that good health played a key role in promoting an experience of life satisfaction.

Although the studies reviewed above have contributed significantly to the field of gerontology, they almost all used quantitative methods to measure life-satisfaction levels. We decided to include a qualitative aspect to our study. Thus, rather than establishing purely quantitative relationships between variables, we made space for respondents to describe in their own words the factors that enhance and detract from their experience of satisfaction. The use of qualitative and quantitative methods facilitated the triangulation of our results.

In terms of existing literature on Zambia specifically, studies we identified focused on the social impact of the ageing population (Mapoma 2013), care for the elderly (Changala 2015) and attitudes towards the elderly Finch (2014). As far as we are aware, no other studies have investigated the contextual factors related to the attainment of life satisfaction among elderly people.

Why understanding life satisfaction among the elderly is important

While it is fairly obvious that social, cultural and economic differences between countries will influence the ways in which elderly persons experience life satisfaction (Bonsang and Van Soest 2012), identifying and analysing factors that detract or promote quality of life in specific contexts is vital for the effective design and efficient implementation of national ageing policies. At the time of writing, Zambia's National Ageing Policy policy was still in its infancy, having been launched in 2015 (Republic of Zambia 2015). A well-designed and implemented policy on ageing can promote well-being and this, in turn, can promote good health. According to the World Health Organization (WHO 2002) if more individuals reached old age in good health, the rising costs of pensions and welfare payments as well as costs related to medical and social care would be offset by the fact that more of these individuals would be fit and willing to work.

Research design

We opted for a descriptive research design that allows for mixed methods of data collection. Quantitative data were derived from the use of the Satisfaction with Life Scale (SWLS) and semi-structured questionnaires. Qualitative data were gathered via a combination of text and narratives (from interviews and semi-structured questionnaires). Our assumption was that collecting diverse types of data would offer us the best possible chance of understanding of the research problem (Creswell 2003).

Population sample and sampling technique

The population for the study comprised persons aged 65 years and over living in the Solwezi District. We settled on the age of 65 because this is the usual retirement age in Zambia, and our sample included both male and female subjects, regardless of whether or not they were actually retired from formal or informal employment. Since the local social worker is responsible for the welfare of the vulnerable, including the old, he was asked to provide information regarding the social welfare scheme and social security system. Staff from the National Pension Scheme Authority (NAPSA) in the North-Western Province were asked to help provide information related to pensioners and the district medical officer for Solwezi was consulted because he was in a position to provide health-elated information regarding the aged. This provided us with information on social security in Zambia.

The sample thus comprised 101 elderly people, one staff member from NAPSA, one from the local social welfare scheme and the district medical officer for Solwezi. Purposive sampling[1] techniques were used to select the elderly respondents from the total population. The distribution of elderly respondents in terms sex and age categories is shown in Table 11.1.

TABLE 11.1   Sex and age-groups of respondents

Sex	Aged 65–75	Aged 76–85	Aged 85 and over	Total
Male	29	15	3	47
Female	31	18	5	54
Total (n)	60	33	8	101

Data collection instruments

Data were collected and assessed via four instruments: the SWLS, a semi-structured questionnaire, interviews, and observation. The SWLS was triangulated with the semi-structured questionnaire. Triangulation was used to check the results on life-satisfaction levels among elderly respondents as well as to mitigate the inadequacies of both instruments. For instance, the SWLS does not allow respondents to explain their reasons for satisfaction or dissatisfaction with life, but the semi-structured questionnaire did allow respondents to give reasons.

The SWLS was developed by Diener et al. (1985; see also Pavot et al. 1991). The assumption behind the scale is that individuals are the best judges of their present and past life satisfaction (see Neugarten et al. 1961). In this study, the SWLS was translated into the two commonly spoken languages in the study area, Ki-Kaonde and Ki-Lunda. All protocols that go with translation of scales from the original into other languages were followed.

A questionnaire comprised of structured and unstructured questions was used to collect data on life satisfaction as well as data on factors that affected attainment of life satisfaction. The questionnaire asked questions such as, 'Are you satisfied with your life?' Then respondents were asked to give reasons for their answers. From this, the researchers were able to establish the factors that detract from and those that promote life satisfaction.

Finally, we used basic observation to collect data on the adequacy of housing, including latrines. Facilities were considered to be inadequate if rooves were damaged or absent, if windows were too few or too small to allow enough light to see by and if doors were not lockable. The widespread inadequacy of the housing we saw helped increase our understanding of respondents' living conditions.

Training data collectors and collecting data

Prior to data collection, five data-collection assistants were trained to administer the SWLS, the semi-structured questionnaires and in how to collect observations. The research assistants were selected on the basis that they were fluent in English and in the local languages spoken in the study area. During the training, the research assistants were first asked to establish their own level of life satisfaction using the SWLS. This helped them understand the usefulness of the survey. The assistants were then asked to administer the instrument to one another, which help them develop a deeper understanding of the statements on the scale. A similar process occurred with the questionnaire; the research assistants pretested the instruments on each other. This helped us standardise the questions and ensure that the translations remained consistent with the original questions in the English version.

Apart from the literature review, all the other data were collected in the respondents' homes. Ethics clearance was sought and given, and in line with this, the researchers and data-collection assistants explained the purpose of the study and obtained consent from respondents with regard to their participation in the study. Permission to take pictures for use in the report was also sought from respondents. Respondents were assured of confidentiality and their names were not recorded. Once consent was obtained, the age of respondents was confirmed through the national registration cards that all Zambians carry.

Respondents were asked if they preferred to complete a self-administered SWLS or if they would like the researcher to read out the statements and record their responses. Similarly, the respondents were asked to choose to respond in English, Ki-Kaonde or Ki-Lunda. The SWLS and the questionnaire were then administered in the respondents' language of choice. Respondents were encouraged to be honest in their responses and were informed that the aim of the study was to obtain and collate valuable information in a way that might benefit them in future.

Data analysis and limitations of the study

Commensurate with the research design, the quantitative data were analysed using SPSS Statistics software. Qualitative data from the interviews were transcribed and analysed by identifying key themes that recurred throughout the data. Respondents' reasons for the non-attainment of life satisfaction were grouped into categories that facilitated the presentation and interpretation of findings in relation to the study's objectives.

The fact that the study leaned more towards qualitative research, especially in terms of choice of population, sample and sampling techniques, poses something of a challenge when it comes to generalising the results. Researcher subjectivity is inherent in qualitative research as it heavily relies on the thinking and choices of the researcher that can lead to bias (Subramanien 2013). Researcher reactivity is another possible limitation of the study. This occurs when interviewees are torn between giving genuine answers and saying what they think the researchers want to hear (Subramanien 2013). For these reasons, the generalisation of the results obtained from this study are offered with caution.

Problems encountered in data collection

Two main challenges were encountered in the data-collection process. First, as mentioned, some respondents seemed to be torn between telling the researcher what they thought the researcher wanted to hear and what they really felt about themselves or their situation. Second, some respondents who were in the care of family members seemed torn between giving answers that they thought would either please or displease their care-givers and saying what they were really experiencing. This problem was especially pronounced regarding the life-satisfaction measurement. Responses to questions such as: 'are you satisfied with your life?' and to statements such as: 'the conditions of your life are excellent'; 'in most ways, your life is close to your ideal'; 'you are satisfied with your life' proved a little difficult to elicit. On noticing the respondents' predicament, the researchers and all the research assistants insisted that interviews take place out of hearing range of respondents' caregivers. Caregivers were informed that the questionnaire was aimed at the elderly people only, and that the respondents' honest responses were more likely to ensure that the results of the study would benefit both themselves and their elderly relatives. Respondents and caregivers were also assured that their personal information would not be divulged to anyone, and that the exercise was not a test in which they should attempt to either attain a high or low score. This intervention helped the researchers to collect information that was to some extent more bias-free.

Findings and discussion

The major finding from the SWLS was that 59 per cent of the elderly respondents were on the dissatisfied side of the scale; 37 per cent were found to be on the satisfied side. Details on levels of life satisfaction are shown in Table 11.2.

Similarly, the major finding from the semi-structured questionnaire was that the majority of respondents were not experiencing life satisfaction. See Table 11.3.

TABLE 11.2   SWLS findings on life-satisfaction among respondents, by sex

Sex	Extremely satisfied	Satisfied	Slightly satisfied	Neutral	Slightly dis-satisfied	Dis-satisfied	Extremely dis-satisfied	Total
Male	1	9	10	2	8	7	10	47
Female	0	5	12	3	9	16	9	54
Sub-total	1	14	22	5	17	23	19	101
Total (n)	37			5		59		101

Sex	Satisfied	Not satisfied	Total
Male	13	34	47
Female	9	45	54
Total (n)	22	79	101

The finding that more people were not experiencing life satisfaction than those that were is not unique to this study. What is unique, however, is the high percentage of dissatisfied respondents. By contrast, in Mauritius, Subramanien (2013) found that 45 per cent of the respondents were not experiencing life satisfaction.

We grouped the factors reported by the elderly respondents as promoting or driving life satisfaction into four categories: economic, independence, family, and age (see Table 11.4). The factors reported as detracting from or constraining the attainment of life-satisfaction were sorted into eight categories (see Table 11.5).

TABLE 11.4 Contextual factors promoting life satisfaction among elderly respondents

Factors	Promotors/drivers
Economic status	Ability to afford to eat three meals a day Enough income to live a decent life Ability to afford to feed oneself Ability to meet most of life's challenges Not worrying about what to eat tomorrow Not having to go to sleep hungry Not starving Success gained from hard work
Independence	Ability to take care of oneself Ability to meet most of life's challenges
Family ties	Having well-behaved children Having educated one's children Being cared for by one's children and extended family members Having family who are employed Having successful children
Impact of age	Proud of living into old age

TABLE 11.5 Contextual factors constraining life satisfaction

Factor	Constraints
Economic status	Having no option but to work regardless of age Limited resources The inability to satisfy basic needs Inability to afford essential commodities Lack of money, too little money Inability to afford three meals a day Economic hardship High cost of living Rising price of commodities Inability to buy good things for self and family Inability to carry out plans due to insignificant funds Inability to make decisions due to lack of money Transport problems due to lack of money Difficult life Lack of money as a factor in all activities No income of one's own
Unmet wants and needs	Not having achieved things one wanted to Not having lived the life one wanted
Health status	High blood pressure Tiredness Weakness due to heart problems Joint pains especially when walking Inability to engage in desired activities Lack of physical fitness
Impact of age	Lack of strength Inability to engage in desired activities Inability to do what one wants due to age Lack of physical fitness
Functionality	Inability to walk without a walking aid Inability to provide own meals
Bereavement	Loss of husband Loss of wife Loss of children
Dependency	No own income Having to ask for everything one needs and waiting a long time for it to come Inability to provide own meals
Depression	Seeing nothing worth enjoying in life

The findings of this study are consistent with those of previous research; specifically, our findings on economic-related factors are consistent with Wang and Hesketh et al. (2012), Fisher (1992), Subramnaien (2013) and Motjuwadi (2013). The key point is that poor economic status detracts heavily from the experience of life-satisfaction. In this study, the majority of respondents were very poor. Their major sources of income are shown in Figure 11.1.

FIGURE 11.1: Respondents' sources of income

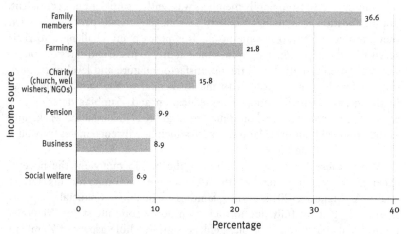

Most respondents reported that their income was insufficient. For instance, at the time of the study in 2016, the average monthly pension for respondents was K390 (approximately US$39). However, some individual respondents were receiving as little as K57 (US$5.7) per month. To provide some context for these amounts, a bag of mealie meal, which is the staple food in Zambia, cost K114 (US$11.4).

One partial explanation for this could be that the Zambian state pension system is insensitive to inflation and only a small percentage of elderly Zambians receive pensions. In this study, only 10 per cent of respondents had pensions and just 7 per cent received social welfare payments. The reason why so few elderly persons receive pensions is that very few were ever formally employed. Our findings on those who benefit from social welfare assistance are consistent with the findings by Mukuka et al. (2002), who reported that the social security coverage in Zambia is insignificant, echoing the finding of the ILO (2001), which estimated that only 5 to 10 per cent of the working population in sub-Saharan Africa had access to social security. The ILO study noted that the majority of African countries spent an average of only 4.3 per cent of their (already low) GDP on social security, as compared to 16.6 per cent of GDP spent by high-income countries, which also have social security coverage of close to a hundred per cent (ILO 2001). Between 1994 and 2006, Zambia allocated as little as 1 per cent of budget funding to social welfare (Kaputo 2010).

A massive 93 per cent of respondents in our study revealed that income they might receive from family members was neither sufficient nor consistent. The implication is that many elderly persons experience periods in which they have access to no income at all. This poses many challenges to their survival, and completely undermines their ability to make and carry out plans. Kamwengo (2004) attributed the unsatisfactory nature and level of families' support for their aged relatives to the weakening of the family bonds due to the strains of urbanisation, mass education and Zambia's deteriorating economy. In a study focused on India, Brijnath (2011) blamed the weakening of the extended family on Westernisation which heavily encourages the values of individualism and nuclear families.

While these factors are certainly applicable, in our view, the poverty experienced by family members themselves largely accounts for this state of affairs. As Mapoma (2013) argued, families are unable to financially support their aged relatives fully due to their own poor economic status. Mapoma pointed out that respect for one's elders is an indelible aspect of Zambian culture, and where resources are available, families would endeavour to take care of their elderly relatives. The results of Zambia's 2010 national population census also testified to the fact that poverty levels are high, with over half (61 per cent) of the Zambian population living below the poverty datum line and 42 per cent of the population considered to be extremely poor (CSS 2012).

The majority (58 per cent) of these extremely poor people live in the rural areas (Rasmussen et al. 2014), and as noted, our study was conducted in a rural area. Our observations were consistent with the census report (CSS 2012) and Rasmussen et al. (2014). Extreme poverty was evident in the inadequacy of housing and latrine facilities, particularly in the informal settlements in Zambia. The photographs in Figure 11.2 were taken in an informal settlement within the study area, and are an example of the facilities that many elderly people in these areas have access to.

As regards health-related factors, our findings were also consistent with previous research. Wang and Hesketh (2012) showed how physical health positively affects the physical, psychological and fiscal well-being of retired or elderly persons while a decline in physical health has a negative impact in all the same aspects of life. Bonsang and Van Soest (2012) found that people with fewer health problems enjoyed higher levels of life satisfaction than those with a lot of health problems. In our study, respondents were asked to indicate if they suffered from any of four chronic diseases, namely: diabetes, high blood pressure, tuberculosis, and general body pains. A shocking 99 per cent of respondents reported that they suffered from one or more of the four ailments; this was true for both male and female respondents irrespective of age.

Our findings on functional disability as detracting from life satisfaction are consistent with those by Good et al. (2011) who conducted a study in New Zealand. Similarly, our finding that unsatisfied wants and needs impact negatively on life satisfaction in late adulthood was in line with the work of Yirmibesoglu and Berkoz (2014) in Turkey. The finding that aging itself detracts from life satisfaction is consistent with those of Gretchen et al. (2011) who show that the diminishing reserves of energy that ageing adults have access to causes them to cease to engage in activities they have previously engaged in and enjoyed or received some positive feedback for. The resulting discord between what a person can do and what they might desire creates dissatisfaction. Our findings related to depression echoed the work of Dhara and Jogsan (2013) who assert that the many challenges faced by people as they enter old age may contribute to their risk of depression. Depression is treatable but in communities where geriatric support services are non-existent, as they are in our study area, depression in elderly people often goes unnoticed.

As noted, older children and extended family members often provide material and financial support to ageing parents or relatives. For this reason, the loss of adult children represents a loss of social security. This is true in our study area, and indeed in the whole of Zambia and most of Africa. The high prevalence of diseases such as HIV and Aids, tuberculosis and malaria, means that a large number of elderly people suffer the loss of children, grandchildren and other young relatives.

Summary and conclusions

Our major finding was that a greater number of elderly adults in our study were dissatisfied with their lives than those who were satisfied. In addition, our findings are consistent with previous research in terms of the factors or categories that promote or constrain life satisfaction (income levels, general health, independence, functionality, etc.). However, the *experiences* linked to these factors reflect the specificity of the Zambian context and, we suggest, might highlight the vulnerability of elderly populations in other African and other low-income countries.

Constraints such as having no option but to work in old age, the inability to plan or make decisions due to lack of money, having no independent source of income, being unable to access sufficient food, and not seeing anything worth enjoying in life are clear indicators of this vulnerability. However, the experiences that our respondents mentioned as drivers of life satisfaction are similarly revealing of the fragility of their support systems: being able to afford to eat three meals in a day, not having to go to sleep hungry, having well-behaved and well-educated children, being cared for by family members, etc.

As indicated in the introduction, the activity theory of ageing suggests that maintaining high levels of physical and social activities into old age brings about life satisfaction, continuity theory posits that being able to continue enjoying our favourite activities into retirement will result in life satisfaction and disengagement theory suggests that what brings about life satisfaction in late adulthood is the ability to voluntarily reduce activity levels and social roles. However, in this study, apart from one finding that supported activity theory – loss of loved ones as a detractor from attainment of life satisfaction – our findings are inconsistent with these three theories of ageing. For many respondents, the factors that detract most from life satisfaction are related to their economic status, and their need to have to work into old age in order to make ends meet.

It seems possible that the developers of the activity theory of ageing did not have elderly people in low-income countries such as Zambia in mind. Zambia, like many other countries, is socially, culturally and economically vastly different from the US, where the activity theory of ageing originated. The majority of elderly Zambians, whether they have retired from formal employment or not, are struggling to fulfil their basic needs for food and shelter. In view of this, we propose that a theory of ageing is required, which takes into account the differing social, cultural and economic status of elderly persons in different contexts.

The implementation of SDG 3 requires governments and other stake-holders to put in place interventions that promote the well-being of all ages. Our findings offer insights that are crucial to the design of appropriate interventions to both counter factors that constrain the attainment of life satisfaction and enhance the well-being of elderly persons in a range of different contexts. In our view, North–South collaboration between researchers and institutions will be critical to the development of a theory of ageing that is more inclusive.

In addition, North–South collaboration between scholars and/or institutions would not only facilitate the execution of research that is critical to the successful implementation of all 17 SDGs, but also bring about a deeper understanding of issues within and between different countries so that interventions devised are similarly more inclusive of different realities and more appropriate to the conditions they aim to address. As the old adage says, this would be like 'killing two birds with one stone'. But this can only be achieved with adequate material and financial support. Many research projects that could have made valuable contributions have had to be abandoned halfway due to lack of resources.

It is also worth mentioning that the contextual factors that affect the attainment of life satisfaction and well-being are varied and many. Consequently, we recommend that more research on the life satisfaction of elderly populations in different contexts within and outside Zambia be undertaken.

Note

1   Two types of purposive sampling were used in this study – namely, sampling to achieve representativeness and sequential sampling. More specifically, homogenous sampling and snowball sampling (Biernacki and Waldorf 1981) were used.

References

Biernacki P and D Waldorf (1981) 'Snowball sampling: Problems and techniques of chain referral sampling' *Journal of Sociological Methods and Research* 10 (4): 141–163.

Bonsang E and A van Soest (2012) *Satisfaction with Daily Activities after Retirement in Europe*. Netspar Discussion paper 35, Network for Studies on Pension, Ageing and Retirement. Available online.

Brijnath B (2011) 'Why does institutionalization care not appeal to Indian families? Legislative and social answers from urban India' *Journal of Ageing and Society* 32 (4): 697–717.

Changala M (2015) Caring for the Aged in Old People's Homes in Zambia: Implications for Adult Education Programmes, PhD thesis, University of Zambia.

CSS (Central Statistical Office, Zambia) (2012) *Zambia 2010 Census of Population and Housing National Analytical Report*. Lusaka.

Dhara RD and YA Jogsan (2013) 'Depression and psychological well-being in old age' *Journal of Psychology and Psychotherapy* 3: 117. Available online.

Diener E, RA Emmons, RJ Larsen and S Griffin (1985) 'The satisfaction with life scale' *Journal of Personality Assessment* 49: 71–75.

Finch F (2014) An Assessment of the Knowledge, Attitudes and Practices in Lusaka Urban District of Zambia Towards the Aged: The Case of Chipata and N'gombe Compounds, master's dissertation, University of Zambia.

Fisher BJ (1992) 'Successful aging and life satisfaction: A pilot study for conceptual clarification' *Journal of Aging Studies* 6 (2): 191–202.

Good GA, S LaGrow and F Alpass (2011) 'A study of older adults: Observation of ranges of life satisfaction and functioning' *New Zealand Journal of Psychology* 40 (3): 96–102.

Humpert S (2013) *Gender Differences in Life Satisfaction and Social Participation*, Working Paper 276, Institute of Economics, University of Lüneburg, Germany.

ILO (International Labour Organization) (2001) *Social Security: Issues, Challenges and Prospects*. Proceedings of the 89th International Labour Conference, Geneva.

Kamwengo MM (2001) *Ageing and the Elderly in Zambia: Perspectives and Issues*. New Delhi: Sterling.

Kamwengo MM (2004) *Growing Old in Zambia: Old and New Perspectives*. New Delhi: Sterling.

Kaputo C (2010) *Assessing Administrative Capacity and Costs of Cash Transfer Schemes in Zambia: Implications for Rollout*. Brasilia: International Policy Centre for Inclusive Growth.

Mapoma CC (2013) Population Ageing in Zambia: Magnitude, Challenges and Determinants, PhD thesis, University of Zambia.

Motjuwadi CL (2013) Life Satisfaction and Adjustment of Retired Migrant Workers, PhD thesis, University of South Africa.

Mukuka L, W Kalikiti and DK Musenge (2002) 'Social security systems in Zambia' *Journal of Social Development in Africa* 17 (2). Available online.

Neugarten BL, RJ Havighurst and SS Tobin (1961) 'The measurement of life satisfaction' *Journal of Gerontology* 16: 134–143.

Nuehs HP (1990) 'Retirement self-efficacy: The effects of socioeconomic status, life satisfaction, health and readiness for retirement' *Journal of the New York State Nurses Association* 21 (1): 15–20.

Osborne JW (2009) *Essential Retirement: Psychological Concerns.* Possum.

Pavot W, E Diener, CR Colvin and E Sandvik (1991) 'Further validation of the satisfaction with life scale: Evidence for the cross-method convergence of well-being measures' *Journal of Personality Assessment* 57 (1): 149–161.

Prieto-Flores M-E, A Moreno-Jiménez, G Fernandez-Mayoralas, F Rojo-Perez and MJ Forjaz (2012) 'The relative contribution of health status and quality of life domains in subjective health in old age' *Social Indicators Research*: 106, 27–39.

Rasmussen PE, K Munkoni and G Lwanda (2014). 'Zambia' in African Economic Outlook 2014. Available online.

Republic of Zambia (2015) *National Ageing Policy: Ageing with Dignity.* Lusaka: Ministry of Community Development, Mother and Child Health.

Subramanien S (2013) Enhancing the Well-being of Older People in Mauritius, PhD thesis, Tilburg University, Germany. Available online.

UN (2015) *Transforming our world: The 2030 agenda for sustainable development.* Resolution 70/1 adopted by the UN General Assembly, 25 September 2015. Available online.

Wang M and B Hesketh B (2012) *Achieving Well-being in Retirement: Recommendations From 20 Years' Research.* Bowling Green, OH: Society for Industrial and Organizational Psychology. Available online.

World Health Organization (2002) *The Impact of Aids on Older Persons in Africa.* Geneva.

Yirmibesoglu F and L Berkoz (2014) Social and physical activity and life satisfaction among Turkish elderly women *International Journal of Business, Humanities and Technology* 4 (4): 146–154.

Chapter 12

Home–school relations and the role of indigenous knowledge in early literacy learning: A case study from a rural school in Zambia

Anne Marit Vesteraas Danbolt, Dennis Banda, Jørgen Klein and Geoffrey Tambulukani

IN OUR VIEW, EDUCATION LIES at the core of development. In the United Nations' 2030 Agenda for Sustainable Development, Sustainable Development Goal (SDG) 4 aims for inclusive and equitable quality education for all (UN 2015). In this chapter, we describe a joint project implemented through master's programmes at the universities of Namibia[1] and Zambia in co-operation with the Inland Norway University of Applied Sciences (previously Hedmark University of Applied Sciences) that has prioritised finding ways to improve the quality of literacy education. Co-operation between our institutions has improved our understanding of the difficulties involved in literacy education in general and in sub-Saharan Africa in particular. The project has also contributed to capacity building, and enhanced our understanding of effective North–South collaboration in teaching and research.

In this chapter, we focus specifically on home–school relations in the development of literacy in the context of primary education in Zambia. We use the term home–school relations in the sense of a *mutual and collaborative partnership* between parents/caregivers, teachers and school management, that aims to provide a good learning environment for the pupils (LaRocque et al. 2011). Parental involvement has been proved to have positive effects on learning achievement (Desforges and Abouchaar 2003), and there is much evidence that good home–school relations are conducive for learner well-being (see, for example, Epstein 2009; Patrikakou 2008). However, mismatches between the nature and uses of literacy at home and at school can also cause difficulties for children in learning literacy (Baker 2011; Brooker 2002; Heath 1983/2006).

Existing research has revealed a lack of parental[2] involvement in children's schoolwork (Clemensen 2011), and a study conducted by the Southern and

Eastern Africa Consortium for Monitoring Educational Quality (SACMEQ) in Zambia found that less than 35 per cent of learners report that they receive assistance with homework sometimes or most times (Musonda and Kaba 2011b). In general, the challenges related to education in Zambia are high. For instance, pupils' performances in reading and mathematics are among the lowest in sub-Saharan Africa, and declined from 2000 to 2011 (SACMEQ 2017). Improving home–school relations might offer one way of meeting these challenges.

Before the advent of formal schooling, most children learned the skills they needed for their lives in their homes and local communities. This form of indigenous education was passed on from one generation to the other, so that growing up and learning was the same thing (Banda 2008; Banda and Morgan 2013). With the development of formal schooling, the link between the home and children's learning weakened, and the learning done at home and at school became more separate (Banda 2008). In post-colonial countries such as Zambia, the schooling system is based on the remnants of colonial education that was run by missionaries and overseen by their colonial masters, even though it was adapted after Zambia won back its independence in 1964. With independence, the government selected English as the language of instruction throughout the educational system, thus adding to the disparity between home and school. Because so much indigenous knowledge is embedded in language, the switch to English prevents learners from being able to use the local or indigenous knowledge that they have already acquired as a foundation for the formal school knowledge and literacy development that they obtain throughout their years at school. Indigenous forms of knowledge may be lost or discarded when an unfamiliar language is used as the medium of instruction at school.

In this chapter, we present a pilot study conducted in a rural school in Zambia. The primary objective is to explore how parents and teachers perceive the relationship between home and school in relation to the role of indigenous knowledge, with specific reference to early literacy learning. We also discuss how implications of the language policy may affect this relationship.[3]

Home–school relations

Internationally, a huge body of research exists on the effects of home background on children's attainment in school. One seminal work is the ethnographic study conducted by Shirley Brice Heath in the United States in the early 1980s. Her study was one of the first to illustrate how literacy practices in families influence children's schooling (Heath 1983/2006). In the United Kingdom, Liz Brooker (2002) described how immigrant families tend to remain on the peripheries of the schools their children attend, and are not involved in the practices and ideas that guide the teaching principles. A compilation of research by Desforges and Abouchaar (2003) demonstrated the significant effect of 'at home good parenting'[4] on children's educational attainment. They concluded that to a major degree, forces outside of the control of the school shape achievement, and social factors play a large role.

Studies like these have raised awareness about home–school relations and literacy intervention programmes among educators as well as researchers (Paratore et al. 2010). According to Patrikakou (2008), there are three broad types of parental involvement: involvement at home, involvement at school and home–school communication. LaRocque et al. (2011) defined parental or family involvement as the extent to which parents or caregivers' invest in the education of their children. This investment can take many forms, including parents volunteering for assistance with practical tasks at school, assisting their children with homework or engaging in events and activities initiated by the school. The form of interaction is not the key factor; what is important is that schools and parents share the same views on what constitutes a good relationship between home and school (LaRocque et al. 2011).

Another term used to describe home–school relations is *school outreach* (Galindo and Sheldon 2011). This puts more emphasis on the actions of the school management and teachers. In our opinion, a mutual relationship between home and school must include school outreach and parental involvement. The distinction between proactive and reactive relations is also a useful one (Desforges and Abouchaar 2003). An example of proactive involvement is when parents and schools co-operate on a regular basis to build a good relationship. A reactive involvement means that parents act only in response to an initiative from the school; typically, this will involve a problem that requires their attention.

Joyce Epstein (2009) developed the most comprehensive model for home–school relations. Her concept of 'overlapping spheres of influence' as a theory for explaining the shared responsibilities of home, school and community has been highly influential. Her model describes six types of partnership: *parenting, communicating, volunteering, learning at home, decision-making* and *collaborating with the community* (Epstein 2009). In our pilot study, we applied Epstein's types of partnership to the analysis of our data, to provide a well-established theoretical framework and key definitions (Yin 2014), but also to find out whether our case corresponded to this widely acknowledged model.

In South Africa, Lemmer (2011) and Lemmer and Van Wyk (2004a, 2004b) have conducted research on family involvement. They identified several impediments to home–school co-operation (Lemmer and Van Wyk 2004a), but also provided many examples of schools reaching out to parents in a systematic and engaged manner (Lemmer and Van Wyk 2004b). Lemmer and Van Wyk (2004b) argued that broader strategies for parental involvement should be adopted in South African schools, and Lemmer (2011) has since documented examples of formal educational provision for in-service teachers on the topic of home–school relations.

An ethnographic study in a rural community in the southern province of Zambia provides another interesting insight into the relationship between home and school. In the study, Clemensen (2011) showed that despite generally affirming the importance of schooling, parents paid little attention to the daily aspects of children's schooling and spent little time assisting them with homework. In addition, several master's theses submitted to the School of Education at the University of Zambia have also focused on the relations between home and school. Kapambwe (1980) investigated the home background of two hundred Zambian junior secondary pupils in relation to a number of variables and found an association between home environment and scholastic achievement. Variables included: parental education, reading habits in the home, parental income, parental occupation, housing conditions, parental attitudes to education, parental encouragement and support at home. Another relevant study is Musonda's research on literacy behaviours among preschoolers in Lusaka (Musonda 2011). Musonda concluded that teachers seldom recognise the emergent literacy knowledge that children acquire in their early years and that parents tend to be left out of their children's education. Musonda recommended designing adult literacy programmes to empower parents to help their children become literate (Musonda 2011).

Yet another master's level study conducted in Zambia focused on the relationship between home and school. Kangómbe (2013) investigated the strategies or techniques that teachers use to promote partnerships with parents in high-density residential areas in Lusaka. The specific topic was collaboration in support of literacy development in selected basic schools. Kangómbe found that a homework policy was the most common approach used by teachers. His study also revealed several constraints on home–school partnerships, such as high illiteracy levels, high levels of poverty, lack of English proficiency among parents and low attendance at school meetings. However, some parents also felt that teachers were unwelcoming, and mentioned the lack of communication between them and the teachers.

Another research report on Zambia (Ginsburg et al. 2014) provides a quantitative study of interschool factors affecting pupils' opportunities to learn. In this case, the researchers looked for effects on learning outcomes in relation to a number of variables. They found that only low attendance among learners (including late arrival and early departure) had a significant effect on learning outcomes at the school level. The researchers recommended that future research direct attention towards learners' opportunities to learn *outside* of school, thus pointing to the findings by Desforges and Abouchaar (2003).

Indigenous knowledge and education

Indigenous knowledge is not a clear-cut concept and is defined in various ways in the literature. Most definitions include notions about knowledge derived from the way people live in a given sociocultural context over a period of time (Shizha and Abdi 2014). Avoseh (2012) stressed that the holistic worldview of traditional African systems of knowledge places a strong emphasis on achieving an equal relationship between life and learning. According to Akena (2012), indigenous knowledge is a complex accumulation of context-relevant knowledge that embraces the essence of ancestral knowing as well as the legacies of diverse history and culture. Those who have published work about research done in Africa often use the terms 'indigenous knowledge' and 'traditional knowledge' interchangeably. Interestingly, Dei's (2000) conceptualisation of indigenous knowledge as a body of knowledge associated with both traditional norms and values combined with a long-term occupancy of a certain place can apply to both terms.

In the context of this chapter, it is relevant to consider the relationship between indigenous knowledge and educational systems. UNESCO (1999) refers to indigenous knowledge as a large body of knowledge and skills that has been developed outside the formal education system, and which enables communities to survive. Several authors, including Breilid (2013) and Mkosi (2005) distinguish indigenous knowledge from Western knowledge. They emphasise that indigenous knowledge is not produced by following prescriptive regulations or methods, but is developed by people seeking solutions to everyday problems. Another characteristic is that indigenous knowledge is often orally transmitted and passed on, and much of it refers to daily habits linked to our subsistence activities (how we live). By contrast, much Western knowledge tends to be written down in books and found in educational curricula.

However, this dichotomisation of knowledge has been widely critiqued. For instance, Stephens (2015) explained that it is theoretically problematic to characterise knowledge as Western or indigenous. Stephens argued that it makes more sense to talk about multiple domains and types of knowledge, with differing logics and epistemologies, rather than two distinct categories. Klein (2011) pointed out that in all societies, knowledge is constantly hybridised and mediated in the local context. Thus, by considering indigenous knowledge as pragmatic and flexible, negotiable and dynamic, we arrive at a more precise and useful concept (Briggs 2005).

Regardless of these theoretical debates, however, the need to link education to children's real experiences is urgent. Banda (2008) described how the school system can alienate children from their home culture when their language, skills and knowledge are rendered invisible, irrelevant and unintegrated into their experience of schooling. Banda and Morgan (2013) showed how traditional education among the Chewa people in Zambia consists of specific training stages that youth have to complete. These stages include aspects of both formal and non-formal learning, but are not recognised by the education authorities. Interestingly, the country's 2013 Education Curriculum Framework (Ministry of Education 2013: 19–20) encourages the inclusion of traditional knowledge in education as follows:

> In making the curriculum flexible and responsive to learner and societal needs, institutions of learning, teachers and teacher-educators are encouraged at all levels of our education systems to localise some aspects of the school curriculum…In this way, the curriculum will provide some compensation for the indigenous knowledge, values, attitudes and practical skills that learners would have acquired in their home environment if they had not been attending school.

Despite these good intentions, Banda and Morgan (2013) argue that traditional knowledge is still not skilfully included in Zambian school curricula. They suggested that, for instance, Chewa folklore could be seen as complementary to and supportive of formal schooling, especially during early childhood education. They argue that including traditional teachings regarding morals, attitudes and values could help form some common ground between formal schooling and Chewa indigenous knowledge systems. Traditional teachings could also provide a basis for several formal school subjects, such as science, geography and agricultural science. Several studies have found that including traditional knowledge in formal education has the potential of reducing dropout rates and disciplinary problems, as well as improving learner literacy (see for example, Klein 2011 and Nungu 2014).

Literacy learning and the choice of language as medium of instruction

Literacy is regarded as key to a successful education, and crucial for economic, social and political participation (UNESCO 2006). The concept of literacy has developed from a relatively restricted view of reading and writing as individual skills to a broader perspective in which literacy is regarded as social practices that vary according to time and space (Street 2003). However, literacy can still be said to comprise text-related activities and concerns the ways in which reading and writing as social practices play a role in people's lives (Barton 2007).

With regard to literacy learning, the most valuable resources that children bring from their home are their oral language skills and early literacy experiences, such as storytelling, songs, rhymes and riddles, occasional writing, like making lists and letters, memorising books or religious verses, etc. Tambulukani (2015) underscored that oral skills, such as songs, games and rhymes, are a strong feature of emergent literacy and should continue to be practised in class when children enter school. Emergent literacy experiences reflect some of the literacy practices embedded in the daily lives of the families and represent the foundations of children's literacy development in early schooling (Brooker 2002; Heath 1983/2006; Tambulukani 2015). Furthermore, since these literacy experiences are embedded in the language practices of the home, if these skills are not given space at school, and if the language of instruction is different to the one(s) spoken at home, the disjuncture between home and school is likely to be felt more strongly by children and to continue to grow as they progress through school.

In multilingual contexts, endeavours to include children's home language/s have also been shown to have a positive effect on parental inclusion (Danbolt 2011). In an ethnographic study of bilingual education in two rural communities in Mozambique, Chimbutane (2011) explored the effects of introducing bilingual education in the first years of primary education. He described how bilingual education facilitated the incorporation of culturally relevant topics into the curriculum, facilitated the involvement of parents in the schooling of their children and, as such, empowered the community. Besides involving the parents, the use of a local language in education also facilitated the involvement of other community members in the school, bringing intellectual resources from outside into the classroom. This study clearly revealed that the choice of language as medium of instruction has significance for the inclusion of parents and of locally embedded knowledge into schooling, and this has the potential to enhance the linkages that both children and parents experience between home and school.

Some basic background on schooling in Zambia

Since gaining independence in 1964, Zambia has followed a monolingual model of language of instruction where English is used as the medium of instruction from preschool to higher education. The seven regional languages of Zambia (zonal languages) were taught as subjects at some secondary schools and as optional subjects taken by a few pupils at others. When the

Primary Reading Programme was introduced (Musonda and Kaba 2011b; Tambulukani 2015), one hour of basic literacy was taught each day in the zonal languages in the first grade. However, the language of instruction was still English.

In 2013, the Zambian government adopted a bilingual and transitional model, using a zonal language as the medium of instruction from Grades 1 to 4 and teaching English as a subject only. English became the medium of instruction from Grade 5 onwards. According to the new language policy, the zonal language is to be used as the medium of instruction in all subjects for the first four years. Studies have shown that children who learn initial literacy in a mother tongue, and move to English when they have reached a level of fluency in the first language, tend to read better both in their mother tongue and in English than those who are subjected to English as medium of instruction from Grade 1 (Banda 2012; Tambulukani 2015).

Free primary education was introduced in Zambia in 2002, in an effort to attain the Millennium Development Goals and ensure full enrolment (Musonda and Kaba 2011b). Previously, parents had to provide school uniforms and learning materials, even for primary education, and many parents struggled to afford these. The introduction of free primary education led to a vast increase in enrolment, thus putting considerable pressure on the country's education system. By 2007, 41 per cent of Zambian learners in Grade 6 did not have basic items such as textbooks, a pen, pencil or a ruler. In government schools, as many as 60 per cent of the learners did not have these items. Clearly, a lack of textbooks is a serious impediment to parental involvement in homework.

Another factor influencing home–school relations is class size. Musonda and Kaba (2011a) also noted that in 2007, the average number of Grade 6 pupils per class was 46, exceeding the national benchmark level of a maximum of 40 learners per class. Being responsible for such large numbers of students makes it very difficult for teachers to reach out to parents, especially on an individual basis.

Under the Primary Reading Programme, a manual was developed to give parents or guardians guidelines on how they could participate in the learning of their children (Mitchell et al. 1999). Parents were encouraged to sit in on classes alongside the children to see how learning takes place, and to help in any ways that they thought would enhance their child's learning. In the document, parents were asked to sign their children's homework exercise books following the completion of each homework assignment. In this way, it was hoped that parents would not just help their children to do their school homework, but also prioritise time away from many household chores for their children. Research has shown that although the reading programme was positively received, many aspects of the programme were difficult to sustain once donor funding ended (Kombe and Herman 2017). There were also reports of teachers being reluctant to invite parents into their classrooms because they felt supervised, or parents asked questions as if they were learners, and thus displayed misconceptions about their roles in the partnership.

Methodology and fieldwork

As in much qualitative research, our project focused on a specific topic. There is limited research on home–school relations within Zambia, so we chose an exploratory case study to investigate this phenomenon within its real-world context (Yin 2014). An exploratory case study is useful prior to more substantial fieldwork, as it allows for small-scale data collection to be conducted before the research questions are fully developed. From the exploratory study, we sought in-depth understanding of the topic from the participants' point of view. We therefore applied a single-case design, examining in detail one case within a limited geographical area. Themes that emerged from this, and that we plan to investigate further, are the multiple causes of absenteeism and the vast potential for integrating local knowledge and practices into schools. Although we did not intend to generalise our findings, we believe that they do have transferability to other small studies in similar contexts.

The data were collected at a government primary school in a rural area in Zambia. When the data were collected, the school had approximately 800 learners and a teaching staff of 17. It can be regarded as a typical case, as nearly 65 per cent of schools in Zambia are situated in a rural area (Musonda and Kaba 2011b), and the average number of learners per class was 47, compared to the national average of 46 (Musonda and Kaba 2011a). Teaching took place in two sessions every day to accommodate the large number of learners. In terms of resources, the school is in the lower range, and was currently building new classrooms to ease overcrowding and improve learning conditions.

The school had previously hosted researchers for visits and observations, and the staff and parents were willing to share their experiences on the issue of home–school relations. We collected data using a mix of methods consisting of focus-group interviews, individual semi-structured interviews and a questionnaire. Focus-group interviews are useful for gathering data from people who share a common experience(Yin 2014). Ours were conducted with parents in one group and teachers in another. This was done because we assumed the parents would speak more freely if the teachers were not present, and vice versa. The questionnaires were distributed to the teachers a few days after they had participated in the focus groups.

We chose not to interview pupils in this pilot, as such interviews ideally should be conducted once researchers have had time to build trust with the children and make them feel confident. In a school context, learners often fear that their statements will be communicated to their parents or teachers. Their vulnerability must be carefully taken into account by researchers when using children as informants. In the full-scale research project, children will be involved to ensure that their perspectives inform the study.

Our data is thus drawn from: a focus-group with 11 parents (1 hour and 26 mins); a focus group with seven teachers, one male, six females (just over an hour long); and an individual interview with the head teacher (also just over an hour). Questionnaires were distributed to the seven teachers.

The interview with the parents was conducted in Chinyanja, the zonal language of the region in which the school is situated, and it was moderated by a member of the research team from the University of Zambia. The other interviews were conducted in English. A member of the research team, who was present at the interviews, transcribed the interviews with the teachers and head teacher, while the interview with the parents was transcribed and translated into English by a research assistant at the School of Education at the University of Zambia. Having members of the research team who could speak the zonal language was of great importance in making communication with parents possible. These team members were also able to compare what was said in the parents' interview with the English translation and helped us to avoid losing any information. The interviews and the questionnaires were analysed by means of content analysis, including juxtaposing data from the three groups of interviewees and searching for patterns that emerged in relation to our research questions. The data from the interviews and the questionnaires were compared for consistency.

Presentation of data and analysis

We explored how parents and teachers perceive the relationship between home and school with a specific focus on early literacy learning in relation to the role of indigenous knowledge. Furthermore, as this was a pilot study, our aim was to test and refine our research instruments and explore the topic in a small-scale setting. We analysed the material using inductive open coding. Five major themes emerged: absenteeism, communication and contribution, behaviour and respect, agricultural activities, and local literacy practices.

While the study was small, and as noted, we did not set out to generalise our findings, we believe it has value in both illuminating the themes that emerged, and in having the potential to generate further hypotheses, and we offer our analysis in this light.

Absenteeism: a strain on the relationship

Parents and teachers mentioned the problem of absenteeism, but the concept has different meanings for the two groups. Parents complained about *teacher* absenteeism several times during the focus group interview, and their words could be quite harsh. One respondent noted that 'many teachers absent themselves from work due to excessive beer drinking but many are also involved in small businesses and other business ventures'. The parents pointed to the challenge teachers face in finding accommodation and noted that most rent places to live some distance away from the school. It must be noted, of course, that the parents were not necessarily speaking about the teachers that took part in this study, but about teachers in general. In any case, the parents' statements point to a problem that is evident in other research, for instance Ginsburg et al. (2014), where teacher absenteeism is estimated to cause on average a loss of almost 14 school days per year.

On the other hand, the teachers focused on *learner* absenteeism. They mentioned that children are absent because they take part in economic activities when it comes to 'the season when it is farming'. Since they live in an area where agriculture is the main means of livelihood, teachers seemed to have an understanding of this. However, learners arriving late or being absent from school is a serious impediment to progress in learning, as documented by Ginsburg et al. (2014). The head teacher also mentioned initiation ceremonies as an example of a practice that causes absenteeism among learners. He expressed concern about this, noting that some parents keep their girls at home for a long period of time when they reach puberty[5]. The government has put initiatives in place to advise parents on this issue, and the teachers stated that it is no longer practised within their community. The teachers seemed thus to be less willing than the head teacher to talk about these challenges, and we may here touch upon what is considered secret knowledge in the community. There may be practices that are kept away from strangers posing questions about issues that are considered private. Parents may, in any case, need to be advised about the drawbacks of their children's absence from school, as they may not be fully aware of the negative consequences. However, as the problem of absenteeism seems to occur on both sides, this issue has the potential to create a stand-off rather than enhance relations between home and school.

Absenteeism thus emerged as a strain on the relationship, and jeopardises a good learning environment for the children. However, the issue also points to more profound challenges: the struggle for both teachers and parents to maintain daily subsistence.

Communication and co-operation: 'quite limited'

The data show few traces of effective communication between the parents and teachers about the school's programmes or the children's progress. Although the parents reported that they could present complaints to the head teacher as well as participate in annual general meetings and parent-teacher meetings, their answer to the question of whether the teachers had invited them to talk about cross-cutting issues or the welfare of their children was negative. Concerning the school's outreach activities, parents said explicitly that the teachers do not invite them. The teachers also admitted that their interaction with parents is 'quite limited'. The head teacher said that the school arranges an open day, usually in the second term. However, they no longer bring the parents into the classroom, 'because some of them do not want to be exposed to the children. They only want to talk to the teacher.'

Apart from the prescribed meetings, communication between home and school seems to take place when there is a problem to be solved. The head teacher stated that teachers call on the parents 'sometimes when they have difficulties with the children'. Such problem-oriented communication is often the norm (Lemmer and Van Wyk 2004b) and must also be considered an impediment to a good relationship, especially if this reactive strategy is not balanced by other more positive interactions.

The extent to which families are involved in decision-making about the school (Epstein 2009) is unclear from our data. The annual parent–teacher meeting is probably the one forum in which parents could exert some influence, but our data indicate that influence from the parents on decision-making is scarce, and they are rarely involved in the everyday life of the school.

Despite this, there are instances of parents contributing to the school. The head teacher noted that some parents helped by making bricks and taking part in the construction of new classrooms at the school. We also learned from the head teacher that some parents are willing to share their knowledge and skills of the local culture with the teachers, but this does not seem to be part of any systematic form of co-operation. *Volunteering* is one of the categories in Epstein's framework, but it seemed to have a limited role in the daily life at this school. The head teacher noted that asking parents to contribute is not straightforward; most are working, and would expect payment if they had to take time off from work. He said that while parents could offer indigenous skills, such as in craft, traditional songs, stories and folklore, the school has no resources to reimburse parents for any loss of income incurred if they help out at the school.

It seems that, at this school, the head teacher plays a mediating role between parents and teachers. He is the one to step in and cover for absent teachers, and the one who receives complaints from the parents. He also maintains close contact with the representatives of the local traditional leaders and attempts to communicate with the parents through these elected representatives. The parents expressed their trust in the head teacher, and he was not a target of complaints in the interview we had with parents. This might imply that the head teacher could play a crucial role in improving the home–school relationship, which would be in line with research findings by Lemmer and Van Wyk (2004b).

Behaviour and respect: concordance of values

A distinct feature of the data is the concordance between statements by parents, teachers and the head teacher on values such as respect for adults and good conduct. The teachers placed much emphasis on good behaviour, as 'an ongoing thing apart from subjects', while the parents explicitly stated that respect should be taught at home and at school. However, some parents complained about some children becoming bullies when they start school, due to negative peer influence. Parents did not seem to relate this to the role of the teachers, however, and seemed to see the teachers as their allies when it came to teaching learners about good behaviour.

Some examples were given of parents and teachers learning from each other, which in Epstein's framework falls within the category of *parenting* (Epstein 2009). For instance, the head teacher reported that some teachers had visited the parents of a child with disabilities, so they could find out how to take care of the child at school. In the questionnaires, the teachers expressed willingness to learn more about traditional child-rearing and parenting practices in the school catchment area. One of the teachers expanded on this by writing: 'As a teacher I move around in the villages to see and learn from the parents.' Interestingly, all the teachers who took part in the group interview were from other parts of Zambia and were not native to the area. They all seemed to see the need to learn about local practices and to comply with the traditional norms and values concerning the children's upbringing. This concordance of values, combined with the teachers' willingness to learn from the parents, could form the basis for an improved relationship.

Agricultural activities: a common experience

As noted, the school is located in a rural area, and the teachers often mentioned agricultural activities as examples of how they link their teaching practice to local knowledge. There seemed to be a positive attitude among the teachers concerning indigenous knowledge as a resource, and the teachers listed many examples of indigenous forms of learning in the questionnaires, including: pastoralism, poultry rearing, chiyato,[6] playing in the soil, drawing and writing, and requesting that the learners bring a specific number of items, for example, bottletops, to be counted as an activity to enhance numeracy. The head teacher mentioned that they previously used a localised curriculum, where the parents contributed by teaching crafts. This curriculum was no longer in place, as it had been difficult to include the contribution from the parents in a systematic way.

Interestingly, one of the teachers challenged the idea of localised curricula noting that, 'At the end of the day, we must educate the children so they fit in the global market.' This statement illustrates a dilemma that both the teachers and parents seem to feel. On this point, the Zambia Education Curriculum Framework gives little more than general guidance, stating that: 'The curriculum development process should take a global view of the new trends, strategies and practices, and embrace indigenous heritage and thoughts that could fit in the local and national situation' (Ministry of Education 2013: 56). The challenge is to adapt elements of indigenous knowledge in ways that enhance learning outcomes, and the teacher's statement revealed that teachers require more knowledge on this issue. For instance, Baker (2011) emphasised how providing early literacy education in a language that is familiar to a child, including content that builds on their primary experiences, provides a better foundation for their educational success at every subsequent level.

Literacy practices in the community: a potential for improved relations

In our study, the parents said that they try to teach the children traditional stories and songs. They also said that they teach their children everyday calculations by checking the amount they return after having been given money to buy something from the market. Some had storybooks, Bibles and calendars but others had no reading material for children in their homes. On the other hand, all seven teachers answered 'yes' to a question about whether they use local games, songs, riddles and tongue-twisters in their teaching.

Under the category described by Epstein (2009) as *learning at home*, we found that parents keep up the traditions and try to infuse their children with oral and/or written texts that form part of their culture. The head teacher emphasised that the teachers try to make use of traditional songs and stories especially in the first few years of schooling. And as previously mentioned, the teachers expressed willingness to learn from the parents. However, co-operation around homework does not occur. This corresponds to findings by Clemensen (2011). The limits on resources available to learners are very evident here as very few children had their own books to take home (Musonda and Kaba 2011a). However, the mutual understanding between parents and teachers of the benefit of building on children's existing oral skills may provide grounds for extending their co-operation.

Final reflections

Despite the limited scale of this study, interesting patterns emerged. In line with research in South Africa (Lemmer and Van Wyk 2004b) and Zambia (Kangómbe 2013) this study uncovered several impediments to good home–school relations. An obvious one is the lack of resources: large numbers of learners in each class, and the need to attend to everyday obligations, leave parents and teachers little time to spare for the extra effort of building a relationship between home and school. Another impediment is the tension in the relationship between parents and teachers, as evident in the parents' complaints about teacher absenteeism and the lack of invitations from teachers to talk about their children. Further research on the causes of absenteeism is needed, as this not only deprives learners of opportunities to learn, but also hampers a good relationship between home and school.

On the other hand, mutual adherence to traditional norms and values concerning the upbringing of children could provide a platform for improving this relationship. In addition, both teachers and parents speak positively of the role of indigenous knowledge related to agricultural activities, and this seems to offer great potential for education in general and for literacy education in particular. Situated and local knowledge embedded in community practices featured in the statements from all participants in the study. The potential for integrating local knowledge and practices into the everyday life of the school could bring the community and the school closer together thus renewing and improving relations between home and school. This also requires teachers and parents to be better informed about the potential benefits for children's success at school and their willingness to collaborate in building an infrastructure for systematic home–school co-operation.

In this study, the head teacher played a crucial role in mediating relations between home and school. Any steps towards improvement of this relationship should involve the school's leaders, as they often possess the key to communication between teachers and parents.

This pilot study revealed the potential for a closer relationship between home and school by including indigenous knowledge in early literacy learning. Furthermore, it informed the design of our larger study by emphasising the necessity of obtaining a deeper understanding of how local communities perceive this relationship. To get a broader picture, schoolchildren will be included in the larger study, and observations of parent-teacher meetings will be added to the data sources.

In our opinion, improved communication between home and school could be a first step towards empowering parents to assist their children with their literacy learning. The conditions for a positive home–school relationship should become more favourable as the language policy changed in 2013, and a familiar local language is now used as the language of instruction for children from Grades 1 to 4. This language policy should also have the potential to create a closer relationship between home and school, to the benefit of learners, parents and teachers.

Notes

1. From 2008 until 2013, the University of Namibia's participation in this project was funded by the Norwegian government's funding agency Norad, under its Programme for Master's Studies. However, as a middle-income country, Namibia has since been removed from the list of partner countries funded by Norad, and became ineligible as a partner in the continued collaboration. This is illustrative of the kinds of challenges facing sustainable partnerships in higher education and shows how vulnerable North–South co-operation is to the political priorities set by donor countries.

2. We use the term 'parent' as defined in the Zambian Education Act of 2011 to include 'a guardian or a person who has the actual custody of the child' (Chapter 1, Definitions).

3. We intend to use the insights obtained from this pilot study in a broader research project under the umbrella of the Literacy Education in Multilingual Settings Project (LEMS) that received funding from the Norwegian Partnership Programme for Global Academic Cooperation in 2016. The LEMS project is an extension of the co-operation between the University of Zambia and Inland Norway University of Applied Sciences, and allows for a more comprehensive research project, involving faculty from the two universities as well as master's and PhD students.

4. This includes parents providing a secure and stable environment, intellectual stimulation that includes spending time interacting with their child, and a set of values to aspire to as well as maintaining contact with schools to share information, etc. (Desforges and Abouchaar 2003).

5. On the practical challenges of managing menstruation in low-income settings, see Nanda et al. (2016).

6. Chiyato is a traditional game that uses pebbles and enhances numeracy skills.

References

Akena FA (2012) 'Critical analysis of the production of western knowledge and its implications for indigenous knowledge and decolonization' *Journal of Black Studies* 43 (6): 599–619.

Avoseh MBM (2012) 'Proverbs as theoretical frameworks for lifelong learning in indigenous African education' *Adult Education Quarterly* 63 (3): 236–250.

Baker C (2011) *Foundations of Bilingual Education and Bilingualism* (fifth edition). Clevedon, Buffalo, Toronto and Sydney: Multilingual Matters.

Banda D (2008) *Education for All and African Indigenous Knowledge Systems: The Case of the Chewa people of Zambia.* Saabrücken: Lambert.

Banda D (2012) *Disabling or Empowering? A Quick Transition from L1 to L2 as LoI: An Evaluation of the Primary Reading Program's (PRP) Quick Transition from Pupils' Mother Tongue to English.* Saabrücken: Lambert.

Banda D and JP Morgan (2013) 'Folklore as an instrument of education among the Chewa people of Zambia' *International Review of Education* 59: 197–216. Available online.

Barton D (2007) *Literacy: An Introduction to the Ecology of Written Language* (second edition). Oxford: Blackwell.

Breilid A (2013) *Education, Indigenous Knowledges, and Development in the Global South: Contesting Knowledges for a Sustainable Future.* Routledge: New York.

Briggs J (2005) 'The use of indigenous knowledge in development: Problems and challenges' *Progress in Development Studies* 5 (2): 99–114.

Brooker L (2002) *Starting School: Young Children Learning Cultures.* Buckingham: Open University Press.

Chimbutane F (2011) *Rethinking Bilingual Education in Postcolonial Contexts.* Bristol, Buffalo and Toronto: Multilingual Matters.

Clemensen N (2011) Children in Ambiguous Realms: Language, Socialisation and Schooling among Children in a Rural Zambian Community, PhD thesis, Danish School of Education, Aarhus University.

Danbolt AMV (2011) 'Bilingual home-made dictionaries as bridges between home and school' *Journal of Teacher Education and Teachers' Work* 2 (1): 7–17.

Dei GJS (2000) 'Rethinking the role of indigenous knowledges in the academy' *International Journal of Inclusive Education* 4 (2): 111–132.

Desforges C and A Abouchaar (2003) The Impact of Parental Involvement, Parental Support and Family Education on Pupil Achievements and Adjustment: A Literature Review. London: Queen's Printer. Available online.

Epstein JL (2009) 'School, family, and community partnerships: Caring for the children we share' in JL Epstein and associates (eds), *School, Family, and Community Partnerships: Your Handbook for Action* (third edition). Thousand Oaks, CA: Corwin.

Galindo C and S Sheldon (2011) 'School and home connections and children's kindergarten achievement gains: The mediating role of family involvement', *Early Childhood Research Quarterly* 27: 90–103.

Ginsburg M, D Balwanz, D Banda, J Park, G Tambulukani and W Yao (2014) 'Opportunity to learn and its consequences for student learning outcomes in basic education schools in Zambia' *African Educational Research Journal* 2 (4): 123–156.

Heath SB (1983/2006) *Ways with Words: Language, Life, and Work in Communities and Classrooms.* Cambridge: Cambridge University Press.

Islam MR and D Banda (2011) 'Cross-cultural social research with indigenous knowledge: Some dilemmas and lessons' *Journal of Social Research and Policy* Journal of Social Research and Policy 2 (1): 67–82.

Kangómbe D (2013) Home-School Partnerships in Literacy Development in Selected Basic Schools of Lusaka District, master's thesis, School of Education, University of Zambia.

Kapambwe GM (1980) An Investigation into the Relationship between Home Background and Scholastic Achievement of a Group of Junior Secondary School Pupils in Zambia, master's thesis, School of Education, University of Zambia.

Klein J (2011) 'Indigenous knowledge and education: The case of the Nama people in Namibia' *Education as Change* 15 (1): 81–94. doi: 10.1090/16823206.2011.554847

Kombe CLM and C Herman (2017) 'Can education be sustained after the end of donor funding? The case of a reading intervention programme in Zambia' *Educational Review* 69 (5): 533–553. Available online.

LaRocque M, I Kleiman and S Darling (2011) 'Parental involvement: The missing link in school achievement' *Preventing School Failure* 55: 115–122.

Lemmer E (2011) 'Making it happen: A grounded theory study of in-service teacher training for parent involvement in schools' *Education as Change* 15 (1): 95–106.

Lemmer E and N van Wyk (2004a) 'Home-school communication in South African primary schools' *South African Journal of Education* 24 (3): 183–188.

Lemmer E and N van Wyk (2004b) 'Schools reaching out: Comprehensive parent involvement in South African primary schools' *Africa Education Review* 1 (2): 259–278.

Mitchell C, M Blaeser, B Chilangwa and IM Maimbolwa-Sinyangwe (1999) 'Girls' education in Zambia: Everyone's responsibility: A policy framework for participatory process' in C Soudien and P Kallaway (eds), *Education, Equity and Transformation.* Dordrecht: Springer.

Ministry of Education, Science, Vocational Training and Early Education (2013) Zambia Education Curriculum Framework 2013. (Prepared and published by the Curriculum Development Centre. Localised 15 December 2016.) Available online.

Mkosi N (2005) 'Surveying indigenous knowledge, the curriculum, and development in Africa: A critical African viewpoint' in AA Abdi and A Cleghorn (eds), *Issues in African Education: Sociological Perspectives.* New York: Palgrave Macmillan.

Musonda MG (2011) Literacy Behaviours which Pre-schoolers Exhibit in Selected Households of Lusaka, master's thesis, School of Education, University of Zambia.

Musonda B and A Kaba (2011a) *Quality of Primary School Inputs in Zambia*, SACMEQ Policy Brief, SACMEQ, Gaborone.

Musonda B and A Kaba (2011b) The Sacmeq III Project in Zambia. A Study of the Conditions of Schooling and the Quality of Education. Gaborone: SACMEQ. Available online.

Nanda G, J Lupele and J Tharaldson (2016) Menstrual Hygiene Management among Schoolgirls in Eastern Province of Zambia: Qualitative Research Final Report. Washington, DC: USAID/ WASHplus Project.

Nungu M (2014) 'Reclaiming the education for all agenda in Africa: Prospects for inclusive policy spaces' in E Shizha and AA Abdi (eds), *Indigenous Discourses on Knowledge and Development in Africa*. London: Routledge.

Paratore JR, B Krol-Sinclair, M Páez and KP Bock (2010) 'Supporting literacy learning in families for whom English is an additional language' in G Li and PA Edwards (eds), *Best Practices in ELL Instruction*. New York: Guilford.

Patrikakou EN (2008) The Power of Parent Involvement: Evidence, Ideas, and Tools for Student Success. Lincoln, IL: Center on Innovation and Improvement. Available online.

SACMEQ (The Southern and Eastern Africa Consortium for Monitoring Educational Quality) (2017) Reading and Math Achievement Scores. Gaborone. Available online.

Shizha E and AA Abdi (2014) 'Indigenous discourses on knowledge and development in Africa' in E Shizha and AA Abdi (eds), *Indigenous Discourses on Knowledge and Development in Africa*. London: Routledge.

Stephens (2015) Book review: Education, indigenous knowledges, and development in the global South: Contesting knowledges for a sustainable future' *Comparative Education* 51 (2).

Street B (2003) 'What is "new" in new literacy studies? Critical approaches to literacy in theory and practice' *Current Issues in Comparative Education* 5 (2). Available online.

Tambulukani GK (2015) First Language Teaching of Initial Reading: Blessing or Curse for the Zambian Children under Primary Reading Programme? PhD thesis, University of Zambia. Available online.

UN (2015) *Transforming our world: The 2030 agenda for sustainable development*. Resolution 70/1 adopted by the UN General Assembly, 25 September 2015. Available online.

UNESCO (1999) *Cultural Challenges of the International Decade of the World's Indigenous People, 18–20 October*. Paris.

UNESCO (2006) *Education for All: Literacy for Life. EFA Global Monitoring Report*. Paris.

Yin R (2014) *Case Study Research. Design and Methods* (fifth edition). Los Angeles, London, New Dehli, Singapore and Washington, DC: Sage.

Chapter 13

Relocation of the homestead: A customary practice in the communal areas of north-central Namibia

Antti Erkkilä and Nelago Indongo

SINCE THE SECOND WORLD WAR, there has been a shift in development practice and theory from centralised, technically orientated solutions towards participatory initiatives often focused on poverty alleviation (Agrawal 1995). The current paradigm for sustainable development science emphasizes transdisciplinarity, involving both scientists and non-scientists (Komiyama and Takeuchi 2006; Scholz and Steiner 2015). It is evident that the consideration of a broader range of knowledge, and particularly the inclusion of indigenous knowledge, is critical to the implementation of the United Nations Post-2015 Development Agenda (UN 2015).

The concept *indigenous knowledge* appeared in the debate on sustainable development in the early 1980s (Briggs 2005) and it refers to terms such as traditional ecological knowledge, community knowledge, and local knowledge (see WIPO 2002). Indigenous knowledge is considered cultural knowledge in its broadest sense, including all the social, political, economic and spiritual aspects of local ways of life (Langill 1999). Such local knowledge is passed on from generation to generation by word of mouth (Warren 1991). Thus, indigenous knowledge can be defined as locally bound knowledge that is indigenous to a specific area and embedded in the culture, cosmology and activities of particular peoples (McIntyre et al. 2009: 67).

Many farming systems in Africa and elsewhere are based on a profound knowledge of soils, vegetation, climate, and pests. Peasants and small farmers have long understood the benefits of intercropping agricultural crops with trees, a land-use system defined as agroforestry (Nair 1989; Olofson 1983).

In the most densely populated areas of north-central Namibia, agroforestry dominates the landscape, where the original forest cover has gradually changed into on-farm fruit-tree cover (Erkkilä 2001). Indigenous fruit trees, such as bird-plum (*Berchemia discolor* Hemsl.) and marula (*Sclerocarya birrea* Hochst.), are commonly found growing among cultivated crops, especially pearl millet (*Cenchrus spicatus* L. Cav.), which is known locally as *mahangu*.

In 1851, the English explorer, Francis Galton, commented on north-central Namibia's 'charming' agroforestry landscape (1853: 204–205). Kalle Koivu (1925), a Finnish missionary, was most likely the first to write about the abundance of fruit trees within cultivated fields occurring as a result of human activities. He argued that this particular landscape is not natural but a man-made park. Accordingly, an agricultural production unit should rather be called a garden, not a field.

Traditionally a homestead is placed within a cultivated field, and relocated frequently a few metres within the same field area. This process is called *oludilu*, and it should not be confused with shifting cultivation, where the field in cultivation is rotated. According to Koivu (1925), the homestead was relocated every second or third year. Tönjes (1911/1996) observed that the transfer interval was three to four years.

There are three major reasons for *oludilu*. First, soil fertility at the site and around the homestead is improved by household litter and other debris, including smashed mud blocks from old hut walls. Thus, the relocation of the homestead is a way of improving soil fertility on degraded spots within a cultivated area. Second is the gradual deterioration of constructions, and need for renovation. The third reason is related to the change of ownership of a homestead.

Namibia's 2011 Population and Housing Census defined a traditional dwelling as 'a compound consisting of a hut or a group of huts walled or un-walled with sticks, poles with or without thatch or grass' (NSA 2014a). (In this study, we use the term 'homestead' instead of 'dwelling'.) Traditional homesteads provide a favourable environment for the germination and growth of trees due to the fact that seedlings are protected from browsing animals. *Oludilu* has therefore been an important factor in creating the agroforestry landscape typical of north-central Namibia and southern Angola (see Erkkilä 2001). Despite the central role it has played, not only in crop cultivation and tree growing, but also culturally and spiritually, the practice of *oludilu* has hardly been studied.

The objective of this study was to increase awareness and understanding of this customary practice, which is still carried out in the communal areas of north-central Namibia and southern Angola. It forms part of a research project on 'Demographic Change and the Resilience of the Social and Ecological Systems in North-Central Namibia' carried out by the University of Eastern Finland (UEF) and the University of Namibia (UNAM) in 2012–2016.[1]

Study area

North-central Namibia is located in the southern part of the Cuvelai Basin, and consists of Ohangwena, Omusati, Oshana and Oshikoto regions (see Figure 13.1). The area is bordered by Angola in the north, Kunene Region in the west and south, Otjozondjupa Region in the south-east and Kavango West Region in the east. The southern part of north-central Namibia contains Etosha National Park and freehold farmland of the Oshikoto Region. The area north of latitude 18°30' south is communal land, which consists of eight traditional authority areas.[2] The main language spoken is Oshiwambo, which has two predominant dialects, Oshindonga and Oshikwanyama.

The Cuvelai Basin has sustained relatively high populations compared to the surrounding areas (Calunga et al. 2015; Erkkilä 2001; Mendelsohn et al. 2000, 2013; Mendelsohn and Weber 2011). This has been possible predominantly because of highly integrated agropastoral farming practices, where plots of land are cultivated permanently. The population of the Cuvelai

FIGURE 13.1 Population distribution in Namibia

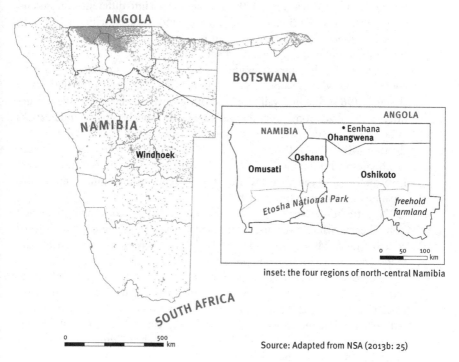

inset: the four regions of north-central Namibia

Source: Adapted from NSA (2013b: 25)

Basin amounts to about 1.2 million people, of which two thirds live in Namibia. Almost all the people of the area belong to one ethnic group, known as Owambo in Namibia and as Ambó in Angola.

According to the 2011 national census, the population of north-central Namibia amounted to 0.8 million, of which 17 per cent were urban (NSA 2013a). The area is vulnerable to the impact of climate change due to the inherent water deficit and high temperatures during the spring and summer months (Government of Namibia 2015). Increasing drought and flood damage caused by climate change multiply the challenges to farm sustainability.

In the 2011 census, 165 000 private households were counted in north-central Namibia, of which 130 000 were rural (NSA 2013a; 2014b; 2014c). Average household size was 5.1 people. The total number of rural traditional homesteads was 113 000.

As mentioned, traditional Owambo homesteads are placed within a cultivated field. A homestead has a continuous outer palisade, usually two to three metres in height, consisting of tightly packed vertical wooden poles or laths, which are partly buried in the ground. In large homesteads there are inner stockades, which separate the household area into different sections and enclosures: for social life, sleeping, cooking and storage facilities. Typically, there are some two thousand wooden poles in the outer palisade and more than a thousand poles in inner stockades and hut walls.[3]

Enclosed by the outer palisade are round huts and shelters, which have conical roofs with a wooden frame, thatched using grass or millet stalks (Urquart 1963). The hut walls are built of tightly packed vertical poles or air-dried mud blocks. Sometimes the walls are made using bundles of millet stalks lashed together and installed between a mud wall plinth and the underside of the roof (Mills 1984). The floor of a hut may be daubed with clay. The surface of a homestead compound is earth, similar to the surrounding cultivated field. Livestock pens, if there are any, are either attached to the homestead or form separate enclosures in the same field.[4]

Non-traditional building materials include cement blocks and corrugated iron sheets, which are used in modern buildings among traditional constructions. Mesh wire, cement blocks and corrugated iron sheets are increasingly replacing wooden poles in the outer palisades.

The relocation of a traditional homestead, *oludilu*, means pulling up thousands of poles and carrying them up to two hundred metres to a new place in the same field. The homestead is then rebuilt on a new spot reusing old construction materials, as well as freshly cut poles, new millet stalks and grass, wherever needed. Modern cement block-buildings and walls are difficult, if not impossible to relocate.

Neighbours and others from the village are invited to assist in the *oludilu* process (Ndeutapo 2014). Men help by moving poles, huts and granary baskets from the old site to the new, while women prepare foods and drink in the new homestead. This kind of voluntary group work is called *eendjabi*.

Data collection

A specific case study area was selected from the eastern part of the Ohangwena region, 20 km south of the border between Angola and Namibia, and 10 km south-west of Eenhana, the regional capital. The study area consists of a cluster of fifty small-scale farms in Egambo and Otaukondjele villages. Egambo is located within the northern margin of the Ondonga Traditional Authority area and Otaukondjele at the southern limit of the Oukwanyama Traditional Authority area. Oshikwanyama is a common language spoken in both villages.

The objectives of the research project were explained and agreed at the beginning of 2012 with the incumbent councillors of Ondobe and Eenhana constituencies, while they visited the UNAM main campus in Windhoek. The councillors then contacted the headmen in the study area, and spoke on the radio in order to explain the objectives of the research to the community and to request their participation. Subsequently, the research team met with the councillors in Eenhana. In addition, they paid a courtesy call to the headman of Egambo village and contacted the principal of Egambo Combined School.

The household survey was conducted between 30 July and 6 August 2012 using a semi-structured questionnaire. The interview team consisted of three senior UEF scholars and two UNAM research assistants. Two of the interviews were conducted in English, and the rest in Oshikwanyama. The duration of the interviews was 90 minutes on average, and a total of 38 households were visited.

Most of the respondents said they were either Lutheran or Anglican. The main respondent was usually the head of the household, some were relatives of the head of the household, and in two homesteads, a domestic worker was interviewed; 24 female and 14 male respondents were interviewed. The median age was 50 years for female and 54 years for male respondents. In one household, a male respondent of 15 years was interviewed, whereas 25 respondents were 20 to 59 years of age and 12 respondents were 60 years or more. In Egambo village 27 interviews were carried out and 11 interviews took place in Otaukondjele.

Aerial photography of 10 to 12 June 2011[5] was used as reference data to assess possible changes in the homestead location. During the fieldwork, co-ordinate data on homestead locations were obtained using handheld global positioning system (GPS) devices. Thus, *oludilu* practices were assessed for the period between June 2011 (date of aerial photography) and August 2012 (ground truth). The period consists of two dry seasons suitable for *oludilu*. The interviews included questions related to *oludilu*, such as: how frequently does the practice take place; why is it still carried out; and do householders intend to relocate their homesteads in the future.

Results

A total of 38 homesteads were visited in the villages of Egambo and Otaukondjele (Table 13.1). On-site GPS recordings proved that eight homesteads had been relocated and seven homesteads were in the middle of a transfer process during the visit. Thus, in August 2012, 15 homesteads had been relocated or were in the middle of a transfer process.

TABLE 13.1   Oludilu in Egambo and Otaukondjele between June 2011 and August 2012

Status of Oludilu by August 2012	Total	Head of household	
		Female	Male
Completed	8	3	5
Ongoing	7	4	3
Not relocated	23	10	13
Total	38	17	21

The death of the owner of the homestead was given as a reason for *oludilu* in five cases – three husbands and two mothers of the heads of the household had recently passed away. A large number of respondents mentioned that a homestead site is changed in order to obtain access to more fertile soil. Other reasons given were that the site was unsuitable due to waterlogging or an abundance of termites.

Reasons mentioned for not relocating a homestead were: the head of the household was getting old, permanent structures cannot be moved, shortage of construction poles, shortage of grass for thatching, no suitable site available, no need to move since the land is fertile enough. Four homesteads had never been relocated. These homesteads had been established in 1998, 2000, 2007 and 2009. In two cases, both the head of the household and his wife were migrant workers. One homestead included permanent houses and one was headed by a 95-year-old woman.

One 62-year-old male head of the household stated that he had cleared the land and established his farm in 1979. He had relocated his homestead quite a number of times:

> We first stayed in the same location for two years, and then we moved to new place for four years, and then for three years, five years, two years, and lastly we came to the current location in 2004.

Another respondent, a 40-year-old female head of the household, had moved from her mother's nearby homestead about a year before the interview took place. She had cleared the land from dense woodland and established her first homestead, *oshihambo*. She regarded her current site as temporary, saying it would not be a proper place to perform family functions, such as giving birth, celebrating weddings or having funerals. At the time of the interview she was busy relocating her homestead to a new place nearby.

A 54-year-old widow, the head of the household, had relocated her homestead in 2011, a year after the death of her mother, who had been the previous head of the household. She said that her current homestead was temporary and that she would soon relocate the homestead to a new site nearby. Another respondent, a 56-year-old female head of the household, said:

> We came here and stayed for two years, and then we moved again and stayed for a year and then we moved to a place, where we stayed for four years, and then a year, and then for seven years and lastly here.

Her husband had died in October 2011 and, in August 2012, the homestead was relocated about 150 metres to the west. Old poles were used for the outer palisade, but fresh ones were cut for the hut roofs. During the interview, many of the huts were still under construction. The widow mentioned that she was too old to relocate her homestead again, *oludilu* would require at least a month's work.

The husband of one 60-year-old female head of the household had died just a few days before her interview took place. After his death, cattle were brought in ceremonially through the main entrance. The widow's sleeping hut, *ondjuwo*, was destroyed, as were three U-shaped benches (logs) and an ox-skull rack (an indicator of prosperity) at the homestead's main meeting place, *olupale*. The main entrance to the homestead was closed and a new one created. Traditionally, it was believed that death cannot find its way into the homestead again, if the entrance was changed (see Shigwedha et al. 2002).

Discussion

According to Owambo tradition, a homestead is located within a cultivated field (Koivu 1925) and it is headed by a man (Williams 1991). In order to become the head of a household, men are expected to be married (ELC 1930–1932). A homestead headed by a man is called *eumbo* in Oshikwanyama and *egumbo* in Oshindonga.

In the past, according to the matrilineal customary system, a wife and children were not legally related to the husband and biological father; thus the children were considered kin only to the family of their mother (Hinz and Namwoonde 2010). As a consequence of this, widows or divorced women (and their children) were often evicted from the land and forced to return to their matrilineal family (Siiskonen 2009). Movable property, such as cattle, was not inherited by the widow, but by her husband's brothers and sisters (Gordon 2008).

According to pre-Christian tradition, the deceased was buried within or next to the homestead (ELC 1930–1932; Shigwedha et al. 2002). The death of the head of a household changed the name of the homestead to *oshiumbo* in Oshikwanyama and *oshigumbo* in Oshindonga. After the death of her husband, the widow was supposed to wait for the rainy season, and cultivate and harvest the fields once more before vacating the farm. The next occupant of the farm relocated the homestead away from *oshiumbo* but still within the same field.

Soon after Namibian independence 1990, customary laws on inheritance were changed to allow widows to remain on the land (Hinz and Namwoonde 2010). The 2011 Population and Housing Census showed that 54 per cent of rural households of north-central Namibia were headed by women, most of them never married (NSA 2014b). Widows represented 24 per cent of female-headed households. The analysis of preliminary communal land registration data showed that 43 per cent of landholders were women (MLR 2014). Both data illustrate the important role of rural women in household and farm management.

The findings of the present study confirm that the terms *oshiumbo* and *oshigumbo* are still used in north-central Namibia. Even though the deceased are nowadays buried in a cemetery, the relocation of homesteads is still carried out. Accordingly, a widow is required to cultivate the fields once before relocating the homestead to a new place.

The first study on the relocation of homesteads based on aerial photography was conducted by Erkkilä (2001) using images acquired on 9 October 1992 and 31 August 1996. A total of 246 homesteads were counted in the Ondobe–Eenhana area of the Ohangwena Region. Of these, 45 per cent had been relocated between 1992 and 1996, four of them had even been relocated twice. The results of the present study prove that *oludilu* is still practised in the eastern part of the Ohangwena Region.

The forestry authorities, referring to the Forest Act 12 of 2001 and Forest Amendment Act 13 of 2005, discourage the excessive use of wood. The shortage of wood increases the use of cement blocks and other permanent construction materials. The availability of locally harvested building materials, especially construction poles, together with the prevalence of permanent houses, is a major determinant of *oludilu* frequency.

The introduction of modern building materials, such as cement blocks, obviously makes the relocation of a house impossible. However, if a permanent house is attached to the traditional homestead, palisades and stockades made from wooden poles, as well as other non-permanent structures, are sometimes relocated. In addition, homestead and livestock pens are relocated independently; that is, even if the homestead is not relocated, livestock pens are moved frequently (Erkkilä 2002).

Another reason for the declining frequency of *oludilu* seems to be related to the old age of the heads of the household, and in general the shortage of labour. Many of the households are headed by female pensioners taking care of a large number of grandchildren, whose parents have moved to urban areas. It can be assumed that these elderly heads of the household have great difficulty in carrying out frequent relocations of the homestead.

The findings of the present study indicate that *oludilu* has still a strong cultural connotation. It is practised not only to increase the soil fertility, but also after the death of the head of the household. Nowadays widows continue to occupy the farm and the homestead, and they are not evicted as they often were before Namibia's independence. Nevertheless, a previously male-headed homestead still needs to be relocated to be seen as a fully fledged female-headed homestead. The practice of *oludilu* seems to continue, at least to a certain extent, despite the changes in family and land-tenure systems.

New agricultural and housing practices are increasingly being introduced, and *oludilu* is becoming less common. This may have a negative impact not only on the production of grain, but also on the regeneration of fruit trees.

The United Nation's 2030 Agenda for Sustainable Development highlights resilient agricultural practices that increase productivity and production. Therefore, the impact of *oludilu* on soil productivity should be better known. The relocation of a traditional homestead can be regarded as a successful implementation of indigenous knowledge. Before introducing new policies and programmes to develop existing farming systems in Namibia and elsewhere in Africa, it is essential to recognise this kind of indigenous knowledge.

Acknowledgements

The study was kindly facilitated by the Hon. Mandume Pohamba and Hon. Nehemia Haufiku, councillors in the constituencies of Ondobe and Eenhana, as well as Tatekulu Petrus Nghoshi, headman of Egambo village and Mr Dumeni Matheus, principal of Egambo Combined School. Supplementary data were provided by the Namibia Statistics Agency and the Ministry of Land Reform in Namibia. The study was funded by the Kone Foundation, Finland.

Notes

1 The academic collaboration between Namibian scholars and UEF dates back to a Finnish government scholarship programme for Namibian students established in the 1980s. The first research collaboration was on 'Cultural and Social Change in Ovamboland 1870–1915', a project funded by the Academy of Finland from 1984 to 1987, which involved one Namibian and three Finnish PhD students. In 1990 and 1991, a research project on 'Forests and Woodlands in the Development of Namibia', funded by the Ministry for Foreign Affairs of Finland in 1990–1991, preceded a long-term Finland–Namibia bilateral development collaboration on forestry. UEF and UNAM first began to work towards an academic partnership in 1991. Joint research interests have included issues as diverse as fertility, mortality and migration, precolonial and colonial history, landscape change, land use, oral histories, tourism, information society and education. At the time of writing, the two universities are working to increase their collaboration in teacher education, healthcare and pharmaceutical studies.

2 Communal land is vested in the state by the Constitution (Malan 2009). Individuals cannot own communal land, but may have customary land rights or rights of leasehold with regard to certain areas. According to the Communal Land Reform Act No. 5 of 2002, individuals may obtain rights to customary land for residential and/or farming purposes or rights of leasehold to certain areas of land. The rest of the communal land is commonage, and is traditionally used for the common grazing of stock.

3 For a more detailed description, see Erkkilä (2001: 38–42).

4 In the 2013/2014 agricultural census, 34 per cent of agricultural households had livestock (NSA 2015).

5 The aerial photography was part of mapping processes related to the Namibia 2011 Population and Housing Census (P Minnaar, GeoSpace International, personal communication).

References

Agrawal A (1995) 'Dismantling the divide between indigenous and scientific knowledge' *Development and Change* 26: 413–439.

Briggs J (2005) 'The use of indigenous knowledge in development: Problems and challenges' *Progress in Development Studies* 5 (2): 99–114.

Calunga P, T Haludilu, J Mendelsohn, N Soares and B Weber (2015) *Vulnerability in the Cuvelai Basin: Angola* (translated by M Lopes). Occasional Paper 12, Development Workshop, Angola. Available online.

ELC (Emil Liljeblad's Collection of Owambo Folklore) (1930–1932) Afrikan amboheimojen kansantietoutta (typed manuscript, translated by E Liljeblad and A Glad). National Archives of Finland.

Erkkilä A (2001) 'Living on the land: Change in forest cover in north-central Namibia 1943–1996' *Silva Carelica* 37. Available online.

Erkkilä A (2002) 'Homestead site change in the Owambo farming system' in E Lusepani-Kamwi and P Chikasa (eds), *Proceedings of the First National Forestry Research Workshop*, 12 and 13 March. Windhoek: Directorate of Forestry.

Galton F (1853) *The Narrative of an Explorer in Tropical South Africa*. London: J Murray.

Gordon RJ (2008) 'Widow "dispossession" in northern Namibian inheritance' *Anthropology Southern Africa* 31 (1&2): 1–12.

Government of Namibia (2015) *Republic of Namibia: Third National Communication to the United Nations Framework Convention on Climate Change*. Windhoek: Ministry of Environment and Tourism. Available online.

Hinz MO and NE Namwoonde (eds) (2010) *Customary Law Ascertained, Volume 1: The Customary Law of the Owambo, Kavango and Caprivi Communities of Namibia*. Windhoek: Namibia Scientific Society.

Koivu K (1925) *Amboneekerin jokapäiväinen leipä: Kuvauksia ja mietteitä ambokansan taloudellisista oloista*. Helsinki: Suomen Lähetysseura.

Komiyama H and K Takeuchi (2006) 'Sustainability science: Building a new discipline' *Sustainability Science* 1 (1): 1–16.

Langill S (1999) *Indigenous Knowledge: A Resource Kit for Sustainable Development Researchers in Dryland Africa*. Ottawa: IDRC. Available online.

Malan J (2009) *Guide to the Communal Land Reform Act (No. 5 of 2002)* (English version, second edition). Windhoek: Legal Assistance Centre.

McIntyre BD, HR Herren, J Wakhungu and RT Watson (eds) (2009) *Agriculture at a Crossroads* Washington, DC: Island. Available online.

Mendelsohn J, A Jarvis and T Robertson (2013) *A Profile and Atlas of the Cuvelai: Etosha Basin*. Windhoek: Raison and Gondwana Collection.

Mendelsohn J, S el Obeid and C Roberts (2000) *A Profile of North-Central Namibia*. Windhoek: Macmillan.

Mendelsohn J and B Weber (2011) *The Cuvelai Basin: Its Water and People in Angola and Namibia*. Occasional Paper 8, Development Workshop, Luanda, Angola.

Mills GT (1984) An Inquiry into the Structure and Function of Space in Indigenous Settlement in Ovamboland, master's thesis, University of Cape Town, South Africa.

MLR (Ministry of Lands and Resettlement, Namibia) (2014) *Data Set: Customary Land Rights, Namibia Communal Land Registration*. Acquired January 2014, Windhoek.

Nair PKR (ed.) (1989) *Agroforestry Systems in the Tropics: Forestry Sciences Series 31*. Dordrecht: Kluwer.

Ndeutapo N (2014) *Ondjokonona yombadja, ovakalimo nomikalo davo*. Windhoek: Kuiseb Verlag of the Namibia Scientific Society. (In Oshikwanyama).

NSA (Namibia Statistics Agency) (2013a) *2011 Namibia Population and Housing Census: Main Report*. Windhoek. Available online.

NSA (2013b*) Namibia 2011 Census Atlas*. Windhoek. Available online.

NSA (2014a) *Namibia: Namibia Population and Housing Census 2011*. Report generated 24 April 2014. Available online.

NSA (2014b) *Data Set: Persons Records, 2011: Namibia Population and Housing Census*. Acquired January 2014, Windhoek.

NSA (2014c) *Data Set: Housing Records, 2011: Namibia Population and Housing Census*. Acquired January 2014, Windhoek.

NSA (2015) *Namibia Census of Agriculture 2013/2014: Communal Sector Report*. Windhoek. Available online.

Olofson H (1983) 'Indigenous agroforestry systems' *Philippine Quarterly of Culture and Society* 11: 149–174.

Scholz RW and G Steiner (2015) 'Transdisciplinarity at the crossroads' *Sustainability Science* 10 (4): 521–526.

Shigwedha V, J Pemberton and L Beaty (eds) (2002) *Keep our Fire Burning! The Traditional Homestead*. Oshakati: University of Namibia History Project.

Siiskonen H (2009) 'Land use rights and gender in Ovamboland, North-Central Namibia, since the 1930s' *Fennia* 187 (1): 5–15.

Tönjes H (1911/1996) *Ovamboland, Country, People, Mission: With Particular Reference to the Largest Tribe, The Kwanyama* (translated by P Reiner). Windhoek: Namibia Scientific Society.

UN (United Nations) (2015) *Global Sustainable Development Report* (Advance unedited edition). Available online.

Urquhart AW (1963) *Patterns of Settlement and Subsistence in Southwestern Angola*. Report 18. Foreign Field Research Program, National Academy of Sciences, Washington, DC.

Warren DM (1991) *Using Indigenous Knowledge in Agricultural Development*. Discussion Paper 127, World Bank Washington, DC.

Williams F-N (1991) *Precolonical Communities of Southwestern Africa: A History of Owambo Kingdoms*. Archeia 16. Windhoek: National Archives of Namibia.

WIPO (World Intellectual Property Organization) (2002) *Traditional Knowledge: Operational Terms and Definitions*. Third session of the Intergovernmental Committee on Intellectual Property and Genetic Resources, Traditional Knowledge and Folklore, Geneva, 13 to 21 June. Available online.

About the contributors

Dennis Banda is assistant dean of research in the School of Education at the University of Zambia.

Karin Bengtsson is a senior lecturer in special education in the Department of Education Studies at Karlstad University in Sweden.

Anne Marit Vesteraas Danbolt is a professor at the Inland Norway University of Applied Sciences.

Hartmut Domröse is a lecturer at the Hochschule Wismar University of Applied Sciences in Germany.

Erlend Eidsvik is an associate professor in the Department of Social Sciences in the Faculty of Education at the Western Norway University of Applied Sciences.

Antti Erkkilä is a senior researcher in the Department of Geographical and Historical Studies at the University of Eastern Finland.

Henri-Count Evans is a PhD candidate in the Centre for Communication, Media and Society at the University of KwaZulu-Natal in South Africa.

Roddy Fox is an emeritus professor in the Department of Geography at Rhodes University in Grahamstown, South Africa.

Tor Halvorsen is a senior researcher at the University of Bergen Global, an associate professor in the Department of Administration and Organisation Science at the University of Bergen, and a senior researcher at the FAFO Institute for Labour and Social Research in Oslo, Norway.

Hilde Ibsen is an associate professor of history in the Department of Environmental and Life Sciences at Karlstad University in Sweden.

Nelago Indongo is an associate professor in the Department of Statistics and Population Studies at the University of Namibia.

Jørgen Klein is vice-rector for research at the Inland Norway University of Applied Sciences.

Regina Krause is the chief executive officer of the Robert Schmidt Institute at the Hochschule Wismar University of Applied Sciences in Germany.

Thembinkosi E Mabila is director of the Research Administration and Development Department at the University of Limpopo in South Africa.

Stephen Mago is an associate professor in business management and entrepreneurship at the Durban University of Technology in South Africa.

Evgenia Mahler is a project co-ordinator at the Hochschule Wismar University of Applied Sciences in Germany.

Suriamurthee Maistry is a professor in the School of Education at the University of KwaZulu-Natal in South Africa.

Robert L Martin is executive director for strategic alliances at the Vaal University of Technology in South Africa.

Emmy H Mbozi is a senior lecturer in the School of Education at the University of Zambia.

Rosemary Musvipwa is a lecturer and researcher at the University of Swaziland.

Martha T Namutuwa is the acting director of the Cooperative Education Unit at Namibia University of Science and Technology.

Erik J Olsson is Professor and Chair of Theoretical Philosophy at Lund University in Sweden.

Sharon Penderis is acting director of the Institute for Social Development at the University of the Western Cape in South Africa.

Kate Rowntree is an emeritus professor in the Department of Geography at Rhodes University in Grahamstown, South Africa.

Rachel J Singh is Deputy Vice-Chancellor for Research, Innovation and Partnerships at the University of Limpopo in South Africa.

Mubiana K Sitali-Ngoma is a lecturer in the School of Education at the University of Zambia.

Jens Stilhoff Sörensen is an associate professor in peace and development studies at the University of Göteborg's School of Global Studies and a senior research fellow in the Institute for Security and Development Policy in Stockholm, Sweden.

Geoffrey Tambulukani is a senior lecturer in literacy and language education at the University of Zambia.

Carina van Rooyen is a senior lecturer in the Department of Anthropology and Development Studies, and visiting fellow at the Africa Centre for Evidence, at the University of Johannesburg.

Printed in the United States
By Bookmasters